D1035915

Interpreting
Revelation

Other books by Dr. Tenney —

THE NEW TESTAMENT: AN HISTORICAL AND ANALYTICAL
SURVEY

JOHN: THE GOSPEL OF BELIEF

THE GENIUS OF THE GOSPELS

GALATIANS: THE CHARTER OF CHRISTIAN LIBERTY

PHILIPPIANS: THE GOSPEL AT WORK

Interpreting Revelation

By

MERRILL C. TENNEY, Ph.D.

DEAN OF THE GRADUATE SCHOOL
WHEATON COLLEGE, WHEATON, ILLINOIS

WM. B. EERDMANS PUBLISHING COMPANY
GRAND RAPIDS, MICHIGAN

INTERPRETING REVELATION
by MERRILL C. TENNEY

Set up and printed, May, 1957

LIBRARY OF CONGRESS CATALOGUE CARD NUMBER: 57-7391

S+ H
T 25

To My Sons
ROBERT AND PHILIP
Who May Live To See
The Apocalypse Fulfilled

PREFACE

For nearly nineteen centuries the book of Revelation has been both an inspiration and a mystery to the Christian church. In hours of darkness it has given courage to its readers, enabling them to endure persecution and death for the sake of Christ. In periods of ease and prosperity it has been the battleground of exegetes who have endeavored to fashion its strange pageant into a consistent eschatology. From the seemingly desultory assortment of seals, trumpets, beasts, and bowls they have sought to derive a systematic program of the present or of the coming age. All of these interpreters have found some true insights, even though not all of them can be right in every detail.

The purpose of this volume is not to add one more variation to the prevailing schools of interpretation nor to advocate some novel fancy. The depths of Revelation, like those of any other part of Scripture, will never be plumbed completely by the unaided human intellect. If, however, a fresh approach can open a different avenue of study or shed some new light on old problems, the effort will be worth while.

This study is built on the thesis that Revelation had a definite message for those to whom it was first written, and that the meaning which they found should be the initial clue to its interpretation. Their comprehension would have been shaped by several factors: the structure of the book, which would declare the progress of the thought; the imagery, which would have to be interpreted in terms of the concepts and literature familiar to them, particularly the Old Testament; and the phenomena of the contemporary social, political, and religious scene which are reflected in allusions and prophecies.

Today the contemporary setting of Revelation is difficult to recover, but the resources of archaeology and the understanding of the Greek speech of the first century afforded by the papyri have shed additional light upon the ancient Christian world. This study attempts to integrate the book as a whole and to apply broad interpretative principles which will enable the reader to think through the Revelation for himself and to formulate his own conclusions. The book has been treated from a premillenarian and moderate

futurist standpoint. The writer makes no apology for his views,
though he would not press them arbitrarily upon the subject or
upon the reader. He has sought to state all views fairly without
submerging his own.

Acknowledgments are due to *Bibliotheca Sacra* and to *Moody
Monthly* for the privilege of reproducing the substance of some
articles which first appeared in their pages. Sincere thanks are
offered to the author's many friends for their suggestions and
crticisms.

M. C. T.

Wheaton College
Wheaton, Illinois

CONTENTS

LIST OF CHARTS

CHAPTER I

THE BACKGROUND OF REVELATION

THE CHARACTER OF REVELATION

One need not be an expert theologian to recognize that Revelation is different from the other books of the Bible. Weird imagery, lurid predictions of judgment, and the final gleaming picture of the city of God arouse the curiosity of the student. No other part of Scripture has proved so fascinating to expositors, and no other has suffered so much at their hands. To many people Revelation is an insoluble puzzle, the meaning of which was forgotten long ago, if, indeed, it was ever known at all.

Notwithstanding its mysterious nature, the book was not written to frighten or to bewilder its readers, but to aid them in understanding God's program for their time. The symbols were significant, and were intended to be the vehicle of a very definite and important train of thought. However elusive the meaning of that thought might be, the sincere purpose and the prophetic gifts of the writer must be acknowledged. The uniqueness of the book does not consist in its weird pictures only, but also in many other distinctive characteristics.

Probably the most prominent of these unique features is the *symbolism*. The candlesticks (1:12), the stars (1:16), the precious stones (4:3; 21:19, 20), the sealed book (5:1), the horsemen (6:1-8), the locusts (9:3), the measuring rod (11:1), Babylon (17:5), and numerous other objects are used as symbols of powers and principles operative in the judgment of the earth. Many of these may be found in the prophetic language of the Old Testament; some may be taken from the current life of the period; others may be new; but all of them unite the imagery of divine revelation in a pictorial drama with a vivid climax.

The *language* of Revelation is unique. The symbolism introduces odd figures of speech, but even the average vocabulary of the Apocalypse is extraordinary. There are a number of passages in which the author seems to violate the simplest rules of Greek grammar and to express himself awkwardly, yet none of these are the result of ignorance or of carelessness. In several instances

13

these ungrammatical expressions are the unavoidable consequence
of attempting to put into Greek a concept which that language
cannot easily express. For instance, this phrase, "from him who
is and who was and who is to come" (1:4) should be translated
literally: "From he who is, and from he was, and from he who is
coming." The case of the noun after the preposition "from" is
wrong; the second expression is a finite verb and not a participle;
and the third expression is used in the same way as the first. The
reason for this strange rendering is that the Greek had no past
participle of the verb "to be," and so the author used a finite form.
Furthermore, the case did not change because evidently the entire
expression had become stereotyped as a title, and so did not alter
the construction to fit the context. The writer translated a Hebrew
title directly and literally into Greek without attempting to con-
form to the Greek idiom. He thought in Hebrew or Aramaic; he
wrote in Greek. The relative certainty of this fact shows that the
Apocalypse does not emanate chiefly from Greek and pagan
sources but that it has a literary connection with the apocalyptic
writings of the Old Testament and of the inter-testamental period.
The author was putting Christian truth into the literary vessels
which were already used by the devout people of that era.

In literary type the Revelation belongs to the class of apocalyptic writings, and is the only specimen of this kind in the New Testament. There are similar passages, such as Matthew 24 and 25,
or II Thessalonians 1, but there is no other one book which belongs entirely in this classification. While such writing is not generally characteristic of the modern day, it is not unknown in English literature. Milton's *Paradise Lost,* though largely Biblical in
its imagery, is apocalyptic in style and scope, and so also are the
mystical writings of William Blake.[1]

Apocalyptic writing has certain well-marked characteristics.
The style is generally figurative. Many of the characters and
much of the phraseology are drawn from Biblical writings. Information is conveyed by the announcement of angels, by visions, and
by other supernatural means. There is an attempt to portray
vividly the unseen world that lies behind the action of this present
world. The sovereign intervention of God on behalf of His people
and in judgment on His enemies concludes the action, which is
usually represented as in the future. In most of these writings
the author's name is pseudonymous; the real author took the
name of some famous Biblical character in order to give author-

ity to his production. In the case of the Apocalypse there seems to be an exception, for the author assumes that he is writing under his own name and that he is well known to the churches of Asia.

The apocalyptic character of Revelation does not necessarily mean that its content is fanciful or unreal. Apocalypse was a distinct type of writing like essays or drama; the form did not necessarily affect the truth or usefulness of the content. While the majority of apocalypses known to us are of little real prophetic value, and while a number of them were obviously written to foster some peculiar doctrine, the Revelation seems to be free from these drawbacks. The author's use of his own name as a recognized leader in the church speaks for his genuineness of purpose and for the truthfulness of his work.

THE AUTHOR

Few details are given by Revelation concerning its author. His name was John (1:4,9; 22:8), and he is classed among the "prophets" of the church (22:9). He did not claim apostleship, but called himself "your brother and partaker with you in the tribulation and kingdom and patience *which are* in Jesus." He wrote the book while he was staying in Patmos, a rocky isle in the Aegean Sea where the Roman government had a penal colony to work the mines. Revelation asserts that he "was in the isle that is called Patmos, for the word of God and the testimony of Jesus" (1:9). The text does not state positively whether he meant that he had been exiled as a result of persecution, or whether he had gone to Patmos voluntarily as a missionary. The language of Revelation could apply to either alternative, although tradition affirms that John had been arrested under the persecution of Domitian, and that he had been condemned to work in the mines.[2]

The verbal composition of the book itself adds a few pertinent facts. The language that the author uses in the letters to the seven churches shows that he was familiar with the topography of Asia, and that he was acquainted with the churches to whom he wrote. Presumably he had been a leader among them. He was thoroughly versed in the Old Testament, as his frequent allusions to its text and imagery show. Probably he was one of the earlier disciples of Jesus, since the Aramaic influence did not last long in the early church.

ITS PLACE IN THE CANON OF THE NEW TESTAMENT

The book of Revelation was not instantly and uncritically accepted as canonical by all the churches. The earliest historical allusion appears in the works of Justin Martyr (c. 135), about the middle of the second century. Quoting it verbatim, he attributed its authorship to John, an apostle of Christ.[3] Irenaeus (c. 180) quoted at least five passages and definitely mentions John as the author.[4] There are also possible allusions in the writings of Papias (c. 100)[5] and in the *Shepherd of Hermas* (c. 140),[6] but neither is a clear quotation. Clement of Alexandria (c. 200) cited the Apocalypse as authentic Scripture,[7] and Theophilus of Antioch (c. 175) referred to Revelation in one of his writings. There is no doubt that it was known and used widely in the church of the second century from Rome to Alexandria and from Carthage to Antioch. The Muratorian Canon indicates that by the end of the second century Revelation was accepted in the church as a canonical book, while the Apocalypse of Peter was not.

The canonical status of the book was questioned by Eusebius, whose motives may have been affected by his theological bias. He stated that Dionysius of Alexandria (A.D. 231-265) rejected Revelation, holding it to be a forgery by Cerinthus, a Gnostic heretic, because it taught the advent of a material kingdom. Dionysius, however, did not really reject the book on these grounds, but offered other reasons. He contended that John, the writer, was not the son of Zebedee, because he stressed his own name which the author of the Gospel and Epistles did not do. In addition, Dionysius noted that there was a marked difference of vocabulary and grammar between the Apocalypse and the Johannine writings, and thus concluded that both could not be attributed to the same author.

Marcion (c. 140) also excluded Revelation from the list of authoritative books of the New Testament, but Marcion omitted others as well. His action was not prompted by information or by tradition so much as by his antipathy to anything Jewish.[8]

In the Western churches of Rome and of Gaul, in Asia Minor, and in North Africa the Apocalypse was received as canonical. Origen, who preceded Dionysius in the church of Alexandria, included Revelation in his list of accepted books, although he disputed the authorship and canonicity of Hebrews, II Peter, and II and III John. Inclusion in the canon of the Eastern churches was not general until the year 500, about which time it was first brought into the Syriac Bible by Philoxenus.

Eusebius (c. 325), whose quotation of Marcion and Dionysius
has been mentioned, admitted that Revelation had been accepted
by some, but only in the list of works that he regarded as doubtful.[9] By the end of the fourth century, however, it appeared in all
the lists of the Biblical books and in the canons officially promul-
gated at the councils of the church. Curiously enough no other
apocalypses were included, although the Apocalypse of Peter was
quite popular in the second century among Christians in Egypt.
The inclusion of Revelation in the canon indicates that it was recognized by the majority of the church as a genuine disclosure of
prophetic truth and that it deserved a place with the Gospels and
the other writings which constituted the written platform of the
new covenant in Christ.

THE HISTORICAL BACKGROUND AND DATE

Although the book of Revelation, being genuinely prophetic,
deals in large measure with events subsequent to the time of its
composition, it can, nevertheless, be understood best against the
background of its own day. Prophecy is always given to interpret
the present in terms of the future, and unless the present conditions are understood clearly, the meaning of the future as expressed in prophecy will remain obscure. While one should not
attempt to confine prophecy to an explanation of the present in
language that seemingly applies to the future (*vaticinium ex
eventu*), one must always be aware of the conditions which necessitated the prediction.

Probable Dates

Revelation was written in the last third of the first century of
the Christian era, at some time between the opening of the reign
of Nero (A.D. 54-68) and the close of the reign of Domitian
(A.D. 81-96).

The argument for the early date[10] of Revelation in or shortly
after the reign of Nero is based chiefly upon certain internal allusions in the book. In the description of Babylon given in Revelation 17, the city is symbolized by a harlot seated on a beast
having seven heads and ten horns. The symbolism is explained as
follows:

> Here is the mind that hath wisdom. The seven heads are
> seven mountains, on which the woman sitteth: and they are
> seven kings; the five are fallen, the one is, the other is not
> yet come; and when he cometh, he must continue a little
> while. And the beast that was, and is not, is himself also an

eighth, and is of the seven; and he goeth into perdition.
(17:9-11)

The only politico-religious power of the day that could correspond to Babylon, the harlot, is Rome. The seer adds,

> And the woman whom thou sawest is the great city, which reigneth over the kings of the earth. (17:18).

This statement confirms the idea that Rome was the immediate parallel to the harlot, regardless of whether or not a more exact counterpart should appear in the future. If, then, the "kings" referred to the succession of the individual emperors, of which five were fallen, Revelation, so it is argued, must have been written after the decline and fall of the first five: Augustus, Tiberius, Caligula, Claudius, and Nero.

Furthermore, the passage contains a prediction: "the beast that was, and is not, is himself also an eighth, and is of the seven; and goeth into perdition" (17:11). A corresponding passage in Revelation 13 speaks of the beast that had a stroke of the sword, and lived (13:14). Apparently one of these rulers was killed, but later returned from the dead to take his throne, with the result that all the world was astonished and awed (13:3,4). There is a parallel between these passages and the "Nero-redivivus" myth. Nero did not die publicly in battle, but committed suicide privately on his flight from Rome. A rumor arose that he had fled to the Parthians and that he would return at the head of a Parthian army to recover his domain. The idea that Nero could and would return from death or exile to reign in Rome was naturally strongest during the period of anarchy under Galba, Otho, and Vitellius in 68-69, rather than later under the settled government of the Flavians.

Another factor that might postulate an early date for Revelation is the allusion to the temple in Revelation 11:1, as if it were still standing. The building was destroyed by Titus in A.D. 70. Of course, the passage may be regarded as completely predictive of a future rebuilt temple; but if the allusion is historical, the writing would have to be dated early.

Another bit of evidence cited for the early date of Revelation is the meaning of the number 666 (13:18). In antiquity letters were used as numbers. The first letter of the alphabet stood for 1, the second for 2, and so on. By using the numeric values of the letters in a person's name, they could be added together so that the total would make one number which thus stood for the person.

In this fashion the numeric value of NERON KESAR in Hebrew is 666; and thus the beast of Revelation 13 is supposed by some to be an allusion to Nero. There is, however, as T. Zahn points out, [11] no evidence that the Apocalypse was written for Hebrews or in Hebrew. All allusions to the Old Testament ideas in this book are stated in Greek. The disciples of John from whom Irenaeus derived his information concerning the use of this symbol denied that it referred to a Roman emperor. Besides, the usual spelling of Caesar must be changed in order to fit the explanation — a device which makes the interpretation dependent upon it at least suspicious.

One other argument for an early date has been advanced. The language of the Apocalypse is rough Greek, written by a man who thought in Semitic construction. It has been suggested that if the Apocalypse and the Gospel and Epistles of John were written by the same person, he wrote the Apocalypse early when he had a less perfect command of Greek than he had acquired when he wrote his other works.

Dating the writing from its style of language is precarious, however. The content of the visions would make description difficult no matter when it was written, and an amanuensis could smooth out the written style at an early date as well as at a late date. The apparent awkwardness of expression in some of its language is therefore not a final criterion for judging the time of publication.

The later date has the advantage of being confirmed by definite historical evidence. Irenaeus stated specifically that the Apocalypse was written in the reign of Domitian.[12] Victorinus (c. 270), [13] Eusebius (c. 325),[14] and Jerome (c. 370) [15] all agree with Irenaeus.

Internal evidence for the late date is confused and not very clear; nevertheless there are some factors which point to a later origin for Revelation.

The letters to the churches presuppose a period of development followed by decline which in some cases was rapid, yet these churches were not founded until late in the sixth decade of the apostolic age and were still flourishing when Paul was imprisoned in the early sixties. By the reign of Nero there could scarcely have been time for the growth of complacency and the ensuing declension of which the letters speak, but by the reign of Domitian a second generation would have arisen who would not have shared the convictions of their fathers. Loss of first love, acceptance of libertine doctrine, worldliness, and idolatry could easily have crept into these churches exactly as these letters indicate. On the whole the later of these two dates for the writing of Revelation seems preferable.

Conditions in the Empire

Under the Flavian emperors, Vespasian (69-79) and his sons, Titus (79-81) and Domitian (81-96), Rome prospered. The Flavians strengthened the integrity of the empire by suppressing revolt and by improving internal organization. Vespasian quelled uprisings among the Bataviae, the ancestors of the modern Dutch, and the Gauls, while Titus effected the capture of Jerusalem after a long siege, and established Roman supremacy over Judea. In addition, the military organization was improved by moving national soldiers, such as the Gallic legions, out of their own territory where they might find inducement to revolt, into other lands where they were strangers. Vespasian paid especial attention to securing the frontiers. He annexed new territories along the Rhine and the Danube, and re-enforced the military posts there. New garrisons were stationed on the upper Euphrates, and the kingdom of Commagene was added to the Roman territory. The praetorian guard, which had been disbanded under Vitellius, was reorganized and re-established.

Under Domitian new territories were seized in Britain and in Germany. He was less successful in Dacia, where Decebalus, the reigning king of the Dacians, fought him to a draw and compelled a compromise settlement.

Imperialism under the Flavians took on a new aggressiveness and the Roman grip on the civilized world was greatly strengthened. Their universal dominion seemed inevitable; all nations and all languages were destined to be under their control.

Judaism Under the Flavians

Numerous references to Judaism in Revelation (2:9, 14; 3:9; 5:5; 7:4-8; 11:1, 2; 21:12) indicate that important developments were taking place during this period. The fall of Jerusalem terminated the independent existence of the Jewish state, and drove thousands of the survivors of the siege into involuntary exile or slavery. The years immediately following A.D. 70 were a time of adjustment to new conditions of life. Many of the slaves and refugees perished from hardships; others still retained the germ of their faith and united with the exiles of the Diaspora who had already made their homes among the Gentiles.

Until the times of the Flavians the Jews of the Diaspora had enjoyed unusual privileges. They were exempted from participation in worship of heathen deities and even from the state worship of the emperor, nor were they compelled to engage in military service. In some cities, such as Alexandria, they were privileged colonists who possessed their own courts and a measure of autonomous urban government. Proselytes did not always enjoy these privileges, and so were sometimes charged with disloyalty and atheism. Vespasian laid a special tax called the *fiscus Judaicus* upon all Jews and proselytes to take the place of the tax which they had formerly paid to the temple in Jerusalem. Domitian enforced it and singled out especially those who were not Jews by birth or who had concealed their origin. The tax tended to discriminate against the Jews as an economic class and to expose to public attention those of Gentile birth who had espoused Judaism as a faith.

It is quite possible that this procedure brought into sharper relief the Christians who had up to this time been at least partly sheltered under the banner of Judaism. They could no longer claim the exemption the Jews had enjoyed, and their complete repudiation of polytheism laid them open to all the charges of "atheism" that had been levelled against the Jews. The increasing pressure of the totalitarian government made their position precarious, and because of the known character of Domitian the future looked dark.

The Provinces of Asia

Although little direct evidence is available concerning the operation of the imperial policy in the provinces, Rome was generally more strict with the administration of the provinces than in Italy itself. Peter, who wrote to Christians in the northern provinces of Asia Minor in the reign of Nero, spoke of "the fiery trial . . . which cometh upon you to prove you . . ." (I Pet. 4:12), as if the churches were threatened with a full scale persecution at that time. Whether it was ever fully realized is debatable. Nero's attacks upon the Christians in Rome may have been confined to the city, for there is no adequate record of any general proscription of them throughout the empire. On the other hand, the very fact that Peter was apprehensive shows that he fully expected the imperial attitude to be reflected by action against the Christians in the provinces.

The totalitarian government by Domitian may well have looked with suspicion upon the rapid rise of the new sect which had so many political potentialities for revolt. The obstinate refusal of Christians to worship the emperor was undoubtedly interpreted in political as well as in religious terms, and would be regarded much as Americans would look upon refusal to take allegiance to the flag. Domitian's execution of his cousin Flavius Clemens may have been prompted by the fact that Clemens had become a Christian, and that Domitian considered his attachment to Christianity to be subversive. It is still doubtful whether the emperor attempted a wholesale extermination of Christians as a government policy.

Revelation recognized the spiritual forces that lay behind the hostility of Rome's political power. Its pagan might was derived from Satan, and the struggle was thus basically spiritual. The book was intended to arouse the churches to the spiritual conflict that confronted them.

THE SOCIAL BACKGROUND

The late first and early second centuries marked the height of Rome's greatness and the fullest prosperity of her social order. Rome itself was filled with men from all lands, many of whom had their own quarters in the city. Like any modern city there were sharp contrasts of wealth and poverty. The ornate mansions of the wealthy and the squalid tenements of the poor could both be found in abundance. The political levels which were created by the imperial organization were reflected in the social levels: the senatorial aristocracy, the wealthy upper middle class, the plebs, who were dependent upon the urban dole, the freedmen, and the slaves. These classes were constantly changing in size and in constituency. Under Nero and Domitian the senatorial aristocracy had been subject to proscription, confiscation of goods, exile, and even death. The rapacity of the emperors and the low birthrate had reduced their numbers considerably. To some degree the same situation obtained for the wealthy middle class. There had been a rapid increase in the number of freedmen because of the progressive manumission of slaves, particularly at the death of their masters. Many of them were trained workers who were quite capable of earning their own living, and when they were freed they added to the independent skilled workmen of the empire. From this class and from the slaves the largest number of Christians were recruited. Paul and Peter, in the letters to their churches, spoke especially of slaves (Eph. 6:5-9, Col. 3:22-4:1, Philemon, I Pet. 2:18-25), and Paul pointed out that in Christ all racial and social distinctions disappear (Col. 3:11).

The prosperity of Rome was its weakness. The freedmen, who had just been emancipated from a propertyless and hopeless condition, avidly sought the wealth which had previously been denied to them, and many of them achieved it. Some became imperial favorites and members of the court; others prospered greatly in their business and swelled the ranks of the *nouveaux riches*. The senatorial aristocracy who survived the civil wars and the imperial proscriptions luxuriated in their wealth, and wasted it on debauchery.

Trade flourished in this period. A brisk interchange of goods was maintained between Italy and the provinces, and even with more remote countries like Britain and India. Gold, silver, jewelry, silks, ivory, fine woods, exotic foods, and slaves were imported; manufactured pottery, bronze work, lamps, glass, and textiles were exported. Caravans and shipping were the chief means of transportation. The importance of this trade is mentioned in Revelation 18, where the merchants bewail the fall of Babylon, the center of commerce and the source of their riches.

This economic prosperity carried in it the seeds of decline and of ultimate disaster. The extravagance of the emperors, the unfavorable balance of trade which forced Italy to import more than it exported, and the gradual decay of agriculture brought bankruptcy. The coinage lost its value, and bare sustenance of life was all that was possible. The economic pressure of "a measure of wheat for a shilling, and three measures of barley for a shilling" (Rev. 6:6) was well known to the lower classes of Rome, who were threatened constantly with starvation if the supply of cheap grain provided by state subsidy were interrupted.

THE RELIGIOUS BACKGROUND

The primary concern of the Apocalypse is not with social and economic conditions, but with the spiritual interpretation of life. It represents the state not only as a political power and as a social scheme, but also as a manifestation of spiritual force. The thirteenth chapter of Revelation indicates that the ultimate end of human totalitarianism will be an organized rebellion against every standard that God has set for the world, and that the system which leads to that rebellion is under complete condemnation. Rome is only one stage of the development of the system of evil, although it prevailed at the time when the Apocalypse was given, and so was the focal point of application for its truth.

Roman religion was *idolatrous*. Not only was the empire tolerant of the deities of subject nations; it fostered them in order to utilize the religious loyalties of the people as a cement for the empire. In the city of Rome itself could be found shrines and temples to all kinds of foreign deities, and in the other cities local cults flourished. The great altar of Zeus at Pergamum ("where Satan's throne is," 2:13) was still standing at the end of the first century. The cult of Artemis (Diana) of Ephesus which is mentioned in Acts 19 still existed when the letter to Ephesus was written. Idolatry was a definite temptation to the church of Thyatira (Rev. 2:20), and there are other references to it elsewhere (9:20; 21:8; 22:15).

The worship of the emperors, to which allusion has already been made, was the most vigorous and also the most dangerous of the cults. Its vitality depended not solely upon the enforcement of state decree, but also upon the fact that it provided a living, visible, tangible, audible deity for men who had been accustomed to the formal routine of ritual observance. The gods of Graeco-Roman legend had no reality; and their very existence had been challenged by the philosophers. The emperor was the living head of the state and the guardian of its welfare. He could and often did bestow gifts upon the poor and give aid to those who needed it. His abilities and deeds seemed almost superhuman to the ordinary man of the street. Here at last was a real person whose position and powers made him worthy of worship, and the Roman populace acclaimed him as *Dominus et Deus*, though, of course, many were indifferent and skeptical.

The imperial cult became increasingly strong and pointed the way to the totalitarian state which should become not only a political entity but also a religion. Modern fascism and communism are both the logical outcome of a humanism which exalts the highest representative of the state to the pedestal of deity. If the culmination of this tendency is yet to come, the past manifestations have been sufficient to show in what direction humanity travels when it attempts to organize its own affairs without acknowledging God. Revelation is the presentation of a divine philosophy of history at a time when men sought the solution to their political and social problems through a humanly conceived and humanly administered empire.

Judaism, as already noted, had passed through a tremendous change. The fall of the city weakened the nationalist party and drove the learned members of the Sanhedrin into exile. The great colonies of Jews in Rome, Alexandria, and other cities remained undisturbed. The Christian church was closely related to Judaism, for it used the Jewish Scriptures, accepted the main tenets of Jewish theology, and received its first adherents from the synagogue. As the church became predominantly Gentile in character because the larger number of the converts were Gentiles, the breach between it and Judaism widened. The relationship between them, however, never ceased completely. Jewish literature, Jewish imagery, and Jewish theology appear in the book of Revelation, and show that among the churches of Asia a considerable Jewish element was present. Without a knowledge of the Old Testament one cannot interpret Revelation successfully. The book is a mosaic of allusions, quotations, and images taken from the Jewish Scriptures, and it interprets these in terms of the person of Christ.

The rise of the church as a recognized historical body is also apparent in Revelation. The seven churches of Asia were not the only churches of Asia nor of the world of that time. Whether they are typical of successive periods in their significance or not, they stand for a larger body which had permeated the civilization of the eastern Mediterranean world, and which had moved at least as far west as Rome. As a historical movement the church had already clashed with the empire, and it was beginning to be conscious of its own purpose and future. What would befall it in the next few decades? Would it rise, decline, and vanish like so many religious cults that flourished in that period, or would it be more lasting? Was it destined by God to be an expression of His ultimate purpose, creating a faith and a society of its own, or was it simply ephemeral? Confronted with the growing hostility of the great world empire, devoid of military and political defense, possessing few if any learned apologists, what prospects did it have?

The book of Revelation is the answer. It reveals a church that is far from infallible, plagued with invading heresies and sometimes blighted with apostasy, but still in the omnipotent hand of the eternal Lord. It asserts that behind the church is a supernatural purpose which must preserve that church until its mission is fulfilled. By whatever system the book be interpreted, it does predict plainly that the people of God shall be preserved until the Lord Jesus Christ returns to become sovereign of earth and to establish His kingdom.

THE LITERARY BACKGROUND

As already stated, Revelation belongs to the class of literature known as apocalyptic which flourished in periods of depression and defeat. Daniel and Ezekiel were written during the Exile; Zechariah came out of the Restoration; and non-canonical works like the Book of Enoch, the Assumption of Moses, the Apocalypse of Peter, and others were produced in the inter-testamental period or during the early persecutions of the church. The apocalyptic form of Revelation is a sign that it was written during the first serious conflict of the church with the organized pagan world surrounding it, and that it was calculated to present new truth to people who were accustomed to its form of writing.

Another element in the literary background of Revelation is the apocryphal literature of the first two centuries of the Christian era. The word *apocrypha* is a Greek derivative meaning *hidden, concealed,* and consequently *obscure, hard to understand.* Originally the word applied to those works which were written only for an inner circle of readers who could understand them, not for the world at large. In its initial usage it was almost synonymous with *apocalyptic,* but gradually the meaning changed. It became later the term which was applied to the noncanonical books, and was so used by Tertullian. Today the term carries the connotation of "spurious," or "unauthorized."[16]

There were in the early church a large group of works which were not generally considered canonical, but which were used widely for reading whether public or private. Among them were a number of apocalyptic writings, such as the Apocalypse of Peter, the Apocalypse of Paul, the Apocalypse of Ezra, the Apocalypse of Elijah, the Apocalypse of Zechariah, and others. Some of these were never seriously considered as claimants to canonicity; others, like the Apocalypse of Peter, were given a place of authority by some churches. The latter was mentioned in the Muratorian Fragment[17] and was included by Eusebius in his catalogue, although he listed it among the spurious books.[18] Swete remarks that "a study of post-canonical Christian apocalypses serves only to accentuate the unique importance of the canonical books."[19]

The relation of Revelation to the Old Testament is unique, and a more studied treatment of the subject will be provided in a later chapter. The author of the Apocalypse must have been steeped in the Jewish Scriptures, and probably knew them in the Hebrew text as well as in the Greek. R. H. Charles states that the writer did not quote from any Greek version, though he may have been influenced by one or more of them at times.[20] Undeniably he relied heavily on the Old Testament both in Hebrew and in Greek, and thought largely in terms of its language and teaching.

The relation of the Apocalypse to the New Testament is not so obvious as is its dependence upon the Old Testament. If the late date for its composition be granted, there is no chronological reason why the author could not have known and used many of the apostolic writings which would have been in circulation at that time. Charles thinks that definite references can be traced to Matthew, Luke, I Thessalonians, I and II Corinthians, Colossians, Ephesians, and possibly Galatians, I Peter, and James.[21] The instances which he cites, however, do not necessarily prove direct dependence. They may mean only that the Apocalypse reflected a phraseology current in all the churches, and thus in common use among all Christian writers. Possibly, too, the usages of the Gospels and of Paul had so saturated the Christian speech by the end of the first century that the incorporation of this language was inevitable. For instance, he lists the expression in Revelation 1:4, "Grace to you and peace" as a quotation from Colossians 1:2 and eight other Pauline epistles. The identity of the expressions is undeniable; but it was probably such a common greeting that he did not need to read the Pauline Epistles to find it. The expression "firstborn of the dead" (Rev. 1:5) because of its uniqueness might be a more convincing instance as a quotation from Colossians 1:18, but in all of Charles' comparative table of citations there are few if any that would demand dependence of the Apocalypse upon the contemporary Christian canon.

To the extent that it coincides in expression with the rest of the New Testament it serves as an integrating factor, especially in passages like Matthew 24, 25, where there is an apocalyptic message. Conversely, the expressions that are found elsewhere in the New Testament may there be defined by their context and so interpreted for their usage in the Apocalypse. The parallels of both the Old Testament and the New Testament are quite helpful in comparative study.

CHAPTER II

THE THEME OF REVELATION

The correct interpretation of any book of the Bible depends chiefly upon a proper understanding of its main theme. The central theme of the Apocalypse is declared by the title which is given to it in the first line of its text: "The Revelation of Jesus Christ, which God gave him to show unto his servants, *even* the things which must shortly come to pass. . . ."

If the book was intended to be read to a listening congregation, as the initial beatitude states (1:3), the opening verses must have contained some directive for thinking to make it intelligible. The audience would have to know the theme in order to follow it as the various details of action are presented in quick succession. Although there may be other approaches to the book of Revelation, this one is the most direct and the most logical.

First, the title states that the book is intended to be a revelation. The Greek word *apokalypsis*, translated "revelation," means an unveiling, a disclosure of what previously had been concealed. In the New Testament it is most frequently employed to describe God's self-disclosure of truth to man. It implies that from the fulness of a knowledge which man does not possess, God imparts to him some aspects of the divine mysteries in the form of plain truths. Man may not understand all that is behind them, but the revelation insures that what God does disclose is comprehensible and reliable. Paul used the same word in Galatians 1:12 where, in speaking of the gospel which he preached, he said:

> For neither did I receive it from man, nor was I taught it, but *it came to me* through revelation of Jesus Christ.

However difficult of interpretation the Apocalypse may be for its modern readers, it was not designed to mystify, but rather to explain the truth of God more clearly. For this reason one should approach it with the expectation of learning, and not with the expectation of being confused. The theme should make a difference in one's initial attitude toward the book.

Secondly, the theme is declared to be "the Revelation of Jesus Christ." A great deal of ink has been expended in discussing

whether this means that Jesus Christ is the *content* of the
revelation or whether He is the *giver* of the revelation.[1] Grammatically the latter interpretation is preferable; but in either case
there is a strong assertion of the relation of the person of Christ
to the revelation. He has not only acted as the medium by whom
the unveiling of future events is transmitted; He is also inextri-
cably involved in those events and in the process of which they
are part. He is the arbiter of the destinies of the church and of
the world. As He wills and purposes, so the judgments must
fall. In the language of Jesus Himself,

> . . . neither doth the Father judge any man, but he hath
> given all judgment unto the Son . . . (John 5:22).

The person of Christ is the most important key to the Revelation.
As His place in it is recognized, its main structure becomes understandable and its meaning can be found in terms of the disclosure
of His person and work.

A third element in the theme of the book deals with its *destination*. It was intended for the seven churches of Asia that are listed
in the first three chapters. Just why these seven were selected
rather than any other seven is not stated. There were other
churches in the Asian province: Colosse, near Laodicea, to which
Paul wrote in one of his epistles; Troas, where he held a meeting and restored Eutychus to life (Acts 20:5-12) ; Magnesia and
Tralles, to which Ignatius indited letters at the beginning of the
second century. Colosse and Troas were certainly founded before the writing of the Apocalypse, and probably the others were
also. Perhaps these seven churches were selected because they
were peculiarly representative of the main virtues and weaknesses
of all churches everywhere. One thing is added to the theme by
the phrase, "his servants" (1:1), which seems to be equated with
the "seven churches" (1:4, 11) : the theme concerns the churches
directly. Whether it speaks of the churches or to the churches it
should be interpreted as dealing with their welfare and ultimate
destiny. Actual mention of them ceases with the third chapter
and is not resumed until the last chapter (22:6, 16) ; but the rest
of the material is relevant to the churches' life, since it is addressed
to them.

The last aspect of the theme concerns *events*: "the things which
must shortly come to pass" (1:1). The word translated *must*
(Greek: *dei*) implies logical or mathematical necessity, the inevitable result of the inherent scheme or nature of things. The

phrase translated "shortly" (Greek: *en tachei*) means "without delay," indicating that the judgments of which the book speaks may begin at any time. Revelation, then, is the predictive account of certain great events which shall affect the destiny of the churches as these events are set in motion and governed by Christ.

These events may be related to three great principles which appear through the canon of the New Testament. The first is the principle of *judgment*. John (5:27) states that the Father gave to the Son the authority to execute judgment, because He is a son of man. Revelation announces that "the hour of his judgment is come" (14:7), and it implies that the calamitous visitations upon humanity which it prophesies are the stern judgment of God upon sin. It asserts afresh the law of retribution that "the wages of sin is death" (Rom. 6:23), and paints in lurid colors the fate of a rebellious and unrepentant world.

The second principle which is strongly enunciated in Revelation is *redemption*. The dedication is "unto him that loveth us, and loosed us from our sins by his blood . . . " (1:5). The executor of judgment is a Lamb "as though it had been slain" (5:6). When the great unnumbered multitude in heaven is identified by an elder, they are hailed as those who "washed their robes, and made them white in the blood of the Lamb" (7:14). In the contest with the final manifestation of Satan those who came off victorious "overcame him because of the blood of the Lamb" (12:11). These and other kindred passages emphasize the purpose of redemption which God effects through Christ, who desires not to judge the wicked but to save them and to restore them to His favor. Even the judgments have a redemptive aspect. Several times the statement is repeated that in spite of the severity of the judgments, men "repented not" (9:20, 21; 16:9, 11). The purpose of the judgments is not solely punitive, but is primarily to bring men to repentance.

Last of all, Revelation is the final word on the establishment of the *kingdom of God*. The spiritual constituency of the kingdom is given in 1:6: "he made us *to be* a kingdom, *to be* priests unto his God and Father." The rewards promised to the faithful in the churches are all connected in one way or another with the idea of a coming kingdom. The creation of that kingdom potentially is acknowledged in the prayer of the living creatures:

> [Thou] madest them *to be* unto our God a kingdom and priests; and they reign upon the earth (5:10).

The crisis of the kingdom appears in another prayer of the elders:

> We give thee thanks . . . because thou hast taken thy great power, and didst reign (11:17).

It is finally announced by the great voice in heaven:

> Now is come the salvation, and the power, and the kingdom of our God, and the authority of his Christ (12:10).

At the conclusion of all the terrestrial judgments, when the evil rulers of earth have been remanded to the lake of fire and when the victory of Christ is complete, it is written that the saints "reigned with Christ a thousand years" (20:4). After the last assize at the great white throne and the manifestation of the city of God, it is said that "[his servants] . . . shall reign for ever and ever" (22:5).

Judgment, redemption, and kingdom are interrelated parts of the public establishment of God's salvation. Judgments are the fate of the unrepentant and the unredeemed, as the kingdom is the destiny of the redeemed believers. Redemption exempts one from judgment, and makes him ready for the kingdom. This kingdom is composed of the redeemed, and is the new society to which they belong now and which will be realized in its fulness when God's redemptive work is completed by the return of Christ. All of these interrelated concepts focus around the person of Christ who is Himself Judge, Redeemer and King. The fulfilment of the divine purpose in Christ by the exercise of those three offices constitutes the central theme of the Apocalypse.

Chapter III

THE STRUCTURE OF REVELATION

The book of Revelation is varied and complex in its structure as well as in its symbolism. The bewildering sequence of churches, seals, trumpets, bowls, beatitudes, songs, and other themes leaves the reader wondering whether or not it is an unintelligible jumble of words or whether it does really have some significance for him. The discovery of an underlying theme through the book's literary structure will provide an understandable order that gives some meaning to the whole.

Literary structure is the first and the most obvious approach to any book. The clue to the order may appear in repeated phrases which introduce topics, comparisons, parallel sections, or, as in Revelation, visions. Just as a careful examination of the joints of a piece of furniture will show how the cabinet maker constructed it, so the "joints" of a book will show how the author put it together and will give some hint of his purpose.

The book of Revelation contains a large number of repeated phrases, some of which are significant as marks of progressive thought. They seem to have been intended to lead the reader through the maze of figurative expression to an intelligible pattern of teaching. The first and simplest of these is the phrase "in the Spirit" which occurs in four places:

1:10 — I was in the Spirit on the Lord's day.
4:2 — Straightway I was in the Spirit . . . .
17:3 — And he carried me away in the Spirit . . . .
21:10 — And he carried me away in the Spirit . . . .

Comparison with the context makes it clear that "in the Spirit" is not identical with Paul's declaration, "Ye are not in the flesh but in the Spirit, if so be that the Spirit of God dwelleth in you" (Rom. 8:9), since Paul is contrasting two moral or spiritual states rather than the normal state of consciousness and the state in which visions appear. The seer of Revelation under the power of the Holy Spirit was transported in consciousness to a new scene of action where spiritual realities and future events were disclosed to him, and where he received revelations that were not given under ordinary circumstances.

Each occurrence of this phrase locates the seer in a different place. The first states that he was "in the isle that is called Patmos" (Rev. 1:9); the second, that he was called "up hither" and saw " a throne set in heaven" (4:1,2); the third, that he was taken "into a wilderness" (17:3); and the fourth, that he was carried away "to a mountain great and high" (21:10).

The contrasts and comparisons of these phrases are instructive. They consist of two pairs. Each member of the first pair is introduced by "a great voice" (1:10, 4:1), and each member of the second pair by "one of the seven angels that had the seven bowls" (17:1; 21:9). The first pair contrasts Patmos, where the writer was suffering physical exile and presumable hardship for his faith, with heaven, where he saw the hosts of the redeemed and the sovereign Christ breaking the seals of destiny. In the second pair there is the contrast of the wilderness and the mountain, the harlot and the bride, corruption and purity, doom and destiny, despair and delight. The second pair really gives a double outcome to the book.

Such organization cannot be accidental. If these four phrases are taken as marking the opening of four major sections of the book, it may be divided as follows:

Prologue:	Christ Communicating	1:1-8
Vision I:	Christ in the Church	1:9-3:22
Vision II:	Christ in the Cosmos	4:1-16:21
Vision III:	Christ in Conquest	17:1-21:8
Vision IV:	Christ in Consummation	21:9-22:5
Epilogue:	Christ Challenging	22:6-21

The subject matter in each of these divisions is fairly uniform. The Prologue contains the introduction to the book as a whole. The first vision gives the Lord's view of the churches as represented by the seven churches of Asia. The second vision is the administration of judgment from the standpoint of heaven, beginning with the breaking of the seals and concluding with the "sign" (15:1) of the seven bowls of wrath. The third and fourth visions were evidently intended to be parallel. The third narrates the collapse of godless Babylon, the evil product of fallen man's ambition, while the fourth describes the advent of the city of God, which marks the realization of God's ultimate purpose of dwelling among men (21:3). The Epilogue (22:6-21) makes the practical application of the book.

Such in broad outline is the structure of Revelation as marked by these four repeated phrases, but there are others which contribute further understanding of the structure. A second is "And I saw . . . ." There may be some room for debate as to which use of "I saw" are to be classed as formally introductory to an individual vision, but there are not less than forty in any case. The first occurs in Revelation 1:12, the last in 21:22. In the majority of instances the expression introduces a new item which the writer beheld in his vision, though in others it is used to point out new aspects of the same object (17:3,6).

With the exception of one reference in Vision I in the previous outline (1:12) and one reference in Vision IV (21:22) all of these usages appear in Visions II and III where there is the greatest amount of action. The effect is as if John were reporting on a series of slides which had been thrown on a screen, introducing each one or occasionally making some new observation on the same one with "And I saw . . . ." No clear line of continuity or progress can be established by this phrase, but it helps one to understand the style of Revelation and the way in which the content was imparted to the seer.

A third phrase which recurs four times, and which may serve as a division point is "thunders, voices, lightnings, and an earthquake."

> 4:5 — Out of the throne proceed lightnings and voices and thunders.
>
> 8:5 — . . . there followed thunders, and voices, and lightnings, and an earthquake. (Seals)
>
> 11:19 — . . . there followed lightnings, and voices, and thunders, and an earthquake, and great hail. (Trumpets)
>
> 16:18 — . . . and there were lightnings, and voices, and thunders; and there was a great earthquake . . . . (Bowls)

While these verses are not absolutely identical in content, they are sufficiently similar to warrant a comparison. All of them are in the second vision. The last three mark respectively the conclusions of the judgments of the seals, the trumpets, and the bowls, and have consequently been interpreted by some to indicate that their judgments are concurrent, or at least continuous. Does the repetition of the phrase mean that the same reaction takes place three times, or that there are three types of judgment of increasing intensity converging at the same point? In each case, the statement is connected with some terminal activity (8:3-5, 11:16-19, 16:17-21), and with the altar or temple in heaven. This expression focuses the mind of the reader upon the source of judgment and adds another integrating element to the book.

A second important element in the literary structure of Revelation apart from the repetition of introductory phrases is the arrangement of subject matter by blocks. First and foremost in this classification are the letters to the seven churches, which comprise chapters 2 and 3. The detailed structure of these letters will be treated later in the analysis. As a collection they present the divine estimate of the church and the prescription for its needs. Coinciding with the first vision, they constitute an unmistakable division of the book.

The second grouping is composed of the seals, trumpets, and bowls. These series contain a progression of thought which furnishes the chief action of the Apocalypse. The seven trumpets are introduced by the seventh seal (8:1,6), and the seven bowls are a sequence of the seventh trumpet (11:15, 19; 15:1, 5, 6; 16:1ff.). The last two series are less closely related than the first two, for at least three chapters intervene between them. The content of these chapters is, however, largely explanatory, so that the general continuity of the series is maintained as indicated. In the outline they may be treated as major blocks.

The status of the section on the bowls is difficult to assign exactly, since the bowls are called also by a special title, "a sign" (15:1) In four passages of the Apocalypse (13:13, 14; 16:14; 19:20) "sign" is used in the common Johannine sense of "miracle"; but in 12:1, 3, and 15:1 it refers to a person or to an event that is symbolic in meaning. The bowls thus seem to belong in two categories: in the numerical series of seals and trumpets of which they are the climax, and with the "signs," because they are an indication of God's wrath against sin.

Other subject blocks of shorter length comprise the war in heaven (ch. 12), Babylon (chs. 17,18), the holy city (21:9-22:5). The last of these coincides with the fifth division of the outline. In one or two instances the subject block and the vision do not agree exactly. For instance, Revelation 21:1-8 is related closely by subject matter to 21:9-22:5, and might be considered to form one block, as the customary chapter division shows. In reality, Revelation 21:1-8 is the climax of one vision, while 21:9-22:5 is another vision which elaborates the last detail of the vision preceding. In many instances subject blocks, introduced by "and I saw," are the small units of which the larger integrated visions are built.

The songs of Revelation serve as a commentary on the action of the text, somewhat as the chorus of a Greek tragedy used to explain the action of the principals in the drama. No less than eleven poetic expressions of praise can be counted, though not all are called songs.

TITLE	PASSAGE	PARTICIPANTS	OCCASION
1. Tersanctus: "Holy, holy, holy"	4: 8	Living Creatures	Constant worship
2. "Worthy art Thou" in Creation	4:11	Twenty-four Elders	Worship by Elders
3. "Worthy art Thou" in Redemption	5: 8-10	Living Creatures and Elders	Lamb's assumption of rights
4. "Worthy is the Lamb"	5:11-12	Angels, Living Creatures, Elders	"
5. "Unto him that sitteth"	5:13	Every created thing	"
6. "Salvation unto our God"	7: 9,10	Great multitude	Sealing of 144,000
7. "Amen. Blessing . . ."	7:11,12	Angels	"
8. "The kingdom of the world"	11:15	Great voices	Seventh angel
9. "We give thee thanks"	11:16-18	Elders	Seventh trumpet
10. "Great and marvellous"	15: 2-4	Victors over Beast	Seven last plagues
11. Four Hallelujahs	19: 1-8	Great multitude Elders Living Creatures Great voices	Fall of Babylon Marriage of Lamb

In these expressions may be found the essence of worship which pervades the entire Apocalypse. They breathe a sense of awe at the power of God exercised in judgment, and a deep gratitude for the work of redemption. Their contribution to the structure of the book is not so much division as integration. The eleven single stanzas divide into five groups. The first five stanzas relate to the worship of heaven as the Lamb steps forward to undertake the fulfilment of redemption in the earth. The next two echo the praise of those who, having been redeemed, stand at last in the presence of God. The third group, numbers 8 and 9, announce with thanks the arrival of the consummation. Number 10 is the song of those who emerged victorious from the last conflict with evil, and number 11, the fourfold Hallelujah, is the final song of triumph when Babylon has fallen and when the kingdom of Christ is about to be established.

These declarations of praise by the heavenly host, whether angels or redeemed men, serve to show that there is a constant background for the shifting scenes of the book. No matter how many parentheses and digressions may be introduced, the Revelation maintains the celestial setting for terrestrial events. Behind the changing panorama of human history described under the symbolic pictures abides the unchanging reality of an eternal world in which God's purpose is unfailing and in which His Christ is victorious. The unity of scene persists through the second and third visions of the Apocalypse, and ties them together as dual aspects of the same process and purpose.[1]

Numerical structure is prominent in Revelation; in fact, it is the easiest approach to the composition of the book, though perhaps not the best. Seven churches, seven seals, seven trumpets, seven personages,[2] seven bowls, and seven new things[2] appear in the text. Seven, of course is an important number everywhere in the Scriptures, beginning with the days of creation in Genesis. It is emblematic of completeness or of perfection.

The use of "sevens" in Revelation may be illustrated by the chart on page 38:

Scofield adds the "seven dooms,"[3] but these are not grouped as clearly as the others, and seem more like an artificial enumeration. Those that are listed here can be centered around one topic or are located in one fairly consecutive body of text. Each group contains a complete sequence of its own which may have an independent bearing on the content of Revelation, although they are also interrelated by cross reference.

The chronological aspect of the structure of Revelation is most difficult to interpret. If, however, the sequence of the "sevens" can be established, the interpretation will be greatly facilitated.

The passage most generally quoted as authoritative for the chronological interpretation of Revelation is 1:19:

> Write therefore the things which thou sawest, and the things which are, and the things which shall come to pass hereafter.

THE "SEVENS" IN REVELATION

	SEVEN CHURCHES		SEVEN SEALS		SEVEN TRUMPETS		SEVEN BOWLS		SEVEN PERSONS		SEVEN NEW THINGS	
	CONTENT	REF.	CONTENT	REF.	CONTENT	REF.	CONTENT	REF.	CONTENT	REF.	CONTENT	REF.
1	Ephesus	2:1-7	White Horse	6:1-2	Hail, Fire, Blood	8:7	Sore	15-16:2	Woman	12:1	New Heaven	21:1
2	Smyrna	8-11	Red Horse	3,4	Mountain	8,9	Blood-Sea	3	Dragon	5	New Earth	1
3	Pergamum	12-17	Black Horse	5,6	Falling Star	10,11	Blood-Rivers	4-7	Man Child	5	New Peoples	3
4	Thyatira	18-29	Pale Horse	7,8	Darkened Sun, Moon, Stars	12	Sun	8,9	Michael	7	New Jerusalem	2, 10 ff.
5	Sardis	3:1-6	Souls under Altar	9-11	Horsemen	9:1-11	Darkness	10,11	Beast from Sea	13:1-10	New Temple	22
6	Philadelphia	7-13	Celestial Disturbances	12-17	Angels at Euphrates	13-21	Unclean Spirits	12-16	Beast from Earth	11-18	New Light	23
7	Laodicea	14-22	(Parenthesis) Silence	7 8:1,2	(Parenthesis) Great Voices	10 11:15-19	Declaration	17	Lamb	14:1	New Paradise	22:1 ff.

As the text stands in the ARV it divides easily into three parts: "the things which thou sawest," the past; "the things which are," the present; "the things which shall come to pass hereafter," the future. If this verse be a chronological summary of the book, "the things which thou sawest" would refer to the writer's own circle of experience in the past; "the things which are" might include the present, probably the seven churches; and "the things which shall come to pass hereafter" would comprise the rest of the book.

One other possibility of translation might affect this result. The passage may be rendered:

> Write the things which thou sawest, both the things which are and the things which shall be hereafter.

Such a rendering is grammatically possible, though it is not favored by the majority of expositors. If correct, it means that Revelation relates only to the present and to the future, not to the past at all. The visions, "which thou sawest," are of the present and future only, though the visions as an experience are past.

The question then becomes: Where is the dividing line in Revelation between a symbolic view of the present and a symbolic view of the future? In either translation, both are represented. The answer seems to be contained in 4:1, where the voice of a trumpet summoned the seer to heaven to see "the things which must come to pass hereafter." The division point between present and future in this Book is the time of writing.

The ambiguous point in the chronological interpretation of Revelation is the word "hereafter." Does it mark a definite division in chronology which remained static? If so, the letters to the churches would apply only to the literal churches of their own day, and the rest of the book might be interpreted historically of the entire period from the first writing until the return of Christ. If the word "hereafter" means only a general future, then it may well throw the entire Apocalypse into the realm of ideals to be realized at some indefinite date.

The ambiguity can be cleared partially by reference to the obvious termini of the book. Its first terminus was the time of writing when the author was exiled for his faith and when some of the churches had already felt the heavy hand of persecution. If he were writing in the time of Domitian, then the "things which are" reflect the state of the Asian churches at the end of the first century, while "the things which must come to pass hereafter" may deal with anything in the last eighteen hundred years.

The other terminus is that of the Lord's return. The consummation of judgment bringing the doom of Babylon and of the totalitarian government of evil, the establishment of the reign of Christ on earth, the final assize and the eternal state continuing in the New Jerusalem have not yet taken place and still seem remote. Even if the Apocalypse is symbolic, it must still anticipate an end yet unrealized; it cannot be remanded wholly to the past. If the structure is to be interpreted chronologically, perhaps one should say that the first three chapters belong to the writer's present, while the rest belong to his future. Whether they are to be consigned wholly to our future or not is another question.

Another clue to the structure of Revelation may be found in its Christological passages. According to the title, the Apocalypse is "the Revelation of Jesus Christ," and one key to its content is the development of the teaching concerning His person. Aside from occasional allusions and titles, there are four main portraits of Christ in Revelation. Chapter 1:12-18 portrays Christ in the Church, the critic and counsellor of His people. Chapter 5:1-14 presents Christ in the Cosmos, ordering the affairs of the world as He unfolds the scroll of redemptive purpose. Chapter 19:11-16 depicts Christ in Conquest, the King who is about to overthrow evil and establish His kingdom. The last portrait is given indirectly in 21:22-22:2, Christ in Consummation. Around these four themes can be arranged the whole of Revelation as an exposition of Christ in action in the world today. Each is organically connected with the section in which it occurs, and it sets the Christological emphases of the visions beginning "in the spirit," thus confirming the conclusion that these are the natural divisions of the book.

The aspect of the structure most difficult to explain is the "parenthetical" material which apparently interrupts the logical process of the main action. The more important of these parentheses are:

The Sealings and the Great Multitude   7:1-17
Intervenes between Sixth and Seventh Seals

The Angel and the Little Book   10:1-11
Intervenes between the Sixth and Seventh Trumpets

The Two Witnesses   11:1-14
Intervenes between the Sixth and Seventh Trumpets

The Personages and the Angels   12,13,14
Intervenes between the Trumpets and the Bowls

The last mentioned section may not be a true parenthesis. Introduced by the phrase, "And a great sign was seen in heaven" (12:1), it parallels the same phrase which introduces the bowls in 15:1, "And I saw another sign in heaven." Numerically the bowls parallel the series of the seals and the trumpets; in their own setting they parallel the sign of the war in heaven. The fact that all of these series come to the same general conclusion, climactic judgment and the establishment of the kingdom of God, leads toward the deduction that the various series are parallel, and that they give differing aspects of the same process rather than successive historic stages of it. The so-called parenthetic passages are thus illustrated vignettes, inserted to elaborate upon the development of the action of judgment up to the period when they occur.

Chapter IV

THE INTRODUCTION

REVELATION 1:1-8

In some respects the entire first three chapters of Revelation could be considered introductory, since they characterize the recipients of the book and show the needs that prompted the giving of the visions. Even better reasons could be advanced for regarding the whole of the first chapter as introductory, because it contains the portrait of Christ and because it declares more fully the status of the human author. Structurally, however, the first vision begins with Revelation 1:9, 10, and therefore the introduction proper comprises only eight verses.

These verses are crammed with meaning and give a viewpoint on the whole book that facilitates considerably its interpretation. They could be more aptly called its title page than an introduction, for the sequence of ideas in them resembles closely the title page of a modern book.

THE TITLE

The title is contained in the first verse: "The Revelation of Jesus Christ." Although the communication professes to deal with "things" (1:1), it is notwithstanding a disclosure of and from a person. It is intended to illumine the purpose of God in the ages future to the writer and to the readers as that future is unveiled in the person of Christ by God the Father. The unveiling is given to the Son in order that He in turn may show it to His servants, so that they may be adequately prepared for the "things which must shortly come to pass" (1:1). The "things" are events which may be identifiable with historical occurrences, and which will be of tremendous importance to the welfare of these believers.

There is always a temptation to seek the fulfilment of these "things" in the events of the past or of one's own day. None of these "things" should be interpreted by itself, but all must be viewed in the perspective of the book as a whole. Events that seem of great importance to one generation may shrink to relatively insignificant proportions when compared with the total progress of history. There can be no doubt that the symbols of Revelation are genuinely predictive, but one should not rashly identify them with past events unless they accord in totality as well as in individual resemblance.

The method of imparting this knowledge is stated in two words, "sent," and "signified." A better translation is provided by the RSV: ". . . he made it known by sending . . . ." "Made known," or "signified," is the more important term. It is used three times in the Gospel of John concerning Jesus' death, "signifying by what manner of death he should die" (12:33, 18:32, 21:19). In each of these instances the word is somewhat obscure and figurative. The verb means "to indicate," or "to signify." It was used as a technical term for the response of an oracle, which usually gave its answer to an inquirer in symbolic or enigmatic language. In Acts 11:28 "signify" is connected with the predictive prophecy of Agabus. It can be interpreted as *"sign-i-fy,"* or to convey truth by signs and symbols. Such an interpretation fits Revelation aptly since it is largely written in "signs."

These "signs" were mediated through the seer, John, described by the phrase "who bare witness" (Rev. 1:2). The language is reminiscent of the Fourth Gospel, where the word "witness" is used of seven different attestations of the person of Christ. The last of these, mentioned in John 15:27, says: ". . . and ye also bear witness, because ye have been with me from the beginning." It was Jesus' acknowledgment of the testimony of His own disciples as valid accreditation of His person and work. The seer of Revelation belongs to the succession of the witness, and the use of the past tense of the verb here intimates that he was selected for this function because he had already borne witness. Perhaps by this time the word had begun to gain the significance of "suffer for," since witness for Christ frequently involved suffering. The Greek word "witness" has become our English word, "martyr."

The objects of the witness are stated as "the word of God," "the testimony of Jesus Christ," and "all things that he saw." If, as seems likely, the third phrase is appositive with and includes the first two, it means that the new witness which this revelation contains came to him through the succession of visions which it records, and that those visions were "the word of God" and "the testimony of Jesus Christ."

The two phrases have connotations that go back both to the Old Testament and to the life of Christ. "Word of God" appears frequently in the prophets describing the way in which the revelation of God came to them. "The word of Jehovah" came to Hosea (Hos. 1:1), to Joel (Joel 1:1), to Micah (Mic. 1:1), to Ezekiel (Ezek. 1:2,3), and to others. The term is used also in the first chapter of John's Gospel and in the first chapter of his Epistle to describe Christ as the final revelation of God: "The Word was with God . . . the Word was God . . . the Word became flesh, and dwelt among us" (John 1:1,14). Later in Revelation He is definitely given the name, "The Word of God" (19:13). The seer shows that he belongs to the prophetic succession because he is the agent through whom the thought of God is transmitted to men, and by whom the final picture of Christ, who is God's fullest and last revelation, is to be made plain.

"The testimony of Jesus Christ" (1:2) may mean either the witness which Christ Himself imparts, or the witness of life which John gave to Him. Probably the former is the better interpretation because it makes the grammatical construction similar to that of the phrase preceding. It is the message which includes all of the work of Christ: His preincarnate purpose, His earthly ministry of teaching, death, and resurrection, His present work of intercession, and His future reign and judgments. Christ is God's witness to the world of His holiness, His grace, and His power. This witness is the substance of the things that John saw.

Revelation is therefore a graphic representation of God's redemptive purpose and prophetic message. The truth is not diminished because it is expressed in the form of visions; it is rather heightened. It is a visual aid to the Christian who ponders the future and who wonders how the reverses and contradictions of this present life can possibly eventuate in anything but disappointment and disaster. Revelation is God's panoramic answer to the believer's doubts and fears, and is the pictorial promise of victory.

THE COMMENDATION

Having thus stated the title, having defined the general content, and having introduced the author and his method, the book next presents its appeal to the public:

> Blessed is he that readeth, and they that hear the words of this prophecy, and keep the things that are written therein: for the time is at hand (1:3).

This word of commendation is the first of a series of seven beatitudes which are scattered through the book. Evidently the author felt that his writing needed this special inducement to call it to the attention of the churches. Doubtless numerous commu-

nications of the type of Revelation were current in the church of
the first century.   Perhaps so many of them were extravagant
in language and unsound in teaching that the leaders of the
churches eyed them with suspicion.   Such seems to have been the
attitude of Eusebius in the fourth century, since he looked with
disfavor upon any apocalyptic writing.[1]   The shift of number from
the singular, "he that readeth," to the plural, "they that hear," suggests that the work was originally designed for public use in the
church assembly rather than for private perusal.   One of the earliest tests of canonicity was public reading, for only those works
which the church considered authoritative were read openly to all
the assembly and made the basis of exposition or of exhortation.
Justin Martyr states that the Gospels were so read from the very
earliest times.[2]   To command the public reading of the document
was equivalent to recommending it for canonical standing.   It was
commended to the churches as mandatory instruction for their
future, since the time of fulfilment was imminent.   Revelation,
therefore, was intended to cope with a pressing emergency that the
author expected to burst shortly upon the church, and to give
authoritative instructions for meeting it.

THE AUTHOR

The paragraph in verses four and five connects the human
author with the specific destination, the seven churches, and for-
mulates the greeting.

The identity of the author has already been discussed.   He must
have been well known in the Asian churches and have been regarded as one of their teachers, perhaps the most outstanding leader.   He did not assume a superior or dictatorial attitude, but
called himself a "brother and partaker . . . in the tribulation and
kingdom and patience *which are* in Jesus" (9).   In his writing he
acted only as the agent of the messenger (angel) who instructed
him, and he professed only a secondary authority (22:10).   Nevertheless, he expected that these words would be received and
obeyed, for they carried with them the last appeal of divine authority (22:10-19).

THE DESTINATION

The seven churches must be taken initially as literal.   Whatever
they may represent, they are essentially different groups located
in actual historical cities, with marked individual characteristics.
Ramsay has pointed out that the historical facts which archaeo-

logical research has brought to light about these cities have a bearing on the interpretation of the text, since the Lord appeals to the churches in terms that they would understand best in the light of their local history.[3] The reality of the destination prevents regarding Revelation simply as a piece of poetic idealism, with no reference to place or to time. While it may be intended for the church of the entire age, it is sufficiently concrete in its outlook and purpose so that it has a positive application to an existing situation.

THE GREETING

The greeting, "grace and peace," is a combination found frequently in the epistles of Paul. Probably it does not reflect "Pauline influence" here so much as it does the general church usage which Paul followed in an earlier day, and which he doubtless introduced in the new Christian communities that he founded.

The threefold source of grace and peace marks the Trinitarian teaching in Revelation. "From him who is and who was and who is to come" denotes the eternal nature of God, who ever exists, who always was in the eternal past, and who will continue to exist in the eternal future.

The seven Spirits may represent the sevenfold ministry of the Holy Spirit described in Isaiah 11:2:

> . . . the Spirit of Jehovah shall rest upon him, the spirit of wisdom and understanding, the spirit of counsel and might, the spirit of knowledge and of the fear of Jehovah.

The eleventh chapter of Isaiah refers to the advent of the Messiah to establish His kingdom and to restore His authority over the earth. The enduement of the sevenfold spirit is His special prerogative by which He is empowered for His task. Revelation lays a corresponding emphasis upon the Holy Spirit in the consummation of redemption.

The third source of the greeting is the Lord Jesus Christ, the center of the revelation in this book. Three titles are applied to Him: (1) the faithful witness, (2) the firstborn of the dead, (3) the ruler of the kings of the earth. The titles may be a summary of His work among men in chronological order. First comes His earthly ministry, in which He was "the faithful witness." He spoke of bearing witness of Himself (John 8:18), and of heavenly truths which He had seen and known (3:11). He was faithful because He declared the truth and because He did not hesitate to apply it to the lives of His hearers. To all who would hear and heed He bore direct and pertinent testimony concerning the Father and His claims upon men.

"The firstborn of the dead" (or "from the dead") clearly refers to the resurrection of Christ. The expression parallels Paul's language in I Corinthians 15 where He is called "the firstfruits" (I Cor. 15:20). He is the first manifestation of a new kind of life in which all believers shall ultimately share. The title presents all of Christ's resurrection and post-resurrection ministry. "This Jesus did God raise up . . . . Being therefore by the right hand of God exalted, and having received of the Father the promise of the Holy Spirit, he hath poured forth this, which ye see and hear" (Acts 2:32,33). Thus Peter described the work of the risen Christ in the opening sermon of Pentecost, and throughout the progress of the book of Acts His intervention in the affairs of men and His intercession for them are prominent. The phrase "firstborn of the dead" in Revelation epitomizes both His present power and our future hope.

"Ruler of the kings of the earth" is the title of Christ as the victorious conqueror and establisher of the kingdom of God. As a title its fullest realization is yet to come, for, as the writer of Hebrews says, "now we see not yet all things subjected to him" (Heb. 2:8). Potentially He is Lord of the world, but His reign is not manifest in its perfection. Revelation foreshadows the complete fulfilment of this promise.

These three titles relate also to the general structure of Revelation. "The faithful witness" describes Christ's relation to the churches, whom He warns faithfully of their sins and to whom He gives some of His greatest promises. "The firstborn of the dead" describes His role as the arbiter of destiny, opening the seals and effecting redemption because He died and rose again to ascend the throne of authority. "Ruler of the kings of the earth" is His title as He puts all enemies under His feet and asserts His lasting sway over the world. These titles summarize His entire position in the present period of time.

THE DEDICATION

The dedication (1:5,6) describes the revelation of Christ in terms of His relation to believers. "Unto him that loveth us, and loosed us from our sins by his blood; and he made us *to be* a Kingdom, *to be* priests . . . ." Three activities are mentioned here also: He "loveth," He "loosed," He "made." The first describes His permanent attitude to men; the second states the crisis of

His manifested love; the third is the effect which that love has produced in the work of redemption, making men a kingdom and priests. The kingdom is the sphere of His rule; the priests are participants in His ministry, men brought into direct contact with God. As any author might dedicate a book to one specially interested or to whom he owes a debt of gratitude, so John inscribes his dedication to the Lord Jesus Christ whose redemptive work is the foundation and subject of the book.

THE MOTTO

The motto or keynote of the thought is indicated by verse 7:

Behold, he cometh with the clouds;
And every eye shall see him,
And they that pierced him;
And all the tribes of the earth shall mourn over him.

This verse makes the return of Christ the theme of Revelation and asserts its universality because it shall be witnessed by all men without regard to time or space. "Every eye" transcends geographical limitations; "they that pierced him" carries back in time to the day of crucifixion; "all the tribes of the earth" means that no race or people is excluded. The one great universal event that will focus all places, times, races, and expectation is the return of the Lord, "the one far-off divine event toward which the whole creation moves."[4]

The motto is a mosaic of quotations. "He cometh with the clouds" alludes to Daniel 7:13: "There came with the clouds of heaven one like unto a son of man," who received the kingdom from God. "Every eye shall see him and they that pierced him" recalls Zechariah 12:10: ". . . they shall look unto me whom they have pierced; and they shall mourn for him . . . " The intention of Revelation is to concentrate in its visions the heart of the prophetic teaching of the Old Testament and to bring it to its climax in Christ.

THE PUBLISHER'S IMPRINT

The last verse of the introduction corresponds somewhat to the publisher's imprint at the bottom of the title page of a book:

I am the Alpha and the Omega, saith the Lord God, who is and who was and who is to come, the Almighty.

It asserts the transcendent authority of God, who is both beginning and ending of all history, and whose existence spans all time. Alpha and Omega are respectively the first and last letters of the Greek alphabet, and stand for the beginning and the ending, or for the completeness of anything, as Americans would say "from A to Z." This eternal and omniscient God has set His seal upon the book as His message, and has authenticated its production.

In summary, then, the book of Revelation is a disclosure of Christ and of His relation to the world process of redemption, extending beyond the day in which it was written. It is given especially for the benefit of Christ's servants, that they may be prepared for the strange events ahead of them, and that they may understand God's purpose for them.

Chapter V

VISION I: THE SEVEN CHURCHES OF ASIA

Revelation 1:9-13:22

The part of Revelation on which there has been the greatest amount of agreement among expositors both with regard to the points of division and with regard to the interpretation is the section containing the letters to the seven churches of Asia. Although much of the language is figurative, it is so closely related to actual historical occurrences and institutions that one feels more secure in drawing conclusions than when he is dealing with symbolism that is independent of any known place or happening.

As already noted, this vision begins with the phrase, "I was in the Spirit . . . ." Since the second use of this phrase recurs in 4:1,2, the intervening text, tied together as it is by a common subject, must constitute a unit. This conclusion is confirmed by the inward structure. It opens with a portrait of Christ which dominates and integrates the rest of the text, being mentioned in each of the seven letters that follow in order. The portrait is the description of the Lord of the churches, who dictated the letters to the seer.

The churches to which the letters are addressed are named in a definite order. If one should visit them as they are listed, he would travel in a rough circle along the main trade roads beginning with Ephesus and moving north to Pergamum, then southeast to Laodicea, and presumably back to Ephesus. The location of the churches in this circuit suggests that they may represent the entire cycle of Christian faith and of Christian progress as exemplified by the visible church of all time. The vision is concerned with their state and development, and is an appeal to their faith and expectation.

The letters are related to each other not only by the introductory words of each which connect them with the individual vision of Christ, but also by their own uniformity of outline. The chart of comparisons will show that all the letters usually contain the following parts:

1. *The Commission*: "To the angel of the church at . . . write . . . . "

2. *The Character*: "These things saith he that . . . , " followed by an allusion to the introductory portrait.

3. *The Commendation*: "I know thy works . . . , " with such favorable comments as the Lord can give.

4. *The Condemnation*: "But I have against thee . . . , " with a list of adverse criticisms in sequence.

5. *The Correction*: varied injunctions couched in a sharp imperative mood.

6. *The Call*: "He that hath an ear . . . . " This part is uniform in all seven letters, except that in the last four it takes the seventh place in order rather than the sixth.

7. *The Challenge*: "To him that overcometh . . . . " Each of the letters has a promise for the overcomer who rises above the temptations and perils besetting his particular church.

In one or two instances not all of these features appear, but generally they characterize each letter. The uniformity of the missives enables one to compare them with each other and to ascertain with some degree of satisfaction whether the author were sketching existing churches, or whether he were trying to predict the entire course of Christendom.

THE SETTING

Once again the author orients himself for the benefit of his readers. Contrary to the general practice of apocalyptic style, he names himself as John, not that he may claim the reputation of being an apostle, but because he is known by this name to his readers. Instead of placing himself on a pedestal above them he claims to be a brother and a sharer with them "in the tribulation and kingdom and patience *which are* in Jesus" (1:9). The way in which he states his identity precludes pseudonymity, and shows that he was acknowledged as a spiritual leader whose word carried authority. His fourfold vision "in the spirit" became the pattern for the eschatology of these churches, and the symbolical expression of the nature of his vision.

The vision is introduced by a voice which commissioned the seer to write in a book what he saw, and to send it to the seven churches. Turning to find the source of the trumpet-like voice, he saw a Figure walking in the middle of the seven golden lampstands. The picture is obviously an attempt to describe in words what no artist could paint realistically. Eight similes are used in four verses to describe His features. The similes are:

1. "Like unto a son of man" (13). The Figure was human in form, not some grotesque being unrelated to the human race. Perhaps this is a latent allusion to the Messianic Son of Man in Daniel 7:13.

2. "White as white wool" (14)

3. "[White] as snow"

Similes 2 and 3 apply to the hair of the Figure. Whiteness suggests both age and holiness. The whiteness of wool and the whiteness of snow differ in that the latter is dazzling. The Figure represents One who is always ancient because He is "before all things" (Col. 1:17), and One who is so holy that in the blaze of His glory all others seem soiled.

4. "As a flame of fire" (14)

This awesome holiness is made all the more terrible by the piercing glance of the Son of Man, who can see through the character of each church as the X-ray penetrates and photographs the body. His eyes blaze with righteousness, not with temper; for the wrath of God is not His personal pique against those whom He dislikes, but it is rather the revulsion of His being against sin.

5. "Like unto burnished brass"
    "As if it had been refined in a furnace" (15)

The second pair of similes is applied to the feet of this Figure. Treading on anything means in Biblical language victory and contempt; victory over that which is subjugated (Ps. 91:13), contempt for that which is trodden under foot as worthless (Matt. 5:13). The allusion to brass or bronze is not perfectly clear. The Greek word translated "burnished bronze"[1] may mean "brass of Lebanon" or "yellow frankincense." Probably the former is correct, since the addition concerning its being heated in the furnace implies the peculiarly brilliant radiance of molten bronze. Nowhere else in Greek literature does this term appear; its meaning must be determined entirely by the present context. The feet of judgment mark His measured tread of inspection among the churches.

7. "As the sound of many waters" (15)

Anyone who has visited Niagara Falls or any other great cataract has been impressed by the roar of the water that is

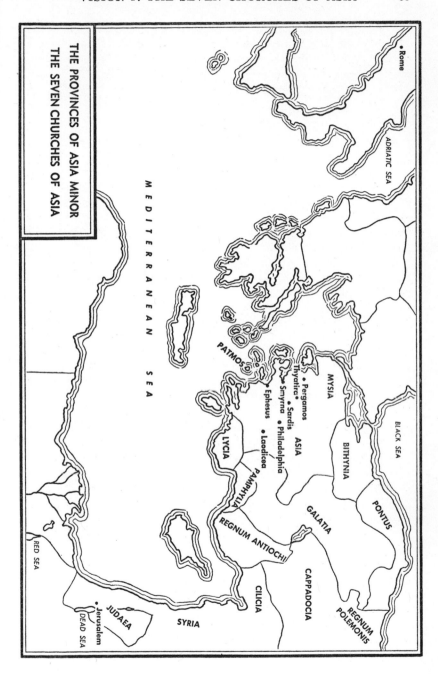

THE PROVINCES OF ASIA MINOR
THE SEVEN CHURCHES OF ASIA

heard above every other sound in the vicinity. On the island of Patmos John would never be out of range of the booming surf along the shore. Its sound would be distinguishable above every other noise. So the voice of Christ rises above the babel of the world, and in solemn majesty makes itself heard in decisive tones.

8. "As the sun shineth in his strength" (16)

No man can look straight at the sun with his naked eye without endangering his sight. Even when the sun is in eclipse it must be viewed through a dark screen so that its rays will not injure the delicate retina of the human eye. The face of the glorified Son of Man cannot be studied by human sight. His glory is too bright to be endured. The simile continues the idea of the eyes as a flame of fire, for the Lord who comes in judgment will act inexorably, irresistibly, and impartially. All of the similes emphasize this aspect of His personality.

Other features of the portrait contribute further to this idea. The long robe was a garment worn by professional men and official dignitaries who were not classed as servants or laborers, but as men of power and authority. A long garment indicated that the wearer was higher than the ordinary class of person, and that he deserved special attention. In the Septuagint this term is used in connection with the priestly garments,[2] or to represent one who is clothed in specially fine material. Probably the term does not of itself denote priestly uniform, but that it was the type of garment that the priest ordinarily wore. It marks the cessation of conflict and the investment of authority in Christ for ministry in the church.

The brilliance and the awesomeness of the manifestation completely unnerved the seer so that he "fell at his feet as one dead" (17). It would seem strange that if John of Patmos was identical with the son of Zebedee he should be overpowered by the sight of One on whose breast he had leaned at the last supper. The appearance was so different from the One whom he had known in the flesh, and the glory was so unanticipated that he was overwhelmed.

Two symbolic features appear in this portrait: the seven golden lampstands and the seven stars in the right hand of the Lord. Both are explained in definite terms, leaving no doubt as to their identity. The lampstands among which the Lord is walking are the seven churches. As lampstands they do not create the illumination; they only hold it. In the Old Testament, the seven-branched lampstand in the Holy Place of the tabernacle represented the testimony of God's truth borne by the united nation of Israel. In the Revelation there are seven separate lampstands, each of which represents one of the churches. They are alike in the nature of their testimony, but each one carries its message independently to its own locality.   The lampstands emphasize symbolically the church's function of witnessing which the Lord is inspecting as He walks among them.

The stars in His right hand are the "angels" of the seven churches. Evidently they are the responsible representatives who are intrusted with the communication of the message which the Lord transmitted through John.   No clear statement is given as to whether they are guardian angels, supernatural beings who were assigned to watch over the individual assemblies, or whether the word *angelos* is to be taken in the non-technical sense of "messenger" as it is frequently used outside of the New Testament.   The context seemingly makes clear that each "angel" is the leader of the church, and so might well be equated with its minister or pastor.

Whatever one's conclusions may be, the fact that the stars are held in the right hand of the Lord shows that they are under His protection and control. In a time of peril He will preserve them and will not let them go. Rigid inspection, powerful protection, and loving evaluation must precede the day of judgment on the world, for judgment must "begin at the house of God" (I Pet. 4:17). Christ cannot judge the world until He has purged His church and made it ready for taking it to Himself.

This portrait is, then, the key to the section. As the various churches are weighed and discussed one can see the living Christ in action among His own people. He does not appear to them as the terrible sovereign on the throne nor as the conqueror riding to battle. He walks among them as a Lord who seeks to commend their virtues even more than to expose and punish their faults. These letters are His particular warning and counsel to the church of all time as its various aspects appear under the guise of their seven historic places.

THE CHURCH OF EPHESUS

The first church of the series is Ephesus, which was located in the largest city of the Roman province of Asia, and which was at the end of the first century a thriving metropolis. It had been originally a prosperous seaport, but the silt brought down from the mountains by the Cayster river was gradually filling the harbor. Careful engineering had kept some channels open, but the port was accessible only with difficulty, and was slowly losing its importance.

The chief cult of the city was that of the goddess Artemis (Diana) whose temple was one of the wonders of the ancient world and the object of intense civic pride. The citizens of Ephesus were fanatically devoted to the worship of the goddess, and cherished her image which was reputed to have fallen from heaven (Acts 19:27, 35). At the instigation of the metallurgists' union they had risen in protest against Paul's preaching when he had visited the city, and had ultimately forced him to leave.

Notwithstanding the troubles that beset the advent of the gospel in Ephesus under Paul's ministry, a strong church was established which became a headquarters for the evangelization of the entire province of Asia (19:26). The same qualities that had made the people fanatical pagans made them enthusiastic Christians. Had not the response to the gospel been great, there would not have been such a protest on the part of the heathen populace. Ephesian Christians had been vigorous witnesses (19:10), and had given up all connection with their old practices, even at considerable cost to themselves (19:19).

An entire generation had elapsed since the founding of the group, and with the passing of the first converts came an inevitable cooling of zeal. The victories which the pioneers won by labor and endurance became the accepted privileges in which their children luxuriated. To this situation the Ephesian letter was directed.

The *character* of Christ emphasized here is His function as a preserver and watchman: "that holdeth the seven stars in his right hand . . . that walketh in the midst of the seven golden candlesticks" (Rev. 2:1). However great may be the failure of the churches, He still retains protective control of their leaders. He has not abondoned them to loss.

The *commendation* concerns chiefly the orthodoxy of Ephesus. The phrase, "I know thy works," as comparison with the other letters will show, is general and inclusive of all that follows. Special notice is taken of the labor and endurance of the church. It has not grown weary in welldoing. Its activities and loyalty have been maintained without interruption in spite of external pressure.

Furthermore, it has tested carefully the authority and truthfulness of the self-styled apostles and has shown that they are false. The word "apostle" has several connotations. It may refer to the group of men who were associated with Jesus from His baptism to His resurrection (Acts 1:21,22). Later it came to mean one who had seen the Lord personally, as Paul did at the time of his conversion (I Cor. 15:7-9, 9:1). The general meaning of the word seems finally to have prevailed as indicating an office or function in the church (Eph. 4:11,12) apart from any relation of the apostle to the earthly career of Christ. Certainly some who could claim the title genuinely were never listed among the Twelve (Rom. 16:7). The designation evidently included those whose spiritual qualities and knowledge made them effective and authoritative administrators of divine revelation.

For this reason it was inevitable that pseudo-apostles should appear, men who arrogated to themselves apostolic authority for the sake of gaining prestige or monetary reward. Paul evidently encountered such at Corinth, for in his Corinthian correspondence he defended himself against attack by them (I Cor. 9:1,2; II Cor. 11:4, 5), and he called his opponents "false apostles" (II Cor. 11:13-15). Charlatans and impostors existed in the first century as surely as they do now.

The spurious claims and false teachings of these pseudo-apostles were tested and rejected by the Ephesian church. There was no sign of departure from orthodoxy on their part: and for their faithfulness the Lord commended them. His *condemnation* was focused upon one fatal flaw: "thou didst leave thy first love" (Rev. 2:4). The word "leave" means to "quit," or to "forsake." The church had departed completely from its initial affection for Christ and had lapsed into a state where its spiritual life had become only an orthodox routine. No great scandals disfigured its reputation, and its organization was still functioning smoothly, but the inner springs of its life had begun to run dry.

For this state the Lord had a *correction* which can be condensed into three words: *remember, repent, repeat.*

"Remember therefore whence thou art fallen" (2:5). Perhaps the decline was so gradual that there would be little noticeable change from day to day, but at the end of a generation the difference between the first love and the existing state would be quite obvious. Christ challenged His church to make a careful reassessment of its spiritual condition in the light of its initial devotion to Him.

"Repent" (2:5) means literally a change of mind, a reversal of a position previously held. It involves a deliberate repudiation of former sins and a complete return to the standards and will of God.

Repeat — "do the first works" (2:5) — calls for a renewal of the works which were the earliest token of the Ephesians' devotion to Christ. Perhaps "first works" refers more to their original quality than to their quantity. The Ephesian church was not inactive, but its activity lacked the warm love for Christ which had originally distinguished it.

The *challenge* to this church promises that the overcomer, the one who meets the conditions laid down by the Lord, shall "eat of the tree of life, which is in the Paradise of God" (2:7). Almost all of the challenges refer to the vision of the heavenly Jerusalem at the close of the Revelation as the characterizations refer to the portrait at the beginning. The "Paradise of God" recalls the first paradise in which man was placed and from which he was expelled because of his disobedience (Gen. 2:9). The tree of life was the expression of eternal vitality and growth. Man was deprived of it after his sin lest he should combine wickedness with eternal existence. With the advent of the new creation in which the redeemed will share, the tree of life is restored "for the healing of the nations" (Rev. 22:2). Of its fruit the overcomer may partake to the enjoyment of everlasting life.

THE CHURCH OF SMYRNA

The city of Smyrna had a long and honorable history. Founded a millennium before Christ as a Greek colony it was conquered by Asiatic Lydians in the seventh century B.C. and regained its Greek characteristics only in the third century B.C. In the second century B.C. it became an ally of Rome, and from that time it prospered. Since the fifteenth century of our era it has been under Turkish rule; but until recent times it was predominantly a Greek city, with a population professedly Christian.

Because of its excellent harbor Smyrna retained its importance, and it is today a large commercial port, through which the trade to and from the interior of Asia Minor passes.

In appealing to this church, the *character* of Christ that is stressed is in the words, "These things saith the first and the last, who was dead, and lived" (2:8). The word "again" does not really belong in the text. Ramsay suggests that this characterization was peculiarly appropriate as an appeal to Smyrna, because after its early destruction by the Lydians it had ceased to exist as a city, but persisted as an Asiatic village-state. After four centuries "it was restored as an autonomous Greek city, electing its own magistrates and administering its own affairs according to the laws which it made for itself."[3] In a sense Smyrna itself was dead and yet lived. Christ, who lived through death and who now is the firstfruits of the resurrection, addressed Smyrna as one who had suffered the worst that evil can inflict and who has triumphed. He is able, therefore, to speak reassuringly to a church under persecution and threatened with the martyrdom of its members.

The *commendation* of the church at Smyrna is more extensive than any other except that of the Philadelphian church. The Lord declares that He is not unmindful of their plight. He knows their tribulation, their poverty, and the opposition of the Jewish population. The synagogue must have been active in its hatred of Christians, for at the martyrdom of Polycarp in Smyrna the Jews brought fuel on Saturday to burn him.[4] John calls them "[they] that say they are Jews, and they are not, but are a synagogue of Satan" (2:9). For him the true Jew was the one who acknowledged the claims of Christ; the rest were false. The allusion is a good illustration of the clear distinction between Judaism and the church that obtained by the end of the first century.

No *condemnation* is recorded for this church, and consequently the *correction* can more properly be regarded as encouragement. "Fear not" (2:10) is the watchword for Smyrna. The prediction of persecution is accompanied with an application of the character of the Lord to the existing situation: "Be thou faithful unto death, I will give thee the crown of life" (2:10). The persistence of life through the enmities and disasters that bring death is the promise of this letter.

The *challenge* follows the same theme: "He that overcometh shall not be hurt of the second death" (2:11). The victor will be delivered from the peril of destruction which awaits the wicked (21:8).

THE CHURCH OF PERGAMUM

Pergamum had been the center of an independent kingdom for many centuries when it finally became the possession of the Romans in 133 B.C. They made it the official capital of the province of Asia and the seat of the imperial authority. "The first, and for a considerable time, the only Provincial temple of the Imperial cult in Asia was built at Pergamum in honour of Rome and Augustus (29 B.C., probably)."[5] This double concentration of civil and religious authority in Pergamum possibly prompted the statement, "I know where thou dwellest, *even* where Satan's throne is" (2:13). One of the prominent symbols on the coinage of Pergamum was the serpent, the emblem of Asklepios, the god of healing, who was worshiped there.

The devout Christian would regard these things with dread and with loathing, and would shrink from the pagan worship which they symbolized. He would need some weapon by which to cope with them. The *character* of Christ supplies just such a weapon, "the sharp two-edged sword." The sword was a symbol of power by which he could meet the Roman authority, and it was also a symbol of the word of Christ, whose penetrative truth could expose, dissect, and slay all falsehood.

The *commendation* is divided into two parts: "I know where thou dwellest, *even* where Satan's throne is," and, "Thou holdest fast my name, and didst not deny my faith . . . " (2:13). The Lord of the church makes all possible allowances for its handicaps. Social and political pressures against Christians were strong in Pergamum, and had even reached the point of persecution. In opposition to this hostility the Pergamenian Christians had adhered loyally to their confession and had not denied the name of Jesus when faced with the alternative of apostasy or suffering, perhaps death. Apparently there had been at least one martyr, Antipas, who had been executed in Pergamum. The account does not say whether he belonged to the local church, or whether he had been brought to Pergamum for trial from some other part of the province. He represented the spirit and the power of the martyr church that was ready to remain steadfast in the face of death.[6]

The *condemnation* of the church at Pergamum betrays a moral laxity which had crept into it. "The teaching of Balaam" recalls the Old Testament episode of Balaam's attempt to serve God and at the same time to please His enemies.[7] Summoned by Balak, king of Moab, to curse the people of God, he refused because God would not give him permission to do so. When Balak offered him richer rewards, he tried again to see whether God would change His mind. God allowed him to go to Moab, but compelled him to utter blessings instead of curses, with the result that Balaam was embarrassed and that Balak was exasperated. Finally, when he could not curse Israel, he taught Balak how to corrupt them so that they brought the judgment of God upon themselves by their immorality and idolatry. Balaam represents those who foster evil and disobedience to God under a guise of piety.

Evidently this error of Balaam was the chief principle of the sect of the Nicolaitans. Aside from the record in Revelation, little is known of them. Irenaeus, who wrote late in the second century, nearly a hundred years after Revelation, said that they were founded by Nicolaus the proselyte of Antioch mentioned in Acts 6:5, and that they "lived lives of unrestrained indulgence."[8]   Irenaeus attributed to them certain doctrinal vagaries which are not mentioned in the Apocalypse.   It is possible that if the sect survived until this day it might have developed new peculiarities; but the main errors stressed here are eating things sacrificed to idols and committing fornication.   These carry out the practices which entered Israel because of Balaam, and illustrate the peril which Paul sought to avert by his warnings to the church at Corinth (I Cor. 10:7,8).   In a civilization where temples to false gods stood on every street corner and in every public square, in which sexual indulgence was not only condoned but was in many of the cults promoted as an act of worship, the Christians who had been brought up in that environment had a hard time to break away from it completely. The teaching of the Nicolaitans was an exaggeration of the doctrine of Christian liberty which attempted an ethical compromise with heathenism.

Whereas in the Ephesian church the Nicolaitans were known by their *works,* in Pergamum they were known by their *teaching.* Sporadic acts had become settled doctrine; and it is possible that the same group was represented in Thyatira by "the woman Jezebel, who. . . seduceth my servants to commit fornication, and to eat things sacrificed to idols" (Rev. 2:20).   In Ephesus they are outside the church, known by their works; in Smyrna they are still an alien sect, but a few hold their teachings; in Thyatira their doctrines are propagated by a person within the group who is at least tolerated as one of them.

This moral decline of the church is sharply rebuked by the Lord who is keenly aware of the peril.   His *correction,* "Repent therefore; or else I come to thee quickly, and I will make war against them with the sword of my mouth," threatens swift matching of His spiritual authority with false ecclesiastical authority, and the consequent purging of the church.   The sword of His mouth is mentioned again in Revelation 19:15 as the means of His judgment upon the unbelieving nations at large.   It is His word of truth put into action, the direct application to divine righteousness.   The judgment of the world at large will be visited upon the churches if they do not sever themselves from its evils by repentance.

The *challenge* to this church is novel:

> To him that overcometh, to him will I give of the hidden
> manna, and I will give him a white stone, and upon the
> stone a new name written, which no one knoweth but he
> that receiveth it (2:17).

Both promises convey special privileges to the overcomer who
resists successfully the temptations previously condemned. The
"hidden manna" is a reference to the manna which was hidden
in the ark as a symbol of the sustenance which God gave to His
people while they traveled through the wilderness to the promised
land (Exod. 16:4-36). In the discourse on the bread of life
(John 6:48-51) Jesus likened Himself to the manna, saying that
He was the true bread from heaven. In Revelation it means the
spiritual food which is the direct antithesis of the food offered to
idols in which the Nicolaitans indulged freely. To those who refuse the allurements of evil God will give the proper satisfaction
of the good.

The white stone with the new name is harder to interpret, and
there is little agreement among commentators. A comparison
with the promise made to the Philadelphian church (Rev. 3:12)
seemingly implies that the new name is not that of the believer but
of God. A name in ancient times stood for character and power.
For example, Jacob was given his name because he was what
the name implied, a supplanter (Gen. 25:26). The power of a
name is well illustrated by the query of the authorities put to
Peter and John after their healing of the lame man: "By what
power, or in what name, have ye done this?" (Acts 4:7). The
knowledge of the name of God gave its possessor power over all
evil forces and over the demonic world. Probably the white
stone with the new name is the overcomer's assurance that he
can live by the power of God here and that he will be assured
of admission to the heavenly city hereafter.

THE CHURCH OF THYATIRA

The *character* of Christ that is emphasized in His dealing with
the church of Thyatira is penetrative judgment. His eyes like a
flame of fire can see through the flaws of the church; the feet like
burnished bronze are ready to trample her sins underfoot.

In *commendation* He recites the list of her virtues: "thy love
and faith and ministry and patience, and that thy last works are
more than the first" (Rev. 2:19). Thyatira was a church of deep
devotion, perhaps also of an emotional character. Its steady growth

was manifest in that its "last works [were] more than the first" (2:19). Into this church, however, the evils of idolatry had penetrated deeply through some prophetess who advocated openly the same apostasy that had appeared in Pergamum. Jezebel may not have been her actual name, but it describes her action perfectly. Jezebel, the daughter of Ethbaal, king of Tyre, was the wife of Ahab, the king of Israel, who made Baalism the official religion of the northern kingdom and hastened its spiritual decline and fall (I Kings 16:29-33). She was responsible in large measure for the collapse of the nation because of the evils which she introduced.

The *condemnation* of this prophetess by the Lord is full and final. Having given her time to repent of the teaching which she had brought to Thyatira, and having seen no evidence of change in her, He is about to judge her by giving her up completely to the way of life which she had advocated. Her moral dalliance will be her downfall; she and her satellites shall taste its full consequence except they repent. They shall receive the penalty of death, which is the inevitable result of sin; and thus the church will be purged.

The *correction* addressed to the rest in Thyatira is simply repudiation of her teaching. The phrase "none other burden" (Rev. 2:24) is reminiscent of Acts 15:28,29, the decree of the Council of Jerusalem, which said that "no greater burden" would be imposed upon the Gentile churches than abstaining "from things sacrificed to idols, and from blood, and from things strangled, and from fornication." The allusion to the "deep things of Satan" shows that what had been an aberrant teaching in the church at Pergamum had become a mystic cult at Thyatira. Perhaps the emotional nature of the Thyatirans made symbolic feasts and rites peculiarly attractive to them as depths of experience in which they could find satisfaction.

The *challenge* to the church is just the opposite of such degenerate mysticism. Keeping his works unto the end will be rewarded by the authority of rulership and with the assurance of hope: "I will give him the morning star" (2:28). Perhaps it is an attempt to recall the loyal Thyatirans from mysticism to action, and from a morbid desire for secret pleasures to a healthy exercise of spiritual power.

THE CHURCH OF SARDIS

The *character* of Christ stressed for the church of Sardis is His possession of the seven spirits of God and the seven stars, His complete wisdom and His complete control of the leadership of the church.

For this church He has almost no *commendation,* and what there is follows the sharply *condemnatory* statements that come first. "Thou hast a few names in Sardis that did not defile their garments" (3:4) seems to be a grudging admission that a small remnant are worthy, but that the church as a whole has failed. This impression is borne out by the initial statement: "Thou hast a name that thou livest, and thou art dead" (3:1). Its profession is hollow and is on the verge of collapse. Its works are unfinished, unfulfilled before God.

The *correction* is similar to that of the church of Ephesus: "Remember, repent." The threat, "I will come as a thief" (3:3) recalls Jesus' words in His parable of Matthew 24:43,44, in which He warned His disciples that if they did not watch He would come at a moment unforeseen and unpropitious to them. The Pauline development of the same idea in I Thessalonians 5:1-11 affirms that the true Christian will be watching for the return of the Lord. If he is not, he is putting himself into the same class with the unbelieving world. Sardis is the picture of the church that has maintained its profession without possession, and its reputation with no works to support it. It possesses a great tradition, but its present task is unfinished. A few faithful souls are in it, and to them the Lord comes with a *challenge.*

Those that did not defile their garments with the evils and compromising faith of their day shall, He says, "walk with me in white" (3:4). White garments were emblematic of purity and of victory (19:8). The overcomers are to be acknowledged publicly as citizens of the city of God and as the personal friends of its ruler (3:5). Overlooked by their fellowmen, these who have kept their purity of life in obscurity shall at last receive their just recognition.

THE CHURCH OF PHILADELPHIA

The *character* of the speaker and the encouragement of the church are merged into one in the letter to the church at Philadelphia.

These things saith he that is holy, he that is true, he that hath the key of David, he that openeth and none shall shut, and that shutteth and none openeth: I know thy works (behold, I have set before thee a door opened, which none can shut), that thou hast a little power, and didst keep my word, and didst not deny my name (3:7,8).

These words are only an indirect reference to the portrait of chapter 1, since nothing is said there about the key to the house of David. Instead of it, there is an allusion to Christ's possession of the keys of Hades and of death. The direct reference applies to Isaiah 22:22, which was a promise to Eliakim the scribe, one of the courtiers of Hezekiah.

> And the key of the house of David will I lay upon his shoulder; and he shall open, and none shall shut; and he shall shut, and none shall open.

The prophecy related to the replacement of Shebna by Eliakim, who would become the acceptable executive in an imperiled land for restoring hope and security. In similar fashion the Lord Jesus Christ is characterized in this letter as the protector of the church of Philadelphia.

The essence of the *commendation* is a promise in three provisions:

"I have set before thee a door opened, which none can shut" (8)
"I will make them to come and worship before thy feet" (9)
"I also will keep thee from the hour of trial" (10)

The first of these, connected directly with the characterization of the Lord, guarantees the preservation of the opportunity for testimony. Because the Philadelphian church maintained its stand in spite of its feeble strength and refused to deny the name of Christ, He will not allow it to be removed.

The second promises the humiliation of the church's enemies. Perhaps the Jews of Philadelphia had attacked the church violently and had denounced the believers to the civil authorities, as had happened in earlier days in Thessalonica (Acts 17:5-9, I Thess. 2:14-16). As in the letter to Smyrna these Jewish antagonists are called the "synagogue of Satan" (Rev. 2:9), men whose claim to belong to Judaism was falsified by their conduct. The language recalls Jesus' utterance to his opponents in Jerusalem: "If ye were Abraham's children, ye would do the works of Abraham. But now ye seek to kill me, a man that hath told you the truth . . . this did not Abraham" (John 8:39,40).

The third promise is preservation from the hour of trial which is to come upon the entire inhabited world. It predicates universality of judgment for men. The Greek phrase, *tereo ek,* is used elsewhere only in John 17:15, and means to preserve from the attack of evil rather than to remove from it by physical separation.

Aside from the implication of weakness in verse 8 there is no adverse criticism of the church. The injunction of verse 11 repeats that of 2:25: "Hold fast that which thou hast." It can scarcely be called a *correction* because there has been no reproof.

The *challenge* to the church is a promise of security and stability.

> He that overcometh, I will make him a pillar in the temple of my God, and he shall go out thence no more . . . (3:12).

To a church which has felt the insecurity of weakness, the accusations of God's reputed people, and the threat of the hour of trial this promise would indeed be good news. The ultimate reward of its loyalty would be the fulness of divine recognition and approval.

THE CHURCH OF LAODICEA

The last of the seven churches is introduced by Christ in the *character* of "the Amen, the faithful and true witness, the beginning of the creation of God" (3:14). The three epithets are drawn from the Introduction rather than from the portrait. As the Amen, Christ is essential truth: "I am the way, and the truth . . ." (John 14:6). Isaiah speaks of the God of the Amen (Isa. 65:16), who seals the veracity of His message with His own character. As the faithful and true witness (Rev. 1:5, 3:14) Christ bears unbiased testimony to the lax state of His own church. He cannot be bribed or cajoled into altering His verdict. As "the beginning of the creation of God" (Rev. 3:14) "he is before all things, and in him all things consist" (Col. 1:17). In Him is the eternal unalterable standard by which institutions and men must be measured.

As He surveys the Laodicean church He sees nothing in it worthy of *commendation*. Viewed externally, it must have been prosperous and powerful. Its treasury was well filled in contrast to the poverty of Smyrna (Rev. 2:9) and to the weakness of Philadelphia (3:8). *Condemnation* is laid upon it because of its smug complacency and because of its lukewarm allegiance. It had not apostatized from the faith into an icy opposition, nor had it become inflamed with heretical zeal. It was drifting, not driving. Consequently the Lord threatened it with complete rejection: "I will spew thee out of my mouth" (3:16).

In addition to its indifference it is ignorant: "[Thou] knowest not that thou art the wretched one . . . " (3:17). The church did not even realize its own state, but assumed that outward prosperity was synonymous with spiritual success. To be "miserable and poor and blind and naked" means beggary; and the Lord was telling the proud and wealthy church that it really was a spiritual pauper.

The *correction* that He commanded showed that there was hope for the church.

> I counsel thee to buy of me gold refined by fire, that thou mayest become rich; and white garments, that thou mayest clothe thyself . . . ; and eyesalve to anoint thine eyes, that thou mayest see (3:18).

Three things were needed by the Laodicean church: gold, clothing, and eyesalve. They represent the true values of life, the true righteousness of Christ, and the vision which brings spiritual understanding.

Gold is an emblem of faith. I Peter 1:7 speaks of "the proof of your faith, *being* more precious than gold which perisheth though it is proved by fire, may be found unto praise and glory and honor at the revelation of Jesus Christ." White garments are figurative of a triumphant righteousness: "the fine linen is the righteous acts of the saints" (19:8). Eyesalve is the corrective that restores vision to eyes diseased or bleared. Faith, righteousness, and vision were the three great lacks of this church.

The nineteenth and twentieth verses of the third chapter are a special plea to the Laodicean church. Nothing exactly like them appears in the other six letters. They may be intended as a summary appeal, climaxing the entire series; but their location before the closing *challenge* of the seventh letter makes them a part of the address to the Laodiceans. As in the other letters, they call for repentance, but they add two new concepts. The first is the love of Christ: "As many as I love, I reprove and chasten" (3:19). Even the lukewarm church of Laodicea is the object of His unfailing love. The second is His immediacy: "Behold, I stand at the door and knock" (3:20). A literal translation would be: "See! I have taken my stand upon your threshold, and I am continually knocking!" He awaits the open door, in order that He may enter. Not only will He take what the tenant of the house can offer Him ("eat with him"), but He will share with that tenant all of the resources that He brings ("eat with me"). Christ outside the door of His own church seems to be an incongruous concept; yet that is exactly what this text implies.

The *challenge,* "He that overcometh, I will give to him to sit down with me in my throne," (3:21), is a curious contrast to the indictment of this church. From poverty to plenitude, from rags to riches, and from the depression of blindness to the altitude of the throne's vision is what the Lord promises to the faithful and obedient overcomer.

The letters to the seven churches close the section of Revelation that relates to the immediate present of the author. To what extent they forecast the development of the historic church may be debatable. The probability that they have a meaning for the church of all time is enhanced by one prominent factor: the increasing imminence of the Lord's coming is reflected in His utterances of correction to these churches.

Ephesus:	"... or else I come to thee, and will move thy candlestick ...." (2:5)
Smyrna:	(None)
Pergamum:	"... or else I come to thee quickly ...." (2:16)
Thyatira:	"Hold fast till I come ...." (2:25)
Sardis:	"... I will come as a thief, and thou shalt not know what hour I will come upon thee." (3:3)
Philadelphia:	"I come quickly." (3:11)
Laodicea:	"I stand at the door and knock." (3:20)

To Ephesus and Pergamum the coming is an alternative, "or else I come"; to Philadelphia it is unconditional, "I come quickly." To Ephesus it is a rather remote contingency; to Laodicea He is present on the threshold. In keeping with the theme of Revelation, "Behold, he cometh with the clouds ..." (1:7), the vision of the seven letters is built around the concept of His coming and of the effect which that coming will have upon the churches. Each representative church is being judged by the living Lord in anticipation of that climax, and the correctives that He seeks to apply are preparatory for His elevation of the church to His side on the throne.

Although the letters are addressed to the leaders of the churches, and hence, presumably, to their congregations, the final challenge is invariably individual. Not "they that overcome" but "he that overcometh" is to be the recipient of reward and blessing. The churches may have sinned as bodies; the repentance must be individual in each member. In the last appeal to Laodicea, the darkest and most hopeless of the churches, He says, "If any man hear my voice and open the door, I will come in" (3:20). The door is not to be opened by unanimous vote, but by one repentant individual. Renewal of fellowship and of power may come to the many through the action of the few, or, perchance, of one.

The coupling of the *character* of Christ, revealed in these seven letters as that character applies to the several needs of the churches, with the challenge to the overcomer which holds out the promise of some aspect of ultimate triumph unifies the churches of all kinds and of all time around Christ's person and kingdom. In Him the churches find both their Head and their future.

CHAPTER VI

VISION II: THE PROCESS OF WORLD JUDGMENT

REVELATION 4:1-16:21

The opening of the fourth chapter of Revelation introduces the second vision describing the process of world judgment. It initiates a second division in the structure of the book which can be established by three criteria: a change of scene, a change of time, and the recurrence of the phrase, "in the Spirit." The change of scene transferred the seer from earth to heaven as the voice of the heavenly summons said, "Come up hither" (4:1). The time of the vision projected him into the future, contrasting with the vision of the churches, which was contemporary with him. The new disclosure concerned explicitly "the things which shall come to pass hereafter." The phrase "in the Spirit" again indicated that a different experience or scene had begun, separating the context that follows from that which precedes, and opening a new unit of the apocalyptic panorama.

The content of the unit embraces all of the text as far as the end of the sixteenth chapter. "In the Spirit" is repeated in 17:3, making 17:1-3 the *terminus ad quem* of the vision under discussion. The termini, however, are not the only clues to its boundaries, for there are at least two pervasive elements that bind it together. The first is the centrality of the throne in heaven, which appears all through the text. Commencing with Revelation 4:2, where it is the most important object that meets the eye of the seer, and continuing to 16:17, where it becomes the source of the pronouncement of judgment, it is the origin of all rule and power, and is the point of reference in relation to which the scenes and the action of Revelation are located.

The second is the figure of Christ, which will be discussed more fully under another heading. In this section He is the "Lamb slain" (5:6), with seven horns and seven eyes, representing the perfection of power and of discernment. His activity of administrative judgment is based upon a redemption already achieved through His death and resurrection, and the judgments that He enacts or permits are to be viewed in the light of that redemption.

In the structure of the section, chapters 4 and 5 are descriptive of the scene in heaven which underlies the process of judgment. Chapters 6 and 7 continue the activity with the breaking of the seven seals, which are immediately followed by the sounding of the trumpets in chapters 8 through 11. The sequence of these two series is uninterrupted, and they maintain a positive connection with chapters 4 and 5, which introduce the total picture.

Chapters 12 through 16 contain "signs." The last "sign" of the angels having the seven plagues (chs. 15,16) constitutes in itself another series of judgments somewhat parallel in character to the judgments of the seven trumpets. They are climactic, for "in them is finished the wrath of God" (15:1). The entire passage on the "signs" seems to be a detailed study of the culmination of judgment taking place at the end of the present era.

This literary structure presents a chronological problem of interpretation. Are the series of sevens — seals, trumpets, and bowls — successive in the sense that each is an enlargement of the seventh item in the preceding series? Are they partially concurrent, each having a narrower scope than the one preceding? Are they simultaneous, being different aspects of the same judgments or of the same period?

The last of these alternatives seems improbable because of the difference in the items that compose them. There is a greater affinity between the judgments of the trumpets and of the bowls than between either of these and the judgment of the seals. Furthermore, the statement of verses 1 and 2 of chapter 8 shows that the series of seals and of trumpets are related by sequence:

> And when he opened the seventh seal, there followed a silence in heaven about the space of half an hour. And I saw the seven angels that stand before God; and there were given unto them seven trumpets (8:1, 2).

The vision of the angels with the trumpets follows the seals directly, and conveys the impression that the seals and the trumpets are successive. The judgments of the trumpets are more specific, more cataclysmic, and more concrete than those of the seals. They deal less with trends or principles and more with material phenomena. They can more easily be compressed into a narrow interval of time than can the seals. The latter deal with broad principles of judgment such as war, economic stringency, and pestilence, which cannot be restricted to any one era of human history, though they may prevail in the last days.

If these first two series be interpreted as successive, they must fill some particular span of time unless, of course, one regards Revelation as completely timeless in its structure, either because it relates only to the present in which the writer and his readers lived, or else because it is purely a symbolic description of the conflict of principles. Neither of these alternatives is perfectly satisfactory. The opening words of the section, "the things which must come to pass hereafter" (4:1) demand some distinction between the temporal present and the temporal future, and assume that there are definite future events which the book is describing, even though figuratively. Again, the close connection of these judgments with the earth and with what goes on in it compels a more concrete explanation of them than an abstract idealism will afford. The seals and the trumpets must be taken as covering a definite period of history.

Whether that period is exclusively future to us, or whether it covers the era of the church age beginning with the end of the first century may be debatable. "Hereafter," literally "after these things" (Greek: *meta tauta*), means after the epoch of the churches described in Vision I. The churches, however, were existent in the writer's own day, so that the "things hereafter" could well begin with the years immediately following the first century and could continue until the coming of the Lord. To postpone the "hereafter" until the events following the days of the reader means that the events of Revelation would always belong to the indefinite future. Somewhere a line must be drawn for the "now" before which are ranged "the things which thou sawest" (1:19) and after which are placed "the things to come." The opening of the fourth chapter marks the point at which the seer received his call to "come up hither" and witness the second vision.

Within the structure of the successive sevens mentioned above are one or two phenomena of lesser importance, but nevertheless worth noting. In each of the sevens the first four episodes are more closely related to each other than they are to the remaining three of the series. The first four seals reveal four horsemen, all of one class of being and representing one general type of judgment. The first four trumpets depict judgments on nature, while the fifth, sixth and seventh are quite different in character. Similarly the first four bowls are concerned with terrestrial judgments, while the last three differ in nature.

Between the sixth and seventh items of each series there is a long or short pause filled with parenthetical visions. After the judgment of the sixth seal comes the sealing of the 144,000 of the tribes of Israel and the appearance of the great unnumbered multitude in heaven. Between the sixth and seventh trumpets intervenes the appearance of the angel with the little book and the two witnesses (chs. 10, 11). The sixth bowl judgment is followed by the appearance of the three unclean spirits like frogs. The explanatory or illustrative visions generally precede the seventh and final judgment in each series.

Two or three general principles aid one in disentangling the strange sequence of symbols in these chapters.

First is the principle that although the language may be figurative, the general order of succession, apart from parentheses and recapitulation, represents a real order of events. However much expositors may differ, for instance, concerning the identity or meaning of the four horsemen in the first four seals, the author intended that they should be understood as following each other in the order that he gave.

Secondly, the unity of a section should depend upon its central concept rather than upon uniformity of events. In the second vision the unity depends upon the Lamb and the throne rather than upon the smooth recital of the episodes as they occur.

Third, temporal sequence must be determined by cross-references within the context, since the Revelation itself does not contain a dated table of contents or schedule of events. When the great uncounted multitude is said to have come out of "the great tribulation," the statement implies that the tribulation must have begun. Obviously the group could not have come out of it if they had not been in it. The events narrated in the section of which the parenthesis of chapter 7 is a part must relate to the great tribulation, or describe it. The dividing points of these eras are not always marked out with mathematical precision, but in most cases a satisfactory approximation can be reached.

With these considerations in mind one may approach the initial interpretation of the vision. The opening stage concerns the transition of the seer to heaven from earth. It involves a tremendous change of perspective. Instead of viewing events from the standpoint of terrestrial relations he sees them in symbol from a heavenly viewpoint. No longer is he confined to specific geographical locations, as in the letters to the churches. The phe-

nomena recorded in the symbols transcend geography, or, if they
do occur in conjunction with the earthly scheme of things, they do
so as part of a cosmic plan.

The scene in heaven presents the throne of God with its inde-
scribable Occupant.　Little is said of His declared will or of
His action; but His presence declares unmistakably His sovereignty.　Behind all the action of the Apocalypse, planning,
regulating, and directing toward the ultimate goal is the person
of the Eternal God.　The forces of evil in this tremendous drama
are not illusory, nor are they merely the puppets with which He
plays.　Nevertheless, He controls them, and in final victory
brings the trimph of the good.

The person of Christ as the Lamb is prominent in all of the
action.　First of all, He takes the book from the right hand of
Him that sat on the throne, thereby indicating His right to
administer the judgments.　At the opening of each seal, the
punitive forces that are released produce successive waves of
judgment that lead up to the ultimate climax.　The sixth seal,
bringing disturbances in the physical world, is identified by
the cry of the inhabitants of earth who fled for refuge to the
caves and the rocks: "The great day of their wrath is come;
and who is able to stand?" (6:17)

If the trumpets and the bowls are to be subsumed under the
seventh seal, or between the sixth and the seventh, then "the
great tribulation" begins with the sixth seal.　The "sealing" of
the seventh chapter and the appearance of the great multitude
before the throne may well indicate the protection of the remnant
of Israel and the universal removal of believers before the horrors
of this final period close in upon humanity.　The latter group
are taken "out of every nation and of all tribes and peoples and
tongues" (7:9).　They stand before the throne of God arrayed
in white robes, and bearing the palms which were emblematic
of triumph.　Their occupation is service, and their destination
is Paradise.

The series of seven trumpets comprises judgments more spec-
tacular and more concentrated than those of the seals.　The seals
are general, and are an introduction to supernatural judgment
rather than the direct manifestation of it.　The trumpets are
specific, drastic, and final.　So strange are they that there has
been a grave question as to whether they should be taken literally
or not.　If they are to be understood literally, it is hard to
comprehend how any life on the earth could survive their ter-

rible onslaught.   If they are to be regarded as figurative, the criteria of interpretation are not clear at all.   What, for instance, would "trees" and "grass" (8:7) represent?   If, as Mauro argues,[1] "Trees are a familiar figure in Scripture for human greatness, for persons of eminence (Judg. 9:8-13; Jer. 7:20; 17:8; Ezek. 31:3; Dan. 4:20-22)," one might also say that "grass" represents the masses (Isa. 40:7).   The symbolic use of "trees" and "grass" in the passages cited is undeniable; but must that symbolism be used in Revelation?   If so, it must extend to all the trumpets if it is to be consistent; and the judgments which professedly affect the world of nature become really judgments on the world of men.

Such procedure is not always safe, because the chance resemblance of terms may inject into the text a meaning which was unintended by the author.   Allowance must be made for the fact that the seer was attempting to describe in ordinary similes events which had no precedent, and which consequently had no adequate terminology for stating them.   Perhaps it is safer to say that these trumpets are actual physical judgments which seem improbable because they have no antecedents in human experience.   The advent of the atomic age, in which the fusion and disintegration of elements have demonstrated the existence of enormous destructive forces resident in ordinary matter and their deadly effect when used on a small scale, makes the idea of a cataclysmic divine intervention in the course of the physical world seem less improbable.

The first four trumpet judgments on the earth are physical in character; the last three are produced by spiritual forces.   The fifth brings an irruption of demonic beings from the abyss under a leader called Apollyon, "the destroyer," whose function is to torment men who have not the seal of God in their foreheads. This judgment must, then, follow the sealing of the servants of God (7:3).   The demons do not engage in united conquest, but behave as pests, for they are likened to locusts and to scorpions. The description of them fits the appearance of a locust, if it were as large as a horse.   These loathsome creatures, limitless in number and apparently invulnerable to any attack, are given power to torment men for five months.   They are really an invasion from another world of malicious embodied spirits whose mission is destruction.

The sixth trumpet (9:13-21) releases the angels that were bound at the river Euphrates, and lets loose a great army of horsemen who attack the world and slaughter its inhabitants. Perhaps the basic concept of this plague came from the menace of the Parthians, who lived east and north of the Euphrates, and who were a potential threat to the peace of Rome during the second half of the first century. In a broader sense the Euphrates was for the empire the boundary between the East and the West, the frontier which the West always had to defend against possible invasion from the warlike hordes that thronged on its border. A second reference to the Euphrates in Revelation 16:12 confirms the idea that the prediction relates to a mass gathering of Oriental peoples by demonic influences against the people of God and the rule of Christ (16:14). The language seems to mingle the elements of the human and the demonic, the natural and the supernatural, in such a way as to make them almost indistinguishable.

The seventh trumpet (10:7, 11:15-19) brings the consummation of the judgments, marking plainly the establishment of the kingdom of God over all lesser dominions in this world. With this announcement of the outward visible divine rulership in the affairs of the nations, the visitation of divine wrath, the judgment of the dead, the reward of God's servants, and the destruction of the wicked, the period of tribulation comes to a conclusion.

The structure of chapters 12 through 16 sets them apart as a detailed treatment of certain aspects of the judgments in this period of final tribulation. They are built around the "signs" which are mainly three: the woman clothed with the sun and with the moon under her feet (12:1); the great red dragon (12:3); and the final judgments of the bowls (15:1). The continuity of the text in this passage shows that it is a detailed presentation of the period generally elaborated under the trumpets. These aspects are centered on a conflict between the totalitarian worship of the dragon and the first beast, and the complete loyalty of the servants of God. The worship of the beast is compulsory, being imposed upon the world by conquest (13:7), by propaganda (13:12), by lying miracles (13:13-15), and by social and economic pressure (13:16-17). This coercion constitutes the last great attempt to unify all religions under one general system with a powerful, visible, personal object of worship who is also the head of the state and in whose hands rests the power of life and death over his subjects. The result is the acme of all dictatorships, uniting politics, commerce, social institutions, and cults in one.

In the days when the Apocalypse was written the Roman empire served as the model for this concept. Its dominion extended to the bounds of the civilized western world, and its authority was unquestioned. Ramsay shows[2] that the worship of the state was promoted by the provincial authorities in much the same way that the "beast out of the earth" promoted the worship of the "beast out of the sea." Ramsay is right in presupposing a definite connection between the trends of society in the first century and the content of Revelation; but the fulfilment of this text can hardly be restricted to the rule of the Flavians. The judgments of the sixteenth chapter are yet unfulfilled, and the actual dominion of Christ on the earth is not yet visible. The historical conditions of the Roman empire in the first century may provide the setting for Revelation and the initial medium for understanding it, but they do not exhaust its meaning nor cover its fulfilment completely. The characteristics of totalitarianism do not change, and it would be small wonder if the last great united rebellion against God under the leadership of a powerful and astute antichrist did not duplicate on a larger scale the iron rule of Rome.

Within the section which portrays the last days in such vivid colors is a new chronological element not previously introduced. Described variously as "a thousand two hundred and threescore days" (12:6), "a time, and times, and half a time" (12:14), "forty and two months" (13:5), it measures the span of the last organized conflict of the people of God with the forces of antichrist. It is the period in which the woman is persecuted by the dragon, and in which the beast out of the sea maintains his authority over the earth. There is nothing to indicate that this period must be taken figuratively; for it has a definite ending with the overthrow of the beast and the false prophet (19:19-21), and by logic the opening of the period should be no less definite.

The period is climactic. The two beasts embody the fulness of political, social, and economic power, which is bent toward the extermination of the believers in Christ and toward the worship of the beast, the incarnation of evil. Constant attacks upon the people of God (12:17) ending in certain martyrdom for all who do not worship the beast (13:15) are predicted. The preservation of some is indicated by the protection of the woman, who is sheltered in the wilderness. For the believers who endure persecution it will be a supreme proof of patience (13:10; 14:12), for they will have to endure tremendous suffering before they see the vindication of their cause in the triumph of Christ.

The "parenthetical" material of chapter 14 consists of a series of short visions which are really commentaries on the various aspects of the main action of the book. They are not intended to describe a series of actions in chronological order, but are glimpses of various phases of the conflict.

The first (14:1-5) is the vision of the 144,000 who were "purchased from among men." They have the names of the Lamb and of the Father written on their foreheads in contrast to those who carry the mark of the beast (13:16); they are located before the throne of God; they are undefiled, without guile, and they accompany the Lamb constantly. If they are identical with the 144,000 mentioned in chapter 7 they may represent Jewish believers who have kept their purity of worship and who have come to know the Messiah through great suffering. The fact that they are "before the throne" (14:3) implies removal from the earthly scene whether by martyrdom or by translation. If they can be identified with the "man child" who was "caught up unto God and unto his throne" (12:5), they are a select group of believers, born in tribulation, and separated from the general body of the people of God by their peculiar faith and piety.

The second glimpse of the period indicates that the final testing and conflict have brought also opportunity for witness. The angel with the eternal gospel (14:6-7) proclaims a message that is universal and that is still valid even in judgment. He asserts that his message is all the more imperative because the hour of judgment has come. Even until the last hour the door of faith is still open.

The proclamation of the eternal gospel is immediately followed by the announcement of the fall of Babylon (14:8), which anticipates the judgment on the city described in chapters 17 and 18. Up to this point nothing has been said about Babylon, and the meaning of the word cannot be defined by any reference in the previous context. One must conclude that the seer is assuming either that it will be defined later, and that the reader will then think back to this allusion for placing the vision, or else he takes for granted that his reader recognizes the symbolism because he has met it in other sources.

Babylon from time immemorial had been the enemy of godliness. The city was founded in rebellion against God, and its greatest period of prosperity under Nebuchadnezzar was marked by the zenith of Gentile pride (Dan. 4:30). Babylon was the constant emblem of high intellectual and commercial civilization and of the mandatory worship of the ruler who represented the state (Dan. 3:1-4). It was the implacable foe of the people of God, under whom they went into captivity. By the first century after Christ Babylon had long ceased to be a world power, but the spirit and domain of Babylon had passed to Rome. The description of Babylon as the harlot, sitting on seven mountains (17:9), reminds one sharply of Rome which occupied seven hills on the Tiber; but the symbolism of chapters 17 and 18 which must interpret this cryptic allusion in chapter 14 transcends the immediate empire of Rome. It stands for the entire world system of man's rulership, the acme of a prosperous but faithless culture. The end time will bring it to its fall, and will supplant it with the kingdom of Christ.

Parallel to the proclamation of opportunity in the everlasting gospel is the proclamation of warning by the third angel (14:9-12). The worshipers of the beast are irrevocably doomed, and will be consigned to everlasting punishment. A clear line of division is drawn on the basis of worship: those who worship the beast (14:11), and those that worship God (14:7). The primary emphasis of Revelation is on this point (19:10, 22:9). God alone is worthy of worship, and any lesser worship is an insult to Him.

The beatitude of 14:13 is really a footnote comment on the dead who pass out of the strife into the presence of God. It has only indirect bearing on the sequence of the action.

The vision of the Son of Man on a white cloud (14:14-16) and the vision of the angel coming out of the temple (14:17-20) are parallel, for both relate to the final harvest of earth. The Son of Man reaps the harvest that belongs to Him; the angel reaps the vine of the earth, the final fruition of evil. In both cases, good and evil are the products of gradual growth. Both have grown until the harvest, and both are terminated by a crisis. The same general figure of speech occurs in the parables of Jesus, who spoke of sowing seed and of reaping the results (Matt. 13:1-43).

The final crisis to which these several parenthetical warning visions point is presented by the climactic judgments of the bowls, "which are the last, for in them is finished the wrath of God"

(Rev. 15:1). The execution of this judgment is preceded by the vision of "them that come off victorious from the beast, and from his image, and from the number of his name" (15:2). They are already in the presence of God, where they praise Him in "the song of Moses the servant of God, and the song of the Lamb" (15:3). Whether they are the martyred dead whose spirits live before God, or whether they are a translated group is not stated. One thing is noticeable: the concluding retribution does not fall until they have been removed from the scene. They may experience the wrath of the devil (12:12) and the persecution of the beast (13:15), but they do not experience the wrath of God.

The seven bowls (chs. 15,16) are a closely knit series following each other in rapid succession. They parallel the trumpets in their spheres of action, but they are more intense. The references to the beast (16:2,10,13) synchronize them with the time of the end, and show that they are at its very terminal. The seventh marks the conclusion of man's present regime: the collapse of the cities of the nation, the fall of Babylon, and the shaking of the entire earth.

Neither at the end of the seals (8:1) or of the trumpets (11:15-19) nor at the end of these bowls is the consummation of judgment described in any detail. It is announced, but its nature and procedure are not given. Each of these series leads up to the point where the reader expects God to assert Himself and to establish the kingdom; but the kingdom does not appear. The section is not complete; it prepares for the end but does not explain it.

The three series are parallel in some respects and not in others. All of them have an identical terminus. The sixth seal says, "the great day of their wrath is come, and who is able to stand?" (6:17). The text that follows shows that the seventh seal introduces the last period of time. The seventh trumpet is accompanied by the voices which say:

> The kingdom of the world is become *the kingdom* of our Lord, and of his Christ: and he shall reign for ever and ever,

to which the elders reply:

> . . . thy wrath came, and the time of the dead to be judged, and *the time* to give their reward to thy servants the prophets, and to the saints, and to them that fear thy name, the small and the great; and to destroy them that destroy the earth. (11:15,18)

Perhaps these series cover three differing but partially synchronous periods. The seals express the historical principles or trends that bring judgment upon the world; the trumpets are the judgments that introduce and effect the acute distress of the end; and the bowls are the intense climactic judgments that close it. Thus the structure of Revelation covers in broad review the entire period between the Lord's assumption of the prerogatives of dominion and judgment (5:5-14) down to the end of earth's story.

CHAPTER VII

VISION III: THE CLIMAX OF JUDGMENT

REVELATION 17:1-21:8

The third vision of Revelation covers a smaller span of time than the second vision and is more definite in its sequence of events, with fewer digressions from the main line of thought. The introduction to this part parallels the scheme of the preceding two. It resembles even more closely the last vision of the book with which it can be balanced and contrasted. Both of these visions have their setting on the earth, one in a wilderness (17:3), the other in a high mountain (21:10); both involve the ministration of one of the angels having the seven last plagues (17:1, 21:9); each presents the symbolic figure of a woman, a harlot (17:3), and a bride (21:9). In the former, the forces of evil are dominant; the latter is the full manifestation of the glory of God. The two visions are symbolic of the dual aspect of consummation: the destruction of evil and the glorification of good.

The figure of the great harlot occupies both chapters 17 and 18, with a transitional passage following in 19:1-10. The identity of the woman is clearly stated: "The woman whom thou sawest is the great city, which reigneth over the kings of the earth" (17:18). The interpretation that applies this passage to Rome has already been noted.[1] A seeming confirmation may be found in 17:9: "Here is the mind that hath wisdom. The seven heads are seven mountains on which the woman sitteth." Rome was built on seven hills, and has been known as "the seven-hilled city."

To say that Rome is the final interpretation of this symbolism would not do justice to the text. The great harlot represents more than one city and more than one era of history. The name assigned to her, "Babylon," might have been a figure of speech concealing the real object of the seer's denunciations; but to the reader it would convey the sum total of pagan culture, social, intellectual, and commercial, that had opposed and oppressed the people of God from time immemorial. Babylon grew from the first settlements in the Mesopotamian valley after the flood (Gen. 10:10), and was the seat of the civilization that expressed organized hostility to God. The ambition of its inhabitants, "Come, let us build us a city, and a tower, whose top *may reach* unto heaven, and let us make us a name; lest we be scattered abroad upon the face of the whole earth" (Gen. 11:4), shows the latent elements of self-sufficiency and pride which appeared later in Nebuchadnezzar's ill-timed boast:

> Is not this great Babylon, which I have built for the royal dwelling-place, by the might of my power and for the glory of my majesty? (Dan. 4:30).

The city of Babylon did not rise to world rulership until the eighth century B.C., when under Nebuchadnezzar and his successors it conquered Assyria and Egypt and assumed the overlordship of the Near East. As the successor of these two great nations it became the chief enemy and oppressor of Judah. The Babylonian soldiers ultimately captured Jerusalem and deported the upper classes of Judah into captivity. The brutality of the heathen armies and the long years of exile left an ineffaceable memory among the Jewish people. Babylon, to them, was the essence of all evil, the embodiment of cruelty, the foe of God's people, and the lasting type of sin, carnality, lust, and greed. The prophets predicted its collapse, which was fulfilled in the days of Daniel when the Medo-Persians captured and plundered the city. From that time to the present day Babylon has declined in power, until now it is only a heap of ruins in a desert waste.

All of this background enters into the use of the term in Revelation. The writer of the book was himself Jewish; he used constantly the Jewish scriptures, and his readers were familiar with them also. Any allusion to Babylon would instantly recall to them the historical significance of the city that had been both the chief glory and the chief shame of heathenism.

The application of the term in Revelation cannot, however, be restricted to the literal Babylon of history, nor even to its counterpart, Rome. The judgment of Babylon depicted here is closely connected with the destruction of the beast and of his kingdom, and that has not yet taken place. Even if a symbolic meaning for Babylon be accepted, the materialism and godlessness for which it stood have not yet disappeared from the earth, nor have they been judged. The term seems to include more than any one city or civilization, though the actual city of Babylon, and perhaps Rome also, were the best examples of it in their day.

Some of the symbolism of this passage is explained in the text, either directly, or by association with the Old Testament. The

frequently recurring allusion to harlotry (17:1,2,4,15,16; 18:3,7)
is an echo of the Old Testament prophets, who used the term to
describe the infidelity of man to God, especially in connection with
idolatry. The first chapter of Isaiah denounced Jerusalem as "the
faithful city become a harlot" (1:21). Jeremiah condemned Jerusalem in almost the same words: "under every green tree thou
didst bow thyself, playing the harlot" (2:20), and the figure was
applied later both to Israel and to Judah in his prophecy (Jer. 3).
Ezekiel, in similar fashion, drew the portrait of the sisters, Oholah
and Oholibah, representing Israel and Judah, who from the beginning of national existence in Egypt had been defiled with the idol-
atries and evils of the nations around them (Ezek. 23). In similar fashion the predominance of lust and sensual pleasure, the
willingness to barter righteousness for commercial advantages, the
love of luxury irrespective of its moral cost, are the characteristics
of Babylon.

The beast of Revelation 17 is identical with the first beast of
chapter 13, the head and personification of godless authority, supported by a diabolical supernaturalism. He is "the beast that . . .
was, and is not; and is about . . . to go into perdition" (17:8).
Three times this same idea is used concerning him (13:14; 17:8,
11), as if to emphasize in the mind of the reader that the beast existed, ceased to exist, and then reappeared stronger than ever. It
is a direct contrast to the Alpha and Omega, "who is, and who
was and who is to come" (1:8), and is at the same time a parody
of His death, burial, and resurrection. The beast is the dominating figure of earth's last empire, in which man-made evil rises
to its greatest ascendancy and then collapses under the judgment
of God.

The "seven heads," explained as "seven mountains," are called
expressly "seven kings: the five are fallen, the one is, and the
other is not yet come; and when he cometh, he must continue a
little while. And the beast . . . is himself also an eighth, and is
of the seven; and he goeth into perdition" (17:10,11). The explanation seems to indicate seven successive rulers, of whom one
will ultimately reappear as the beast. Various attempts have been
made to identify these with world empires or with the emperors
of Rome prior to the time of the writing of the Apocalypse. None
is completely successful; for there had not been five complete world
empires which had fallen prior to the writing of Revelation, nor
can these kings be identified certainly with the line of emperors
beginning with Augustus. The latter possibility might be plausible,

were it not for the allusion to the ten kings (17:12) who played no part in the empire of John's day, and who have not yet appeared on the stage of history. Their dating is determined by the statement, "These shall war against the Lamb, and the Lamb shall overcome them, for he is Lord of lords and King of kings" (17:14). The overcoming is placed by Revelation 19:19 at the end of the age; and since the age has not yet ended, the fulfilment of the prediction is still future.

The "waters" on which the harlot sat are "peoples, and multitudes, and nations and tongues" (17:15). The social, cultural, and commercial sway of the Babylonian system will dominate all civilization that is not committed definitely to God. It will be a thoroughly integrated system, cherished by all who profit from it, but at the same time hated for its restraints. A curious paradox occurs in these two chapters, illustrated by the following verses:

> The ten horns which thou sawest [the ten kings], and the beast, these shall hate the harlot, and shall make her desolate and naked, and shall eat her flesh, and shall burn her utterly with fire (17:16).
> The kings of the earth, who committed fornication and lived wantonly with her, shall weep and wail over her, when they look upon the smoke of her burning (18:9).

Why should the kings both hate her and then bewail her fate at their hands? Perhaps the explanation lies in the difference between religious and commercial Babylon. The secular spirit rebels against the corruption of even a decadent religious authority, while it mourns the loss of commercial and social advantages.

The eighteenth chapter deals at some length with the overthrow of Babylon. The dual viewpoint of heaven and earth is adequately represented. The announcing angel states that judgment has fallen, and that the people of God are called to separate themselves from Babylon that they may not partake of her sins (18:4,8). In contrast, the kings of the earth mourn Babylon's fall because the destruction of that system deprived them of their luxuries and delights. Babylon is godless, materialistic, and immoral; her culture originated in disobedience to God, and she is doomed. The building of a civilization pleasing to God must begin with a new life, the genius of which is expressed in the figure of the city of God, appearing in the next section of Revelation.

The literal existence of a city of Babylon in the last days, embodying all the features mentioned in this passage has been discussed at length by various expositors.[2] At least one argument can be mustered in its favor: the mourning over the burning of the city seems to preclude the restriction of interpretation to an ideal city of civilization. Babylon is the symbol and epitome of a pagan culture, but it may also be a very real place. Perhaps the latter days will see the construction of a great world metropolis, the seat of final world empire and the summation of all that the ingenuity of man can devise. If so, Babylon is yet to come in its final manifestation.

The objection to this hypothesis is grounded in the prophecy of Isaiah:

> And Babylon, the glory of kingdoms, the beauty of the Chaldeans' pride, shall be as when God overthrew Sodom and Gomorrah. It shall never be inhabited, neither shall it be dwelt in from generation to generation: neither shall the Arabian pitch tent there; neither shall shepherds make their flocks to lie down there. But wild beasts of the desert shall lie there, and their houses shall be full of doleful creatures; and ostriches shall dwell there, and wild goats shall dance there. And wolves shall cry in their castles, and jackals in the pleasant palaces; and her time is near to come, and her days shall not be prolonged. (Isa. 13:19-22)

For centuries Babylon has been uninhabited and the prediction of Isaiah has been literally fulfilled. A rebuilding of the city would thus violate the statement that "it shall never be inhabited." In that case, the prophecy of Isaiah applies (1) to the Babylon yet to come, or (2) the Babylon of the Apocalypse is the figurative application of the name to a totally different city, or (3) the use of the term in Revelation applies to a system or civilization rather than to any specific geographical center.

To the world of the first century Babylon was only a name; and it is very doubtful whether the Christians of that time would have regarded it as a serious menace to their material peace. Rome, however, was a major threat, for the imperial policy of tolerance might change at any moment, bringing the social and economic forces of the empire into sudden conflict with the Christians. If they applied the figure of Babylon to their existing situation, they could in measure call it fulfilment, but it would not be the exhaustive or final fulfilment.

The finality of the doom of Babylon is declared unmistakably in the closing words of the eighteenth chapter. Six times the phrase "no more at all" (Rev. 18:21-23) recurs in these verses. Just as the city of Isaiah's day was never to be inhabited again, so the city or system of the world will pass away.

The double view of the fall of Babylon appears in the conduct of the kings and merchants of the earth as contrasted with the injunction of the angel of judgment. The kings and merchants mourn because their luxury and power have been destroyed, and thus their hope of a civilization of complete comfort has vanished. Babylon, their earthly and sensual paradise, has been destroyed, and they are left inconsolable. On the other hand, the angel bids the people of God to rejoice, because God has finally avenged the blood of His people on their chief enemy. Guilty of the blood of prophets and saints, she has at last perished. The removal of Babylon thus makes way for the city of God, the civilization that God produces through regeneration.

Another aspect of the last act of the drama of redemption is the chorus of rejoicing (19:1-10). In the chronology of Revelation there is a close connection between this interlude and the preceding section on Babylon, for the first chorus announces that God "hath judged the great harlot, her that corrupted the earth with her fornication" (19:1,2). Insofar as it deals with action, it implies a time after the fall of Babylon. This short section of text renews the setting of the original heavenly scene, for it is placed "in heaven" (19:1), and the four and twenty elders, the four living creatures, and the throne are all mentioned again. The announcements are twofold, and mark a transition from earth to heaven, from sin to righteousness, from corruption to purity, from death to life. The first announcement (19:1, 2) is the voice of the great multitude declaring that the bride of the Lamb is ready, and that the nuptials are about to be declared. It marks the pivotal point in God's climactic dealing with earth. From this point forward He will assert His power and will bring to pass His long cherished purposes which have been so carefully worked out in the total scheme of redemption.

The "marriage of the Lamb" is certainly figurative of the ultimate union of Christ with His people. The word "church" is not used here, but the bride can scarcely mean anything else. A comparison with Ephesians 5:23-32 will show that Paul had a similar concept; and in the Old Testament Israel was represented as the "wife" of Jehovah, although unfaithful (see Hosea 2:16-23). The intimacy of this relationship is used as a pattern of the love of God for His people and of their obligation to be faithful to Him. The di-

vergent fates of the people of the world and of the people of God
are portrayed in the inherent difference between the status of the
harlot and that of the bride. The former may be repudiated at any
time and may be left to her fate. The bride is cherished and becomes a permanent part of the home.

Unlike the stormy nature of so much of the surrounding context,
the entire tone of this passage is praise and peace. The multitudes
in heaven are not dismayed by the troubles of earth, though they
obviously are aware of what is taking place. Their calm is not indifference, but is rather the understanding of what God is doing,
and is the confidence that victory is sure. One purpose of Revelation is to create this confidence in a church whose political and social status was uncertain and which might be confronted at any
time with full scale imperial opposition. In the perspective of
God's plan for the ages, the troubles of the immediate present seem
less alarming.

The action of the interlude in Revelation 19:1-10 is summed up
in the four Hallelujahs which are arranged so that the two longer
expressions come first and last, with the two shorter between them.
With the exception of the third, they are spoken by the multitude,
evidently the body of the redeemed in heaven. The two longest
expressions contrast with each other. The first contains praise to
God for His righteous judgments on the great harlot; the last expresses praise because of the preparation of the wife of the Lamb.
The second and third Hallelujahs are brief, and echo the attitude
of the others. They are the watershed of action in Revelation;
for before them the book builds up to its tremendous climax of
judgment, and after them the denouement comes swiftly.

The remainder of the vision from 19:11 through 21:8 describes
a rapid succession of events as follows:

1. The appearance of Christ in final judgment, followed by
   the armies of heaven.   (19:11-16)
2. The announcement of the final battle, and the destruction
   of the beast and his armies.   (19:17-21)
3. The imprisonment of Satan.   (20:1-3)
4. The reign of Christ.   (20:4-6)
5. The last rebellion and its overthrow.   (20:7-10)
6. The judgment of the dead.   (20:11-15)
7. The new heaven and the new earth.   (21:1-8)

There is a close unity in the sequence of these events, irrespective of whether or not they must be regarded as a series of occur-

rences rather than as differing or overlapping pictures of the same thing. Beginning with the appearing of Christ at the end of the age to take His throne and to vindicate the saints, they follow through to the final judgment of the dead and to the establishment of God's Paradise, which is described in detail in the closing vision of the book.

If it be granted that these events are successive, and that literally or figuratively they represent the order of the program of judgment, then the millennial kingdom of chapter 20 must be a reality which follows the judgments accompanying the return of Christ.

The purpose of this series is not fully apparent, and consequently its meaning has been challenged frequently. Perhaps one can say that the entire process is one of judgment in which the reigning Christ will dispose of His foes, train His people, give opportunity to surviving peoples to live under His own perfect government, and finally, after His administrative task is completed, will transfer the perfected kingdom to the new heaven and the new earth.

Because of the allusion to the beast and his armies (19:19,20) the chronological order of the passage must begin at the end of the present age when evil has reached its climax and its fullest organization. If that is so, the great battle described here and the inauguration of the millennial kingdom cannot be relegated to the past, nor can the millennium be a description of this present age. The "binding of Satan," by which he is restrained from deceiving the nations (20:2, 3) is hardly compatible with the expression of Ephesians which names him as the "prince of the powers of the air, of the spirit that now worketh in the sons of disobedience" (Eph. 2:2). The binding must consequently be future.

The millennial kingdom is not explained in detail, but enough is said to establish the fact that it is a specially marked reign of Christ following His conquest of the forces of evil at the end of the age. The purpose and character of this reign are not stated fully. One might deduce from the general context that the millennial reign is part of the entire process of judgment beginning with the destruction of the beast and the fall of Babylon, and that it is preparatory to the complete elimination of evil and the establishment of the city of God as the eternal fulfilment of redemption. It is, therefore, an interim between two crises in which good rather than evil is in control, and in which the administration of God's law will be conducted by Christ Himself with the aid of His saints.

The release of Satan and the war with Gog and Magog reveal that even the rule of absolute righteousness is not sufficient to change men's hearts. There are still those who listen to Satanic suggestions and who are ready to follow them. The judgment of the great white throne closes earth's accounts, and removes the last vestige of evil before the new city of God brings into being the eternal state.

The vision closes with a sharp differentiation between the saved and the lost, the believing and the unbelieving. The coming of the New Jerusalem is the antithesis of the fall of Babylon, and the blessings of God for His people are in direct contrast to the calamities that befall the wicked.

CHAPTER VIII

VISION IV: THE ETERNAL CITY

REVELATION 21:9-22:5

The vision of the Eternal City which consummates the prophecy of Revelation is the counterpart and opposite of the third vision. Between the two are a number of clear contrasts.

VISION III	VISION IV
The climax of human rebellion	The fulfilment of divine purpose
The doom of the harlot, Babylon	The crowning of the bride, the New Jerusalem
The ascendancy of the dragon and the beasts.	The triumph of God and of the Lamb
The attitude of weeping and fear (18:9,11,15,19; 19:20; 21:8)	The atmosphere of peace and fellowship with God (21:24-27, 22:5)
The old world passing away under judgment (21:1)	The new heaven and the new earth (21:10)

This last vision of Revelation is intended to portray the eternal city as fully as human language can do it. Undoubtedly the picture is symbolical, yet some analysis is necessary to the understanding of the symbolism. The figure is taken from the cities of John's acquaintance, which were relatively small walled communities, tightly packed with inhabitants. To one viewing such a city from a distance it would appear as a mass of walls and towers, a compact unit rather than the sprawling collection of low buildings that makes a modern residential community. The light colored walls of its houses gleaming under the Eastern sunlight would be visible for miles. Perhaps the writer thought of the earthly Jerusalem which crowned the Judean hills, and which was for the devout Jew the focus of his longing and devotion (Ps. 122:3,4). The New Jerusalem, radiant with the light of the glory of God (Rev. 21:11) will outshine the terrestrial glory of any city of John's day.

The method of description by contrast is carried straight through the entire vision by the use of seven negative statements concerning the New Jerusalem. Unlike the cities of earth, it will lack certain things.

No temple will adorn it. The cities of the Graeco-Roman world were filled with temples dedicated to their patron deities. In these shrines the god supposedly dwelt, and through the priesthood that ministered to him his favor was implored and his protection sought. The people came to the temple to offer their sacrifices and to obtain counsel for their daily affairs. Sometimes the god answered them; but most often he was distant and haughty, nor could men enter into intimate fellowship with him. In the promised New Jerusalem God Himself will dwell with men, and the indirect approach to Him will not be desirable or necessary.

Neither sun nor moon will be needed for illumination. Artificial lighting was almost unknown in the ancient cities. Their tall buildings made the narrow streets gloomy by day, and at night the feeble rays of the moon were not sufficient to light the dark corners and alleys. All kinds of dangers and evils lurked in the shadows. The city of God will be radiant with God's glory, and will not be dependent for light upon the natural luminaries nor upon the lamps and torches that men can supply.

The gates will never be closed. From time immemorial down to fairly recent days fortified cities always closed their gates at night to keep out roving robber bands or military enemies. Each municipality was a small fort which was self-sustaining in time of war, and which was always alert in time of peace. Since all hostile forces will have been destroyed, there will be no need for such precautions in the city of God.

Nothing unclean will find lodgment within the confines of this city. Moral and spiritual uncleanness are doubtless intended, since the word "unclean" is further defined as "anything . . . that maketh an abomination and a lie" (21:27). Only in recent years have sanitary service and proper drainage made modern municipalities comparatively clean, although these devices were not completely unknown in antiquity. The filth and disorder of the past would be almost unbelievable now were there not still a few back alleys in the slums filled with rubbish and garbage. The New Jerusalem will be free from dirt and crime.

Revelation adds, "There shall be no curse any more" (22:3). The allusion properly applies to the early accounts of Genesis, in which a curse was placed on the earth because of sin:

> Cursed is the ground for thy sake; in toil shalt thou eat of it all the days of thy life; thorns also and thistles shall it bring forth to thee; and thou shalt eat the herb of the field; in the sweat of thy face shalt thou eat bread, till thou return unto the ground; for out of it thou wast taken; for dust thou art, and unto dust shalt thou return (Gen. 3:17-19).

Not labor, but gruelling, fruitless toil is a curse. The first recorded city was built by the fugitive Cain (4:16,17) who had "gone out from the presence of Jehovah." It was not a city in the modern sense of the word. It may have been a hamlet of a few inhabitants, but it represented a community living by itself, indifferent to God. The bane of futility and the stigma of rebellion will never touch the city of God. The work in it will be delightful service, and the foreheads of His people will wear His name, and not the mark of Cain.

Night will never fall upon this city. Darkness is the time when evil comes out of its hiding place and when crime flourishes. In the city of God there will be no opportunity for evil to hide itself or to grow unnoticed.

Artificial light will be unnecessary if night never comes. The reiteration of this idea stresses the brilliance and the glory of the new life which is planned for the saints of God.

This sevenfold negative presentation contrasts the city of God with all earthly civilization, and particularly with Babylon. Babylon was devoid of God and of the people of God, and was filled with darkness. Babylon's gates did not defend her from her enemies nor from the judgment of God. She was "a hold of every unclean and hateful bird" (Rev. 18:2). Plagues, mourning, and death were predicted for her, and her doom was inexorably decreed by heaven (18:21). The lights of Babylon will be extinguished forever (18:23).

The positive aspects of the New Jerusalem are even more important than the negative aspects listed above.

The new city will be a memorial to the redemptive work of God. Its gates are inscribed with the names of the twelve tribes of Israel and its foundations bear the names of the twelve apostles of the Lamb. Both the old and the new dispensations are represented in this community of the saints of God who are there by redemption rights. Just as the founders of a city may be memorialized in the statues and buildings which adorn it, so the spiritual ancestors of believers are honored in this city.

Worship will be brought to perfection. Here "God . . . dwelleth not in temples made with hands" (Acts 17:24), and no shrine can really make Him fully accessible to men. In the new city God Himself will be always present, and approach to Him will be direct.

The illumination of the city will be perfect. Light reveals reality; and the more penetrating the light, the more exact the revelation. Candlelight can make some things clear; sunlight will reveal more; and the infra-red or ultra-violet will make visible objects and colors that could not otherwise be seen. The light of deity itself will cast no shadows, and will make all things luminous and beautiful.

The society of the city will be perfect. Without war and without evil there will be a happy fellowship of nations and peoples where interchange of interests will add to its joys and prosperity. Each will be free to make its own contribution to the culture which God will establish.

The environment will be suited to the best development of the inhabitants. The river of the water of life, the tree of life, and the other fruitbearing trees are part of the paradise that was originally possessed and forfeited when man fell from his innocency. Sin entered, and brought with it the suffering and sorrow, the hardships and frustration. The removal of the curse means the restoration of the privileges and powers that God intended man to enjoy when He created him.

The occupations of men will be perfect also, for the text says: "His servants shall serve him" (Rev. 22:3). Fruitless toil will be excluded, and all labor will be constructive and useful. The eternal state will not consist of endless idleness but of constant activity without fatigue and without failure.

The satisfaction of life will be complete, for "they shall see his face" (22:4). Moses' prayer, "show me . . . thy glory" (Exod. 33:18) was not granted because man in his earthly state cannot see the face of God and live. In this eternal world those who have been perfected by redemption shall at last enjoy the unclouded vision of deity.

Security will be guaranteed: "They shall reign forever and ever" (22:5). No foe can unseat them, no evil disturb them. The warfare is finished and the triumph is eternal.

The crowning glory of the city of God is the personality of the "Lamb." The city is His wife (21:9); the names on the foundations are those of His apostles (21:14); He is the object of the worship of the city's inhabitants (21:22); He illuminates it

(21:23). The roster of its citizenry is "the Lamb's book of life" (21:27) ; His throne is the hub of its active life, and His presence will be the permanent delight of His people (22:3, 4).   The redeeming Christ is the eternal Christ, who is all in all to those who love Him.   In the words of a well-known hymn: "The Lamb is all the glory of Immanuel's land."

CHAPTER IX

THE EPILOGUE

REVELATION 22:6-21

The opening words of the Epilogue, "and he said," continue the colloquy between John and the angelic guide who had offered to show him the holy city Jerusalem. The verbs which chronicle his activity keep him within the radius of attention, even though the real interest of the passage is not focused on him. He acts as a reader of script, whose voice persists although the subject matter which he is reading may change. Note the list of the angel's activities:

"There came one of the seven angels . . . "	21: 9
"He spake with me"	21: 9
"He carried me away"	21:10
"And showed me"	21:10
"He measured the city"	21:16
"He measured the wall"	21:17
"And showed me . . . "	22: 1
"And said unto me . . . "	22: 6
"And he saith unto me . . . "	22: 9
"And he saith unto me . . . "	22:10

This continuity shows that the close of the book has unity, and that the final appeal is directly connected with the teaching of the main body. On the other hand, the Epilogue stands separate from the fourth vision for the following reasons:

1. The description of the perfections of the city of God has been brought to an end, and there is nothing further to add.

2. The content of the remaining verses is mainly exhortation about what has preceded, not a new disclosure of truth.

3. The opening words of verse 6 which speak of "the things which must shortly come to pass," summarize in retrospect what 4:1 states for the future, "I will show thee the things which must come to pass hereafter." Consequently they mark the conclusion of the prophecy.

4. The Epilogue possesses a structure of its own, based on the thrice repeated statement, "I come quickly" (22:7, 12, 20).

The first of these statements is an appeal to the will, because it calls for obedience. "And behold, I come quickly. Blessed is he that keepeth the words of the prophecy of this book." In view of the rapidly approaching advent of Christ, the Revelation is to serve as a guide to conduct.

The second exhortation is ethical: "Behold, I come quickly; and my reward is with me, to render to each man according as his work is" (22:12). Moral growth or moral decline are alike inevitable, and as a man improves or deteriorates he will be ready or unready for the coming of Christ.

The third exhortation is emotional. "He who testifieth these things saith, Yea: I come quickly," and the swift response answers, "Amen: come, Lord Jesus" (22:20). The seer was overcome with his own desire to see the Lord, and so he adds his prayer as the last of the reactions to the prediction that is both warning and promise (2:16, 3:11).

These three divisions contain also three different exhortations regarding the prophetic revelation itself: (1) "Keep the words of this book" (22:9) ; (2) "Seal not up the words of the prophecy of this book" (22:10) ; and (in substance) (3) "Neither add to nor take away from the words of the prophecy of this book" (22:18). The revelation is mandatory, immediately applicable, and complete in its scope.

The Epilogue is trinitarian in its theism. God the Father is the author of revelation and the object of worship (22:6, 9). Jesus is "the root and the offspring of David, the bright, the morning star" (22:16). The Spirit is the agent who invites men to partake of the water of life (22:17). It balances the introductory greeting of the Prologue, "from him who is and who was and who is to come; and from the seven Spirits that are before his throne; and from Jesus Christ . . ." (1:4, 5). All three Persons are united in authority and as objects of worship, and are alike God.

The Epilogue brings Revelation to a fitting close. It concentrates the meaning of the symbols in the person of Christ, and it stresses the necessity of action in expectation of His imminent return. It is the final authentication of all the foregoing predictions and commands, for it is signed by the Lord Himself: "I

Jesus have sent mine angel to testify unto you these things for the churches" (22:16).

The title given to Christ in the Epilogue, "the root and the offspring of David, the bright, the morning star" (22:16) has its origin in prophecy. The Old Testament called Him "the root of Jesse" (Isa. 11:10), and in the letter to Thyatira Jesus speaks of "the morning star" (Rev. 2:28). The passage from Isaiah is part of a prediction of the attraction of the Gentiles to Israel's Messiah, and of the restoration of the people to their rightful place (Isa. 11:1 ff.). The morning star is the harbinger of the dawn, which announces that full day will soon come. The message is directed particularly to the churches (Rev. 22:16), and for that reason it should be applied to them. Revelation has little to say directly about the future of Israel; but the references that do appear connect that future with consummation of the age and with its relation to the church. In this closing identification of Jesus with the root of David He re-emphasizes the leadership of Israel, and reveals Himself as the hope of all men, Israel, the Gentiles, and the church.

CHAPTER X

OBSERVATIONS AND CONCLUSIONS

The previous study shows that the Apocalypse is an orderly arrangement of prophetic truth. Although it is symbolic in character and although it is written in the apocalyptic style, it is progressive and has a definite framework of teaching. Beginning with the letters to the churches, which reveal the needs of the typical assemblies and their several relations to the coming of the Lord, it carries the reader straight through the climax of God's dealing with the world process to the final overthrow of evil and the assumption of the kingdom by Christ, who destroys the sovereignty of evil.

Throughout the book there is a pervasive unity that binds it all together. There is a unity of *structure* in the four main visions, introduced by the words, "And I was in the Spirit . . . "; nor is this simply the chance repetition of a catch phrase, for each use of it opens a section with a distinctive character which builds on the one preceding it, and yet differs from it. Cross references from one to the other interweave the themes so that one cannot say that any one section is superfluous or irrelevant. There is a unity of *person* in the revelation of Christ as He appears to His church, to the world of which He is ruler and judge, to the generation in which the process of history comes to its close at His visible appearing, and to the saved who enjoy the bliss of the city of God. There is a unity in the *sovereignty* of God irrespective of what is taking place on earth, as evinced by the perennial throne of God which is mentioned throughout the text. There is a unity of *redemptive purpose and power,* beginning with the statement in the Prologue, "Unto him that loveth us, and loosed us from our sins by his blood" (1:5), continuing with the presentation of "a Lamb . . . as though it had been slain" (5:6), and ending with the Paradise of those whose names "are written in the Lamb's book of life" (21:27). There is unity of *expectation* in the frequently repeated allusions to the coming of Christ and to the hope of His reign to overthrow evil. To every church the promise of reward is attached to His

99

appearing; the praise to the Lamb says that He is worthy to receive power and riches, and wisdom, and might, and honor, and glory and blessing. Judgment is the manifestation of His wrath, His favor will be the delight of His servants. The climax of the final conflict occurs when "the kingdom of the world is become *the kingdom* of our Lord and of his Christ" (11:15).

The reality of this unity has been challenged. Dr. R. H. Charles suggests that[1]

> John died when he completed 1-20:3 of his work, and . . . the materials for its completion, which were for the most part ready in a series of independent documents, were put together by a faithful but unintelligent disciple in the order which he thought right.

While the warning of Revelation 22:18, 19 presupposes that tampering with the text was anticipated, and was therefore theoretically possible, it is unlikely that this book ever underwent wholesale changes by later editors. Even if it did, there is always the question as to whether the judgment of the recent commentator would be more valid than the hypothetical editor's mistakes. With all due regard to the learning and acumen of Dr. Charles, it is better to deal with the text as it stands, and to treat positively its unities rather than to assume interpolations and changes. Difficulties in interpretation should not be overlooked, but they need not always be treated by literary surgery.

One may hold that the Revelation is a series of genuine objective visions given to a seer who transmitted them as accurately as human language would permit. They were supernatural in character, and were couched in symbols which would be interpreted largely by reference to the Old Testament. The people to whom they were read understood them in measure, and could find in these symbols much that was applicable to their own day. The meaning of Revelation was not exhausted in the first century, however; and its complete fulfilment still awaits the triumphal return of the Revelator.

CHAPTER XI

THE OLD TESTAMENT BACKGROUND OF REVELATION

The reader of Revelation will not have perused many of its pages before he realizes that much of its language sounds familiar. It is filled with references to events and characters of the Old Testament, and a great deal of its phraseology is taken directly from the Old Testament books. Oddly enough, there is not one direct citation in Revelation from the Old Testament with a statement that it is quoted from a given passage; but a count of the significant allusions which are traceable both by verbal resemblance and by contextual connection to the Hebrew canon number three hundred and forty-eight. Of these approximately ninety-five are repeated, so that the actual number of different Old Testament passages that are mentioned are nearly two hundred and fifty, or an average of more than ten for each chapter in Revelation.

Only a small number of these references contain more than three or four words in sequence to show that they originate in the Hebrew or Greek Bible. Most of these references are oblique, such as one makes when he weaves some familiar phrase from Shakespeare or Tennyson into the running flow of his conversation or writing. The phraseology is often fragmentary or inexact, as one would make an allusion from memory. Nevertheless in most of these instances the probable source is identifiable; and a definite connection between Revelation and the Old Testament can be established.

The count given for these passages will vary among commentators, since there will inevitably be a difference of opinion on what constitutes a quotation or an allusion. The figures given above are conservative in number and are only approximate. They do, however, afford a fair basis from which to draw the conclusions of this chapter. Swete, in his *Commentary on the Apocalypse*,[1] states that out of 404 verses of the Apocalypse 278 refer to the Old Testament. Whether one counts by individual references to the Old Testament or by the verses in Revelation which may contain more than one quotation or allusion apiece, the resulting list is large enough to show what a tremendous influence the Hebrew canon had on the book.

The difference between a citation, a quotation, and an allusion might profitably be defined. A citation is a fairly exact reproduction of the words of the original text, accompanied by a statement of the fact that they are being quoted and by an identification of the source. A quotation is a general reproduction of the original text, sufficiently close to give the meaning of its thought and to establish unquestionably the passage from which it is taken. The quotation may be loose, and still be a quotation. An allusion consists of one or more words which by their peculiar character and general content are traceable to a known body of text, but which do not constitute a complete reproduction of any part of it.

By way of example, Hebrews 4:7 is a citation from Psalm 95:7,8:

> He again defineth a certain day, To-day, saying in David so long a time afterward (even as hath been said before),
> To-day if ye shall hear his voice,
> Harden not your hearts.

Such direct citations do not occur in the Apocalypse.

A close approach to a direct quotation may be found in Revelation 2:26, 27:

> . . . and he that keepeth my works unto the end, to him will I give authority over the nations: and he shall rule them with a rod of iron, as the vessels of the potter are broken to shivers . . .

Although the quotation is freely adapted to the use in its own context, it is plainly taken from Psalm 2:8, 9, and is more than a chance allusion or an accidental resemblance.

Allusions are legion. A good specimen occurs in Revelation 1:8: " . . . who is and who was and who is to come, the Almighty." The term "Almighty" (Greek: *pantokrator*) is used in the Septuagint of Amos 4:13. It is by no means an unusual word in the LXX, for it occurs frequently in Job, Jeremiah, and the minor prophets, especially Zechariah, from which the Apocalypse draws other allusions. One could not prove that the writer took its use solely from the passages in Amos; nevertheless the context there which identifies the term as the peculiar name of God as sovereign seems to mark it as the probable source. It is the

LXX equivalent of the Hebrew "Jehovah of hosts," or, as it has been translated freely, "Jehovah militant." The interpretation cannot be determined by the single context of Amos 4:13: but the latter affords as good a background as there is for defining it. Certainly the term is an Old Testament concept which must be treated in the light of its earlier usage.

The distribution of these quotations or allusions in Revelation is as found in the charts on page 104.

From these charts one may observe that the largest number of quotations and allusions occur in the symbolic Visions II and III, which are consequently dominated by the concepts and by the atmosphere of the Old Testament. There are references to twenty-four of its thirty-nine books, and every division of the canon is represented. The books most often quoted are Psalms, Isaiah, Daniel, Ezekiel, Jeremiah, and Zechariah. These contain the bulk of predictive prophecy in the era before Christ, and thus they form the framework for the further development of prophecy in Revelation.

Variations in these allusions from the exact language of the originals may be explained in a number of ways. The seer may have quoted loosely from memory as the ancients so often did, giving only the sense of the passage which he had in mind. He may have consciously adapted the language of his source to meet his immediate need without attempting to reproduce its exact content or sequence. He may have quoted from a type of text different from that which has survived to make the basis of our present Septuagint or Hebrew text. In several of his allusions to the book of Daniel the words of Revelation accord more exactly with the version of Theodotion than they do with the Septuagint. There are occasional indications that the seer may have known Aramaic, since he uses Aramaic terms on at least two occasions (9:11, *Abaddon;* 16:16, *Har-Magedon*).

The problem posed by the quotations is this: Does the Apocalypse employ the Old Testament scriptures as a source for literary ornament as a modern preacher uses the phraseology of the King James Version in his preaching because of its familiarity to the minds of his audience? Is it brought in to corroborate the statements of Revelation by its authority, and are the allusions really proof-texts? Is it an integrating factor which, by the connotations and allusions to the ancient framework of eschatological thought, affords a key to the understanding of the Apocalypse?

DISTRIBUTION OF OLD TESTAMENT QUOTATIONS AND ALLUSIONS IN REVELATION

DISTRIBUTION BY SECTIONS

Section	Reference	Number
PROLOGUE	1:1-8	11
VISION I	1:9-3:22	38
VISION II	4:1-16:21	164
VISION III	17:1-21:8	95
VISION IV	21:9-22:5	24
EPILOGUE	22:6-21	16
TOTAL		348

DISTRIBUTION BY BOOKS OF OLD TESTAMENT

Books	Number	Books	Number
Genesis	13	Psalms	43
Exodus	27	Proverbs	2
		POETRY	45
Leviticus	4	Isaiah	79
Numbers	3	Jeremiah	22
Deuteronomy	10	Ezekiel	43
PENTATEUCH	57	Daniel	53
		MAJOR PROPHETS	197
Joshua	1	Hosea	2
Judges	1	Joel	8
II Samuel	1	Amos	9
II Kings	6	Habakkuk	1
		Zephaniah	2
I Chronicles	1	Zechariah	15
Nehemiah	1	Malachi	1
HISTORICAL	11	MINOR PROPHETS	38

Or is the converse true, that the Apocalypse by its allusions to the various prophetic sections of the Old Testament ties them together into one unified prophetic system? Can the quotations be used to interpret the book? There are certain aspects of Revelation on which they give considerable light.

TITLES OF DEITY

The repeated passages often provide understanding for the fixed symbols and terms that constitute the major concepts of Revelation. Seven of them contain titles of deity applied to God or to Christ that describe those aspects of character most fully expressive of sovereignty or of judgeship.

1. "[God,] who created the heaven . . . and the earth . . . and the sea" Exodus 20:11, quoted in Revelation 10:5, 14:7.

As the Creator, God is entitled to be the ruler and controller of all things.

2. "He who is and who was and who is to come" Exodus 3:14, quoted in Revelation 1:4, 8; 11:17; 16:5.

Each of these usages accompanies an assertion of divine intervention in world crisis. The eternal God, whose presence fills all time, is the answer to the shifting fortunes of the world. The original passage is part of God's declaration that He will intervene for His people who are suffering oppression, and that He will deliver them from Egypt.

3. "The Almighty" Amos 4:13, quoted in Revelation 1:8; 4:8; 11:17; 15:3; 16:7; 19:6, 15; 21:22.

This term has already been mentioned in another connection. The title is singularly appropriate, for it speaks of God as a warrior, contending against evil with invincible power.

Each of these occurrences is significant. Revelation 1:8 is part of the introduction to the book, and sets the stamp of God upon its whole character as a motto or theme. Revelation 4:8 gives the title of the enthroned sovereign who rules the universe in holiness and power. Revelation 11:17, 18 expresses the worship of the elders who celebrate the divine assertion of rulership that brings judgment upon evil and that concludes the period of its ascendancy. Revelation 15:3 announces the triumph of the victors in the strife with the beast by the power of God. Revelation 16:7 is the acknowledgment of the justice and the thoroughness of the divine judgment. Revelation 19:6, 15 present the almighty power of God in the consummation of Christ's triumph. Revelation 21:22 makes the almighty God the glory of the eternal city. The whole book is the record of the victory of a righteous omnipotence over evil. The original passage in Amos which is concerned immediately with the judgment of God upon a rebellious Israel prefigures the activity of a sovereign God in the work of judgment, and makes the title of "Almighty" peculiarly applicable to the situation with which Revelation deals.

     4. "The God of heaven" Daniel 2:19, quoted in Revelation 11:13 and 16:11.

This title is peculiar to the later books of the Old Testament,[2] especially to those that deal with the Gentile world. It is used in the vision of Nebuchadnezzar (Dan. 2) as the special title of the God who gave authority to the successive kingdoms represented in the image of Nebuchadnezzar's dream, and who ultimately set up the kingdom never to be destroyed.

In the context of Revelation these two occurrences are curiously contrasted. One quotation says that ". . . the rest [who were not killed by an earthquake] were affrighted, and gave glory to the God of heaven" (11:13). It speaks of repentance on the part of some persons who were terrified by the imminent judgments of God. The other reference (16:11) speaks of the citizens of the kingdom of the beast, who "blasphemed the God of heaven . . . and they repented not of their works." In the former instance the title is connected with repentance; in the latter, with obstinate blasphemy.

The titles applied to Christ are as follows:

     5. "The Alpha and Omega, the first and the last . . ." Isaiah 44:6 and 48:12, quoted in Revelation 1:8, 17; 22:13.

These passages are applied both to God and to Christ, as a comparison of the allusions in Revelation 1:8, 17, and 22:13 will show. Revelation 1:17 and 22:13 occur at the beginning and at the end of the main body of visions respectively, as if to assure the reader that the eternal Christ gives the disclosure of Himself to the seer, and then concludes it by putting on it the seal of His personal assurance. It corresponds to the statement in Colossians 1:17, ". . . he is before all things, and in him all things consist."

     6. "The Root of David" Isaiah 11:10, quoted twice in Revelation 5:5 and 22:16.

This is properly an allusion rather than an exact quotation. Isaiah 11:10 says "the root of Jesse" rather than "the root of David," but the underlying imagery is identical. The two allusions in Revelation stand at the beginning and at the end of the record of Christ's redeeming work in the cosmos. They show His undertaking the task of judgment which the scion of David must assume in order to inherit His rightful kingdom, and His rejoicing in the fulness of His inheritance when the conquest is complete. In this fashion the use of the title explains the prophecy of Isaiah 11, which describes Him initially as a shoot out of the stem of Jesse, a single spear of life from a felled and discredited tree, which flourishes to eliminate wickedness and to bring blessing to the entire earth. The whole concept of the millennial kingdom is related to Christ's work as "the root of David." The first promise of the kingdom in the New Testament (Luke 1:32, 33) states: ". . . the Lord God shall give unto him the throne of his father David: and he shall reign over the house of Jacob for ever; and of his kingdom there shall be no end."

7. "Lord of lords" Deuteronomy 10:17, quoted in Revelation 17:14, 19:16.

The title "Lord of lords" coupled with "King of kings" is applied to Christ in His final conquest as He ventures forth to seize His kingdom from His enemies. The original in Deuteronomy 10:17 is the title ascribed to God by Moses in one of his last orations prior to the conquest of Canaan by Israel. It denotes His terrible righteousness as He administrates justice among the people of Israel. Revelation extends it to God's dealing with the world.

There are many other titles of deity employed in Revelation. These, however, link the thought of the old economy with the promise of the future kingdom, and make continuous those characteristics of God which have always been the assurance of His people.

OLD TESTAMENT CONCEPTS

Among the repeated phrases in Revelation echoing Old Testament expressions are others which contain certain concepts fundamental to the framework of the thought of the book. Not all will be catalogued, but a few specimens will be listed to illustrate their use.

1. "Fire and brimstone"

The burning of Sodom and the cities of the plain described in Genesis 19:24 seems to be the model for the destruction of the enemies of God in Revelation 19:20 and 20:10. The latter are not literal quotations; but they recall unmistakably the elements of the judgment of which Genesis speaks.

2. "The tree of life"

Four times the tree of life (Gen. 3:22) is mentioned in Revelation: in 2:7, where sharing in it is promised as a reward to the overcomer; and in 22:2, 14, 19, where it is a part of the city of God. It symbolizes the restoration to man of the eternal life which he forfeited by his sin, with all of the blessings and privileges which that life can bring. The joys from which he had been excluded by the fall now become his eternal possession through redemption.

3. "The book of Life"
        Psalm 69:28, quoted in Revelation 3:5, 17:8, 20:12, 15.

The concept of a celestial roll book in which the names of the saved are inscribed is not peculiar to Revelation. Comparable phraseology may be found in the words of Jesus in the Gospels (Luke 10:20), and in Hebrews (12:23). The phrase of the Psalms is reproduced in Revelation 3:5, and it underlies the other related passages. It indicates that salvation is not a last-minute invention of God, but rather a part of His eternal purpose for each believer even in the midst of persecution.

4. "Lightnings, thunders, voices"
        Exodus 19:16, quoted in Revelation 8:5, 11:19, 16:18.

The visible and audible terrors of God's presence in Revelation parallel closely the accompaniments of the giving of the law on Sinai. As He appeared then to declare the holiness of His being to His people so will He reappear to enforce His holiness upon a rebellious world. The recurrences of the allusion to "lightnings, thunders, and voices" are at the endings of the judgments of the seals, the trumpets, and the bowls.

5. "The wine of the wrath of God," or "Drinking the cup of wrath"

Isaiah 51:17 and Jeremiah 51:7 appear in Revelation 14:8, 10; 16:19; 17:2, 4; 18:3. The former refers to the wrath of God in judgment; the second to the wine of Babylon's evil, which brings madness and destruction to those who partake. The concepts are closely allied. Both imply a drunken insanity which leads to destruction, a deadly indulgence which brings the inevitable doom of those who participate in it.

      6. "Babylon the great"
          Daniel 4:30, quoted in Revelation 14:8, 16:19, 17:5, 18:2

The meaning of Babylon has already been treated in another connection, and need not be discussed again at length here. It stood not only for the literal city of Chaldea, but also for the whole system of organized godlessness which will have its culmination in the end time and which is to be overthrown at the return of Christ.[3]

The foregoing examples of repeated allusions in the text of Revelation show how heavily the seer utilized the teaching of the Old Testament for the background and imagery of his message. Such use of the Old Testament, however, exceeds the chance of memory. In some instances the similarity to Old Testament concepts is due not to a wholesale borrowing of them, but to the correspondence of the personal experience of the seer to that of the man whose work he quoted. For instance, the words "seated upon a throne" in Isaiah 6:1 appear six times in Revelation. Was the writer of Revelation synthesizing a vision from fragments of the prophets, or was he describing in terms that parallel the prophetic account the same glories which he himself saw? The latter is the better explanation, since the majority of these allusions do not constitute the recollection of one unbroken text, but rather are occasional likenesses of language which establish continuity of concept, but not necessarily conscious quotation.

Only a few conspicuous examples of repeated allusions from the total list of ninety-seven have been given above. There remain about two hundred and fifty others which are mentioned in Revelation.

In some instances two or more Old Testament passages are combined into one verse of thought. Revelation 1:7 affords a good illustration:

> Behold, he cometh with the clouds; and every eye shall see him, and they that pierced him; and all the tribes of the earth shall mourn over him.

A comparison of this verse with Old Testament sources reveals the following similarities:

> I saw in the night-visions, and, behold, there came with the clouds of heaven one like unto a son of man, and he came even to the ancient of days, and they brought him near before him (Dan. 7:13).

> And I will pour upon the house of David, and upon the inhabitants of Jerusalem, the spirit of grace and of supplication; and they shall look unto me whom they have pierced; and they shall mourn for him, as one mourneth for his only son, and shall be in bitterness for him, as one that is in bitterness for his firstborn.
>
> And the land shall mourn . . . all the families[4] that remain . . . (Zech. 12:10, 12, 14).

Only a casual comparison of these passages is necessary to show that Revelation 1:7 is a composite of the thought in Daniel 7:13 and Zechariah 12:10, 12, 14. Although the connection here is more obvious than in many instances, neither Daniel nor Zechariah is reproduced with verbal exactitude, but the reference is unmistakable notwithstanding. The important feature is in the connection which the reference makes between the Old Testament prediction and the New Testament revelation. The same person called "the son of man" in Daniel who is presented before the Ancient of Days as a candidate for the everlasting kingdom, and who in Zechariah speaks in the first person with the voice and authority of Jehovah, is identified in Revelation as the Lord Jesus Christ. In both of the Old Testament passages the setting is eschatological. Daniel deals chiefly with the sovereignty of the Son of Man over the world after the collapse of Gentile government. "His dominion is an everlasting dominion, which shall not pass away, and his kingdom that which shall not be destroyed" (Dan. 7:14). The passage in Zechariah is concerned with the repentance of the Jewish nation and its restoration to God's favor. Jerusalem shall be besieged, to be delivered by the direct intervention of God. The self-disclosure of Israel's Deliverer at that critical moment will evoke from the nation deep mourning and wholesale repentance when they realize that the returning Messiah is none other than Jesus of Nazareth whom they crucified.

In this way the Old Testament background gives content to the Apocalypse, because the implications of the quoted text can be used to amplify the meaning of the allusion. Revelation thus carries more meaning than a superficial glance at the text would indicate. On the other hand, the independent teachings of the passages in Daniel and Zechariah, separated by their different settings and times of writing, are brought into a new perspective of unity by their common use in the passage in Revelation which focuses them upon the person of Christ. Revelation becomes in this manner the unifying guide to eschatology in the New Testament.

Interpretation by a study of Old Testament allusions, then, contains two principles: (1) the Old Testament context should be examined carefully to see whether it connotes a definite predictive basis for the corresponding parallel in Revelation, or whether it is used merely as illustrative language; (2) the passage in Revelation should be studied to ascertain what interpretation it places on the shadows and types of the Old Testament.

The vast size of the body of allusions to the Old Testament in Revelation forbids a minute scrutiny of all of them; but perhaps one more will suffice to demonstrate the method. The picture of the conquering Christ in Revelation 19:15 is a composite of three ideas:

> And out of his mouth proceedeth a sharp sword, that with it he should smite the nations: and he shall rule them with a rod of iron: and he treadeth the winepress of the fierceness of the wrath of God, the Almighty.

The first of these concepts, the sharp sword emerging from the mouth, is paralleled by Isaiah 11:4, where the Messiah's rule in His future kingdom is described:

> . . . he shall smite the earth with the rod of his mouth, and with the breath of his lips shall he slay the wicked.

The second of these concepts is taken from Psalm 2:9:

> Thou shalt break them with a rod of iron; thou shalt dash them in pieces like a potter's vessel.

The third concept is probably a reference to Joel 3:13:

> Put ye in the sickle; for the harvest is ripe: come, tread ye; for the winepress is full, the vats overflow.

All three of these passages have one thing in common: they refer to the terminal judgments of God upon the earth. Individually, the first is a prediction of the inauguration of the Messianic kingdom upon the earth; the second is the heavenly investiture of the Son with the authority to suppress evil and to establish righteous rule; and the third is God's summons of the Gentile nations to judgment in the time of the end. These three aspects of the Messianic office of Christ converge at the time of His appearing as Revelation states it. The prophecies explain the symbolism behind the idealized portrait; the portrait coordinates the prophecies.

By far the largest part of the material used in Revelation comes from the apocalyptic prophets, Isaiah, Daniel, Ezekiel, and Zechariah, and Revelation perpetuates in some measure their content and style. Nevertheless it is more than a mosaic of quotations; for although it employs the Old Testament terms freely, it organizes the thought in its own fashion.

The use of these allusions may have been one of the major clues which aided the first hearers of the book in understanding it. If they were thoroughly familiar with the Scriptures of the Septuagint or of some other Greek version, the imagery of the Apocalypse would not have seemed so strange to them as it does today. They would have been able to bring it into line with their own era, and at the same time to catch the significance of its figures from their original setting in the narrative and apocalyptic of the Old Testament.

Not all of the allusions and figures are immediately plain, and one should refrain from claiming that a study of them is the final key to the meaning of Revelation. The book does become more intelligible as one progresses in the examination of its background. The living creatures, angels, beasts, dragon, etc., are to be understood as the continuation of the predictive imagery of the Old Testament, written in apocalyptic style. When the symbolism of Scripture is explained in its own terms, one feels on safer ground than when he attempts a solution that is founded on purely external criteria.

Although most of the passages mentioned in Revelation are taken from individual verses, there are a few which are either contiguous in the original or else so near each other that they exhibit the seer's familiarity with the entire section from which they are quoted. At least thirty-seven chapters of the Old Testament appear more than once, and sometimes much more frequently. Of these thirty-seven nineteen, or slightly more than half, have been read and used by the seer. With one or two exceptions in which the references are quite vague, the rest are identifiable but indirect. The allusions are sufficiently definite to identify the source, but are not so explicit that a consecutive pattern of thought based on the Old Testament can be detected.

The fullest use of consecutive thought falls in Isaiah and in Jeremiah. In Isaiah the chapters which are most plainly mentioned in Revelation are 6, 34, and a number of others occurring in the second half of the book, between chapters 40 and 66. There are seven allusions to Jeremiah 51 which deals with Babylon and its overthrow. Several chapters in Ezekiel, 1, 2, 9, 27, 37, 38, and 40, Daniel 4 and 7, and Zechariah 12 are heavily quoted.

The use of material from these chapters in Revelation is not so detailed that they can be guides for interpretation; but it does show that the Apocalypse binds together and interprets their unfinished prophecies in relation to the future of Judaism and of the church. The seventh chapter of Daniel, which contains the prediction of the four great Gentile empires that would dominate human culture until the coming of the kingdom of God is not repeated nor explained in detail in the Apocalypse. The connection of these prophecies with Revelation is unmistakable, for the identification of the Son of Man with Christ, and the concentration of Gentile world power in the composite beast of Revelation 13 reveal it plainly. Revelation develops the truth which the prophets realized only imperfectly.

In some instances the text is quoted quite casually, with no particular attempt to reproduce its original meaning. Daniel 8: 9, 10 describes the "little horn" which

> . . . waxed great, even to the host of heaven; and some of the host and of the stars it cast down to the ground, and trampled upon them.

This passage is the prototype of Revelation 12:4.

> And his tail draweth the third part of the stars of heaven, and did cast them to the earth.

The allusion is not exact, for it refers to the dragon, not to the antichrist; the action is accomplished by the tail of the dragon, not by his emissary; the "third part" is specified in Revelation, but not in Daniel; and the setting of the action is quite different. Nevertheless the verbal resemblances make a distinct connection between the two passages. Both speak of the arrogance and power of Satan, and both deal with the devastation brought about by evil in the heavenly realms. It seems unlikely that the seer was applying or interpreting directly the passage from Daniel. More likely is it that he used its phraseology to give a hint of the meaning of his symbolism. "Host of heaven" might apply to angels as well as to stars, and it may be that in his use of figures the two are equated. By this means of comparing the Old Testament passage with the allusion in Revelation, a fair interpretation of many of its symbolic terms may be found.

The allusions make a strong link between the glorified person of Christ in Revelation and the Messiah of the Old Testament. The "Lion of the tribe of Judah" (5:5) relates Him to the patriarchal blessing of Jacob (Gen. 49:9, 10) which constituted Judah the potential leader of his brethren and the vanguard of the camp of Israel (Num. 2:3). The "Root of David" (Rev. 5:5) recalls the prophetic hope given in the period when the house of David was confronted with apparent extinction and when the kingdom was slipping from its grasp (Isa. 11:1). The appearance of Christ in the first portrait of the book (Rev. 1:13-18) coincides in many details with the description of the heavenly messenger that spoke to Daniel (7:13; 10:5,6) and to Ezekiel (9:2 LXX, 11) and with the appearance of deity as given to Ezekiel (1:26; 8:2). The words that he spoke, "Fear not . . . ," occur also in Daniel 10:12, 19, and His identification of Himself as "the first and the last" agrees with the declaration of deity in Isaiah 44:6 and 48:12. The disclosure of truth by the Christ whom the seer saw is thus connected with the previous appearances and revelations of God.

The retributive aspect of redemption that is stressed in the Apocalypse has its counterpart in the Old Testament. The person of Christ in judgment is connected with the second Psalm, in which God's appointment of His Son to judge the rebellious nations is stated (Ps. 2:1-12; Rev. 19:15). Although the entire psalm is not quoted, the allusion is unmistakable, and the underlying theme of authority for judgment is the same in both passages. As in most of these quotations, the Old Testament gives the prophetic content, while the New Testament defines its application.

The interpretation of the twelfth and thirteenth chapters of Revelation may be clarified somewhat by resorting to the related thought taken from the Old Testament. The woman with the crown of twelve stars on her head and with the moon beneath her feet, travailing in birth, has been variously interpreted as Israel bringing forth a believing remnant, or the Messiah;[5] as Mary, giving birth to Christ;[6] or as the professing church[7] which produces the victorious minority who are singled out for special reward. A comparison with the prophets will show that the figure of a woman in travail is applied to Israel (Zion) as the vehicle of God's purpose in producing a holy people. The same figure of speech was used negatively by Hezekiah (Isa. 37:3) to show that birth meant accomplishment of purpose or of destiny. It is significant that whereas Hezekiah confessed that he was unable to fulfill his desires and purposes ("the children are come to the birth, and there is not strength to bring forth"), God declared His competence to bring His purposes to fulfilment. "Shall I bring

to the birth, and not cause to bring forth? saith Jehovah . . ."
(Isa. 66:9).

These passages give some light on the identity and on the meaning of the woman in Revelation 12. She represents the people of God, whether the historic elect from whom Christ has come (Gen. 3:15) according to the flesh, or that body of professing faithful from whom a devout remnant have been born. The scope of this vision seems to indicate that the woman does not represent one ecclesiastical body of a particular era, but that the birth of the man child is the climax for which the people of God have existed and for which they are presently in acute travail. The question as to whether the man child is Christ or a select body of believers has been warmly debated by commentators; but the choice may not be a direct alternative, for Christ and His people are united in the purpose of redemption. The promises of ruling and of victory are applied to both (Rev. 2:26, 27; 19:15 and 3:21; 20:4).

From the standpoint of the total conflict between God and Satan this birth may symbolize the appearance of Christ from a suffering people and the triumph of the Incarnation. Viewing the Apocalypse as predictive of the future, it may prefigure the removal of the church to the throne of God while the Jewish group from which they sprang historically remain under persecution until the Lord returns to bring full deliverance.

The quotations show a strong continuity between Revelation and the Old Testament in the symbolical use of historical and geographical names. The one chapter in Jeremiah mentioned most is the fifty-first, which contains the prophet's denunciation of Babylon and the prediction of its destruction by the Medes and Persians. Several of the concepts employed in this chapter are in the Apocalypse: the cup that made the nations drunken (Jer. 51:7), the summons to God's people to forsake Babylon (51:45), the millstone cast into the Euphrates to illustrate Babylon's disappearance (51:63, 64), and some lesser points. Jeremiah is concerned only with the fall of the literal city, and he predicts accurately that Babylon would become a desolate waste, inhabited only by the wild beasts of the desert (51:37). To him Babylon was the habitation of all evil, the source of destructive power, and the implacable foe of God's people.

In the Apocalypse the concepts taken from Jeremiah are applied to the ideal Babylon contemporary with the seer. The historic Babylon of Nebuchadnezzar and Belshazzar had long since disappeared; but the civilization of the end will simply intensify the same pride, pomp and power that the prophet saw in Babylon. The name, therefore, stands for the continuing system of godless society and commerce that began with Cain and Nimrod (Gen. 4:16, 17; 10:8-14) and that will persist until the final judgment.

The use of Biblical terms in recurring references to the Old Testament shows how prophecy and fulfilment are united, and how new predictions are made intelligible as one views them through the meaning of the older prophecies which have already been interpreted by experience. The principles which the new predictions contain illuminate in turn the events of history as it unfolds.

CHAPTER XII

THE CHRISTOLOGY OF REVELATION

The very name of the book of Revelation means that its content is intended to be a disclosure of the person of Christ. He is not incidental to its action; He is its chief subject. Even in these chapters where signs and symbols seem uppermost, and where the cataclysmic judgments of God eclipse all other interests, the person of Christ is still central.

The Christological character of the book is closely related to the structure. In each of the four main visions there is a portrait of Christ. The first vision presents Him as Lord of the church, walking in the midst of the seven golden lampstands (1:12-17). The second vision reveals the Lamb on the throne, into whose authority has been committed the judgment and rulership of all the world (5:1-14). In the third vision He is the Word of God, the invincible conqueror riding His horse to victory over the nations as a Roman general conducted a triumph (19:11-16). The final vision does not contain a separate descriptive paragraph about Him, but it places Him at the very center of the new creation, the city of God.

This Christological emphasis is one of the most important keys to Revelation. By beginning with the Person as the chief interpretative factor, fruitless debate over detail can be minimized, and the main purpose of the book can be kept constantly in sight. The thread of continuity in its thought may be followed more easily, and the initial interpretation can be non-controversial. Whatever one's eschatological scheme may be, he must agree at the outset that the person of Christ is supremely important. All evangelical schools of interpretation would accept this concept as a point of departure.

THE PROLOGUE: CHRIST COMMUNICATING (1:1-8)

The Christological approach is introduced in the Prologue of Revelation by a threefold title, "the faithful witness, the firstborn of the dead, and the ruler of the kings of the earth" (1:5). Although this passage has already been discussed in its place in the text, it deserves some further consideration because of its importance.

"The faithful witness" is a description of the earthly ministry of Christ as a witness to God the Father. The dialogue between Jesus and the Pharisees in John 5 illustrates the function of witnessing. Pressed for an answer by those who challenged His claims, He said:

> If I bear witness of myself, my witness is not [legally] true . . . . But the witness which I have is greater than *that of* John; for the works which the Father hath given me to accomplish, the very works that I do, bear witness of me, that the Father hath sent me (John 5:31, 36).

Jesus Himself, by His words and works, bore an accurate and loyal witness to the character and purpose of the Father. His righteousness reflected God's holiness; His declarations were an adequate representation of the person and character of God; and His goal in life was to carry out whatever the Father had purposed for Him to do. He united Himself perfectly with the will of the Father so that His life became a miniature in time of God's eternal plan.

As a faithful witness He has not withheld any truth nor has He perverted it. He is the one reliable enduring contact between the present and the future, between the seen and unseen worlds.

"Firstborn of the dead" (1:5) suggests that He is the first to experience the resurrection in the sense of a complete victory over death. Paul stated the same idea in Romans 6:9:

> . . . Christ being raised from the dead dieth no more; death no more hath dominion over him.

The resurrection of Christ is unique because He is the first instance of that transformation which the resurrection effects. It is more than a resuscitation of mortal flesh, such as took place in the cases of Jairus' daughter or of Lazarus, for they underwent no essential change of the body. Consciousness was resumed, and they were restored to their friends; but there is not a hint that they were made physically immortal, or that death did not overtake them at some later date.

The body of Christ, however, seemed to be different after the resurrection from what it had been before. The disciples recognized it only with difficulty (John 20:14, Luke 24:16). It possessed properties different from those of normal men, for He could appear and disappear at will (Luke 24:15,31; John 20:19,20) irrespective of material barriers. The nature of these powers was recognized, for Paul observed in Philippians (3:21) that He possessed a "body of . . . glory, according to the working whereby he is able even to subject all things unto himself." Revelation hails Him as the risen Christ, the head of a new order of beings, the beginning of God's new creation. He is the "firstborn among many brethren" who will be brought to glory by the same road which He Himself has trod. Because He is victor over death His victory may be shared by all those whom He has redeemed.

The third element of this title, "ruler" or "prince of the kings of the earth" foreshadows the coming kingdom. "We see not yet all things subjected to him" (Heb. 2:8). Just as surely, however, as He is the faithful witness and the firstborn from the dead, so surely will He become the ruler of the kings of the earth. His spiritual triumph must eventuate in full sovereignty over the affairs of this world. The process of realizing this sovereignty is the story of Revelation, for it is the unfolding of the authority that is already vested in the Son of God.

Just as the first part of the fifth verse of the Prologue provides a Christological approach in terms of what Christ *is*, the second part of this verse provides an approach in terms of what Christ *does*:

> Unto him that loveth us, and loosed us from our sins by his blood; and he made us *to be* a kingdom, *to be* priests unto his God and Father; to him be the glory and the dominion for ever and ever (1:5, 6).

The three declarations are aspects of His work of redemption. The first describes the constant attitude, "that loveth us." Love seems to bear only a small part in this book. Fiery judgments, prayers for vengeance, persecutions, lightnings, thunders, and voices fill its pages. Nevertheless the progress of judgment is prompted by love that vindicates the persecuted, that preserves the elect, and that prepares eternal blessing for its own. The present tense of the verb speaks of a constant attitude that remains the same now as it always was, a love that is as intense for His present disciples as it was for the twelve of whom it was said that "having loved his own that were in the world, he loved them to the uttermost" (John 13:1, mg.).

The second declaration, "and loosed us from our sins by his blood," is an affirmation of redemption. The reading of the Revised Version, "loosed" instead of "washed," is preferable on textual grounds. Revelation deals with redemption of the cosmos, but it begins with the salvation of the individual. The work of Christ is not only the judgment of a world, but it is primarily the cleansing and liberating of each single believer. The book can appeal only to those who have experienced the deliverance that forgiveness in Christ's blood can bring, and who are thereby prepared for the hope of His coming.

The third declaration, "and made us *to be* a kingdom, *to be* priests unto his God and Father," is the last stage of redemption. First He loves those whom He saves; then He redeems those whom He loves; then He makes His redeemed into a kingdom for Himself. The kingdom is the logical outgrowth of redemptive purpose because those who have been delivered from evil and who have been cleansed for service need some common medium through which they can utilize their transformed powers for God. The kingdom is their reward for faithfulness (Rev. 3:21), and is the final manifestation of divine jurisdiction over the earth. In it they can anticipate security and victory over the evils which they have previously found almost overwhelming.

The combination of kingdom and priesthood is not new, for the same basic idea appears in I Peter. "Ye are an elect race, a royal priesthood, a holy nation, a people for *God's* own possession" (2: 9). As a kingdom, the redeemed constitute the subjects and beneficiaries of Christ's rule: as a priesthood they are the worshipers and intercessors who constantly attend upon Him.

The focus both of the description and of the declaration is the theme of the Prologue:

> Behold, he cometh with the clouds; and every eye shall see him, and they that pierced him; and all the tribes of the earth shall mourn over him (Rev. 1:7).

For the Christian the future is not measured in terms of *what,* but in terms of *whom.* Time, events, and trends are all secondary to the disclosure of the Person who is the Son of God, the King of men, and the Redeemer of all creation.

This theme makes three assertions concerning the person of Christ. "He cometh with the clouds" asserts *the supernatural manner* of His advent. He does not enter the world again by the gateway of human birth as He did the first time, coming among us through the same door by which all the rest of men have entered. At His first advent His birth was both supernatural and natural. It was supernatural because He was conceived by the Holy Spirit; but there was nothing in the actual process of birth itself that was different from that of any other baby. Any observer who knew nothing of the annunciation to Mary would have regarded Jesus as an ordinary child born in the usual way. The supernatural character of this person was first established by indirect evidence: the announcement to the shepherds and the star that appeared in the East.

The supernatural character of His second advent will be immediately apparent, since He will become instantly visible to all observers. The first half of the prediction, "He cometh with the clouds," is a direct reference to Daniel 7:13, which prophesies the appearance of the Messiah before God to receive the kingdom. The second half of the prediction, "and they that pierced him," recalls Zechariah 12:10, which is also an apocalyptic Messianic passage, and which connects the Messianic appearing with the last judgments on the Gentile nations that have besieged Jerusalem. The same combination of passages appears in the words of Jesus quoted in Matthew 24:30; and the concept of a sudden appearance from heaven is repeated in Acts 1:11: "This Jesus, who was received up from you into heaven, shall so come in like manner as ye beheld him going into heaven." The ninth verse of the same chapter says that "a cloud received him out of their sight." He vanished into a cloud; He will reappear in one.

The cloud is probably not to be interpreted as a vapor cloud or as a storm cloud, but as a cloud of glory betokening the presence of God. On the occasion of the Transfiguration, which was the fulfilment of Jesus' promise to the disciples, "There are some of them that stand here, who shall in no wise taste of death, till they see the kingdom of God" (Luke 9:27), Jesus was manifested "in glory." Twice the word "glory" is used, meaning a brilliant, dazzling light. Matthew in describing the same event says that Jesus and the disciples with Him were overshadowed by "a bright cloud," from which the voice of God spoke approval of the Son. The "cloud," then, may be the cloud of the Shekinah, which led the children of Israel out of Egypt and through the desert, and which overshadowed the Tabernacle and the Temple (Exod. 13:21, 22; 40:34, Num. 9:15, 16, II Chron. 7:2, 3).

The second clause of verse 7 asserts *the universality of His appearing*. "Every eye shall see him, and they that pierced him." The words imply that living and dead, good and bad alike, shall witness the reality of Christ's advent. They do not necessarily mean that all men shall see Him at the same moment, nor that His advent will have the same significance for all. They do mean that His appearing will be visible, tangible, and historical in the sense that it will be as definite an event as the battle of Waterloo or as the election of the President of the United States. Although there is much figurative language in Revelation, there is little excuse for not taking these statements literally.

The third clause, "and all the tribes of the earth shall mourn over him" (1:7) is susceptible of two interpretations. One is that the advent of Christ, like the manifestation to Paul on the Damascus road, will cause intense grief to those who rejected Him and who then are driven to realize that He is the Son of God, their Redeemer. "Mourning" in this sense would be equivalent to repentance. Such an explanation seems to be warranted by the language of Zechariah:

> They shall look unto me whom they have pierced; and they shall mourn for him, as one mourneth for his only son, and shall be in bitterness for him, as one is in bitterness for his first-born (Zech. 12:10).

Zechariah predicts that the nation of Israel, suddenly realizing that the rejected Messiah is theirs, will repent bitterly of their wrong, and will eagerly turn to Him. The writer of Revelation extends this to "the tribes of the earth," which includes Gentiles.

There is another sense in which the "mourning" may be understood. The advent of Christ will bring to a sudden terminus the wicked schemes of men, and will frustrate many of their hopes and desires. The destruction of Babylon will be attended by the weeping and the mourning of the merchants whose market is thus ruined (Rev. 18:17-19). Not everyone will be pleased to see the Lord returning. Many will bewail the occasion because it will interfere with their plans.

The Prologue thus presents the person of Christ by a threefold description of His position, a threefold declaration of His redemptive work, and a threefold aspect of His appearing. As the first main vision is introduced, the reader has a fairly clear idea of the Person whose future work is to be revealed.

The four great visions in the structure of the book may also be interpreted Christologically.

VISION I: CHRIST IN THE CHURCH (1:9-3:22)

The first vision of Revelation is concerned chiefly with present institutions and events. While the general framework of Revelation relates to the future, the letters to the churches were intended for persons or groups living at the time when the prophecy was written. The phrase which declares specifically "I will show thee the things which must come to pass hereafter"

(4:1) follows the first vision, as if to say that the material following the letters belongs to the future, but that the letters themselves pertain to the present. If that is so, then the picture of
the person of Christ which is drawn in this vision represents
Him in His present function and character.

The letters are directed to seven historic churches located in
seven cities of the Roman province of Asia. There is no reason
to doubt that these churches are accurately characterized by the
messages which the seer indited to them. They were written
to actual believers to arouse them to renewed devotion, and as
an introduction to the teaching in the rest of the book which
would be applicable to the future of them all.

There are many keys to the interpretation of these letters, but
the one most pertinent to the present discussion is the constant
reference in them to the person of Christ as He is described in
the portrait which makes the frontispiece of this section. Each
letter begins with the statement, "These things saith he that . . ."
or an equivalent phrase, which characterizes the speaker by
some one feature of the portrait. Each feature thus emphasized
has an appropriate connection with the nature of the church, as
if the manifestation of Christ were specially designed for that
church. To the careless assembly at Ephesus He is the inspector
who walks among the lampstands; to the oppressed flock of Smyrna threatened by persecution He is the risen Lord whom death
could not destroy; to the lax church at Pergamum He appears
with the sharp two-edged sword of judgment. Each feature of
the portrait is made significant for the addressees.

One of the strange facts of the Bible is that nowhere in the
historic narratives of the life of Jesus is there a description of
His physical person. The portrait in Revelation is not an attempt
to describe His features in photographic detail, but is rather intended to convey an impression of His glory in terms of its effect
upon the seer of Patmos and in terms of the impact of His
person upon the churches.

The features of this portrait have already been discussed[1] and
their individual relation to the letters to the churches has been
noted. Two general impressions, however, are created by it.
The first is that of holiness; for the gleaming whiteness of the
hair, the lightning-like flash of the eyes, the intolerable glare of
the feet like white-hot bronze, and the countenance like the
noonday sun bespeak the Deity who dwells in light unapproach-
able. The second impression is the likeness of this portrait to the

transfiguration of Christ in the Synoptic Gospels. Matthew says that "his face did shine as the sun, and his garments became white as the light" (Matt. 17:2). Mark states that "his garments became glistering, exceeding white, so as no fuller on earth can whiten them" (Mark 9:3). Luke reports that "the fashion of his countenance was altered, and his raiment *became* white *and* dazzling" (Luke 9:29). The identity of this person with the glorified Christ is confirmed by the words, "I was dead, and behold, I am alive for evermore . . ." (Rev. 1:18), which plainly refer to His death and resurrection. The Christ of the churches is a glorified and omnipotent Christ, in whose hands are the keys of death and of Hades (1:18).

The several messages to the churches which follow the portrait have already been discussed structurally. Their Christological interpretation, however, depends upon the use of the first personal pronoun, I, by which the Christ of the portrait identifies Himself and asserts His peculiar interest in them. His messages to them are founded upon certain relationships implied in their assertions.

First, He is the *observer* of the churches who moves constantly among them to watch over their weakness and to preserve their usefulness. Unlike the devil, who walks about as a roaring lion, seeking whom he may devour (I Pet. 5:8), Christ walks in the midst of the churches to give them His counsel and support. His loving desire is to keep them from failure, His messages contain more pleas than threats. To the persecuted church, fearful of the future, He says, "Fear not" (Rev. 2:10); to the church with a loyal but pessimistic minority, He promises that "they shall walk with me in white; for they are worthy" (3:4); to the feeble church with little expectation of effectiveness, He throws open a door of opportunity "which none can shut" (3:8). The last and greatest invitation of His love is addressed to the Laodicean church, in which He could find nothing to commend:

> Behold, I stand at the door, and knock: if any man hear my voice and open the door, I will come in to him, and will sup with him, and he with me. (Rev. 3:20).

Again, the Christ of the churches is *infallible in His discernment*. The phrase, "I know . . ." introduces a precise diagnosis of the attainments and failures of each congregation. Each group stands before Him exactly as it is, stripped of all pretense and unaffected by the false accusations of its enemies. He is an unerring and incorruptible judge, whose justice is unimpeachable and from whose sentence there is no appeal.

Christ possesses *final authority*. He has the power to remove the lampstand that is giving no light (2:5), and He can also preserve the church from the hour of trial that will try those that dwell on the earth (3:10). Though the weight of responsibility for obedience is laid upon all the churches in all of these messages, yet He reveals that the final cause of their preservation or their judgment is His own unfailing will.

The *personal return* of the Lord is the goal of the churches' existence. The increasing urgency in the predictions of His advent, beginning with the rather indefinite warning to the church at Ephesus and concluding in the emphatic challenge to Laodicea, "Behold, I stand at the door and knock," illustrates this point.[2] As time passes, the urgency becomes greater, for the fulfilment of the promise draws nearer. His return is the final answer to the churches' need and the termination of their earthly services.

The Christ of the churches in the first vision of Revelation is the militant guardian of His people. The portrait of Christ reveals both the holiness which is the standard of His purity and the priestly character of His present ministry.

VISION II: CHRIST IN THE COSMOS (4:1-16:21)

With the fourth chapter there is a sudden transition to a new concept of Christ. The seer was elevated from earth to heaven, and was allowed to gaze upon the celestial side of the cosmic drama in which Christ plays the major role. The content of the book from here through the rest of the section is concerned with the relation of Christ to the process of history as He administers it and brings it to a conclusion. For this reason the title is called "Christ in the Cosmos," because the victory of Christ over the world is stressed rather than the state of the saved.

In this vision there are three prominent features: the sealed book, the opening of which determined the progress of action; the person who is entrusted with opening it, Christ; and the orderly fulfilment of God's purpose, which ends with the great voice, "It is done" (16:17).

The sealed book is the clue to the sequence of the action. The term "book" (5:1) does not refer to a bound volume of individual pages, but rather to a scroll on which the writing was arranged in successive columns. When the scroll was rolled, it was sealed at seven different points, so that as each seal was broken a new column or section was exposed to view. The unrolling of this scroll is the progressive disclosure of the action of God.

Various explanations of this unusual book have been offered by commentators. Those who hold that the Revelation contains the symbolic account of God's dealing with the church generally believe that the roll contained the prefigured history of the succeeding centuries. H. B. Swete suggests that "it is the Book of Destiny, to be unrolled and read only as the seals are opened by the course of events."[3]   By this interpretation the scroll is made to mean that the entire historical process of all the years since Christ is involved in its content. Another interpretation makes it refer to the future. J. A. Seiss in his *Lectures on the Apocalypse* says that it is the "title deed" of creation which had been forfeited because of sin, and which had reverted to its original giver.[4] He thinks that it is the charter of creation, which Christ can take over as the redeemer of the human race, and by authority of which He can assert the right over the estate which Adam and his descendants lost. Seiss holds that Christ's final act of redeeming earth's forfeited title is still future, and that the scene in heaven depicted in this passage is yet to take place.

In any case, the sealed book represents the mystery of God's purpose for the world. Creation was not an end in itself, nor did God make the universe simply as a toy to be enjoyed for a while, and then to be flung aside idly as a child discards a plaything of which he is tired. In the beginning God had made the world and man for a purpose, and sin had blighted both. The world thus posed a problem: if sin were ignored, God's righteousness could be challenged; and if sin were summarily punished, man would be utterly doomed. In dealing with the situation God must have had a plan by which the world process could be brought to a consummation in which sin is removed while man is preserved. The breaking of the seals discloses the final execution of the redemptive purpose.

The possession of this book and the execution of the purpose can be entrusted only to one who is completely worthy. No ordinary man can accept the responsibility of opening its sealed pages. Paradoxically, the person who undertakes this tremendous task must be absolutely courageous and absolutely compassionate. From Alexander the Great to Stalin men have sought to bring in the perfect world by the exercise of authority, but not one has succeeded. They lacked the power to reorganize the disorder of humanity or else they lacked the understanding of the human heart necessary for dealing with it sympathetically.

The only person who is capable of fulfilling the purpose of God and who can execute perfectly His judgments is the Lord Jesus Christ, whose threefold capacity for this work is indicated by three titles assigned to Him.

He is the Lion of the tribe of Judah (5:5). This title is taken from the Blessing of Jacob, which he bestowed on his sons just before his death, and which is recorded in Genesis 49:8-10.

Judah, thee shall thy brethren praise:
Thy hand shall be on the neck of thine enemies;
Thy father's sons shall bow down before thee.
Judah is a lion's whelp;
From the prey, my son, thou art gone up:
He stooped down, he couched as a lion,
And as a lioness; who shall rouse him up?
The sceptre shall not depart from Judah,
Nor the ruler's staff from between his feet,
Until Shiloh come;
And unto him shall the obedience of the peoples be.

These verses ascribe to Judah the ascendancy over his brethren. The scepter and the staff are assigned to him as the ruler of the tribes. The prophecy was partially fulfilled when the Davidic dynasty came to power; for David, as a member of the tribe of Judah, was anointed king over all Israel. To him and to his descendants the promise of rulership was confirmed by God. The Gospel of Matthew introduces Jesus as "the son of David" (1:1). He is heir to the throne of Israel and is the rightful sovereign of the kingdom which God promised to His people. As the lion is the king of beasts, the embodiment of courage and power, so Christ is the king of the nations by divine appointment.

The second title, "Root of David" (Rev. 5:5), is drawn from a prophecy in Isaiah 11:1-4:

And there shall come forth a shoot out of the stock of Jesse,
And a branch out of his roots shall bear fruit:
And the Spirit of Jehovah shall rest upon him,
The spirit of wisdom and understanding,
The spirit of counsel and might,
The spirit of knowledge and of the fear of Jehovah;
And his delight shall be in the fear of Jehovah.
And he shall not judge after the sight of his eyes,
Neither decide after the hearing of his ears;

But with righteousness shall he judge the poor,
And decide with equity for the meek of the earth;
And he shall smite the earth with the rod of his mouth,
And with the breath of his lips shall he slay the wicked.

The picture drawn by the prophecy is that of a tree which has been felled, leaving only a stump decaying in the ground. Out of the stump, however, is growing a healthy young shoot in which the life of the tree is renewed, and which will in time restore its original glory.

The context of this passage in Isaiah interprets its meaning. The preceding chapter describes the Assyrian invasion which devastated the northern kingdom of Israel and threatened the safety of Judah. The prophet indicated that the peril was a warning of more severe judgments to come, and that Jehovah would ultimately destroy the kingdoms of the land, including Judah. As the trees of the forest fell before the axe of the woodsman, so Judah would fall in judgment. Although the royal house of Judah as a ruling power perished in the Babylonian captivity, the Messiah, or the Branch as He is called in the prophecies, will yet come to restore its authority over His people. Revelation (5:5) indicates by the use of this phrase, "the Root of David," that Christ, the ruler of the kings of the earth, is the lawful and lineal successor of David, who will restore the kingdom that has been destroyed by judgment.

Revelation asserts also that the Root of David is worthy to take the scroll of destiny because of His character. Again the passage in Isaiah is applicable, for it describes Him as endued with the sevenfold Spirit of God, devoted to the fear of Jehovah, absolutely impartial in His judicial decisions, and unwavering in His execution of them. His kingdom shall begin a universal reign of righteousness and peace, in which Israel shall be restored to the land, and in which "the earth shall be full of the knowledge of Jehovah as the waters cover the sea" (Isa. 11:9).

The third title applied to Christ is "the Lamb slain" (Rev. 5:6). In contrast to the regal majesty of the lion He has also the gentle meekness of the lamb. His lamb-like disposition, however, is not stressed so much as His sacrificial character. The word "slain" (Greek: *esphagmenon*) means literally "slaughtered," "with its throat cut." It is used in the ninth verse of chapter 6 to describe those who were martyred for the witness of Jesus. In the heavenly songs that accompany His exaltation to the position of arbiter of the universe, the reason for His worthiness is not ascribed to His regal appointment as Lion of the tribe of Judah nor to His lineal descent from David, but rather to His redemptive death on behalf of men.

> Worthy art thou to take the book, and to open the seals thereof; for thou wast slain, and didst purchase unto God with thy blood *men* of every tribe, and tongue, and people, and nation, and madest them *to be* unto our God a kingdom and priests; and they reign upon the earth. (Rev. 5:9, 10)

From this point in the Apocalypse one can trace the broad outline of major developments by reference to the Lamb. As He opens the various seals and introduces the successive judgments, there is increasing terror among the wicked until they cry out to the mountains and rocks: "Fall on us, and hide us from the face of him that sitteth on the throne, and from the wrath of the Lamb" (6:16). Because He has redeemed the world, He has the right to judge it and to cleanse it for His use.

The preservation of the saved also is mentioned in this connection:

> After these things I saw, and behold, a great multitude, which no man could number, out of every nation and of *all* tribes and peoples and tongues, standing before the throne and before the Lamb, arrayed in white robes, and palms in their hands; and they cry with a great voice, saying,
> Salvation unto our God who sitteth on the throne, and unto the Lamb (Rev. 7:9, 10).

> They shall hunger no more, neither thirst any more; neither shall the sun strike upon them, nor any heat; for the Lamb that is in the midst of the throne shall be their shepherd, and shall guide them unto fountains of waters of life (Rev. 7:16, 17).

This security is connected with Christ's redemption in two other passages. In the description of the conflict between the devil and the saints of God, it is said that they "overcame him because of the blood of the Lamb" (12:11). The death of Christ, by which all claims of evil upon believers have been canceled, ends the devil's authority over men. He can bring no effective accusation against them, since God has justified them. Furthermore, the believers have been registered in God's permanent record, "the book of life of the Lamb that hath been slain" (13:8). At times they may feel like displaced persons, but the record of their citizenship is kept on high, and by redemption they are assured of finding that country which they now seek as pilgrims.

The figure of the Lamb persists in the third and fourth visions as well as in the second, though it is less prominent. The triumph of the Lamb (17:14), and the marriage of the Lamb (19:7) continue the concept of a fulfilment of redemption. The latter figure, somewhat akin to the Pauline figure of the wife in Ephesians 5:25-27, points to the reunion of Christ's people with Himself as an eternally joyous fellowship.

The story of the world, then, is not the chronicle of chance, but is the operation of a sovereign God who by redemptive power is making ready for the final doom of evil and for the vindication of His truth. Apostasy and oppression have not thwarted His design for bringing in everlasting righteousness.

The execution of this purpose will be finally effected in climactic judgment. The arrival of the kingdom of God will be cataclysmic, produced by a sudden intervention of divine power. Redemption is not a gradual evolution of good out of evil by forces resident within man, but is the supernatural act of God in answer both to the sacrifice of His Son and the patience of His saints.

VISION III: CHRIST IN CONQUEST (17:1-21:8)

The two concluding sections of Revelation parallel each other, and may be taken together, since they are obviously designed as contrasting studies of world judgment. In both of these aspects of the consummation of world affairs Christ is central, but they differ from each other in the way in which He is presented. For the third vision the portrait is recorded in Revelation 19:11-16.

Three epithets describe His functions as judge. The first of these is "Faithful and True" (19:11). The same title appears in Revelation 3:14 where it is applied to Him as He speaks His mind to the Laodicean church. Because He is faithful He must discharge His office of judge, not shrinking from the administration of discipline or punishment where it is needed. Because He is true He cannot alter the standards of God which condemn sin. Favoritism and laxity cannot be found in Him, for He is the perfect administrator of justice in a world where injustice has long since reigned.

His second title, "The Word of God," (19:13) recalls the familiar prophetic formula of the Old Testament: "The word of the Lord came unto . . . . " Usually the content of the revelation was a warning against the evils that were threatening the people, or else was a declaration of impending judgment for sin. As a title of Christ the term shows that the message has become incarnate. The utterance of God which expressed His holy displeasure against sin is now made manifest in a person bringing retribution upon the enemies of God who have corrupted the earth. Christ has become the manifestation of vengeance as well as of mercy, and the two apparently contradictory characteristics coexist in His person. There is no real inconsistency in the contrast; for the historical Christ could forgive a penitent publican like Zacchaeus, and could also wither hypocritical Pharisees with righteous scorn and drive money-changers from the temple with whips of rushes. The meekness of Calvary and the sternness of Armageddon may seem inconsistent, but wherever sin exists, they may both be found. Grace is not synonymous with tolerance of evil; on the contrary, it can operate to its fullest extent only when evil is destroyed.

This same title occurs in the Prologue of John (John 1:1, 14). There the emphasis is on grace, as John specifically states: ". . . grace and truth came through Christ" (1:17). The *logos* or Word is the expression of God's nature in understandable terms, and whether those terms be mercy or judgment they are both equally the message of God. As He came once to condemn and to forgive sin, so will He come again to condemn it and to judge it.

The name written on His garment and on His thigh is a declaration of His indisputable sovereignty. The titles "King" and "Lord" were widely applied to royalty in the Greek East. "King" seems to have been the title generally used in the New Testament for the emperor (John 19:15; I Pet. 2:13, 17). "Lord," in particular, was employed by oriental peoples who regarded all subjects as slaves of their rulers. In the eastern half of the Roman empire the emperors were hailed as kings and lords from the time of Nero (A.D. 54-58), but in the western half of the empire the title of "lord" was not used until the reign of Domitian (A.D. 81).[5]   The application of these titles to Christ was a mark of the reverence in which the early church held Him, and their occurrence in this passage in Revelation shows that the highest possible place spiritually and politically was accorded to Him by His followers. They expected that He would triumph over all lesser potentates and that the social and political life of the future would be governed by Him.

The third vision represents Christ in conquest, sweeping away the last barriers of evil, annihilating its organized forces, establishing His reign over men, and completing the judgment of the dead before the great white throne (Rev. 20:11-14). He is undisputed sovereign of the world which He has conquered by right of redemption.

VISION IV: CHRIST IN CONSUMMATION (21:9-22:5)

Whereas the third vision was largely negative because it dealt with the judgment and doom of evil, the fourth vision is positive because it presents Christ as the delight of His people. In this vision only one title appears, the same that is used elsewhere in Revelation, "the Lamb." There are seven occurrences of it, each one being important (21:9, 14, 22, 23, 27; 22:1, 3).

The first of these defines *the real significance* of the "city" as "the wife of the Lamb." The idea appears in the former section, for "the marriage of the Lamb" was announced as part of the ultimate victory (19:7). Subsequent to the judgment of the great white throne the seer saw "the holy city, new Jerusalem, coming out of heaven from God, made ready as a bride adorned for her husband" (21:2). The term which denotes the most intimate relationship of human life is thus applied to the communion of Christ and His people, who are symbolized by the city which is their eternal abode. Its real importance therefore derives not from its beauties, but from the Lamb; not its location, but its relationship is stressed.

The *foundations* of the city are inscribed with the names of "the twelve apostles of the Lamb" (21:14). The phrase recalls Ephesians 2:20, which says that the church of God is built "upon the foundation of the apostles and the prophets . . . . " "Behold, the Lamb of God, that taketh away the sin of the world!" was the message that originally brought the disciples to Christ (John 1:29). Discipleship is based on redemption, and the fact that the foundation of faith is in the apostolic testimony and experience means that the eternal commonwealth of God is an abiding monument to the sacrifice of Christ.

The *worship* of God's people is centered in Christ, "for the Lord God the Almighty, and the Lamb, are the temple thereof" (Rev. 21:22). Worship is perfected by redemption, because in the act of the incarnation God came down to man in such a way that He became forever a part of human life. No structure nor ritual will be necessary any longer, for symbolism will be replaced by reality, and buildings will be superseded by the eternal presence of Christ.

The *light* of the city is the Lamb. As light makes plain the things that were mysterious in the dark, so in the light of redemption the present ignorance and uncertainty will vanish. The insoluble paradoxes that have tortured finite minds, the dilemmas that sin has posed and that could not be resolved by any ordinary means, the petty doubts and difficulties will disappear in the blazing glory of a realized redemption. "For we know in part, and we prophesy in part; but when that which is perfect is come, that which is in part shall be done away" (I Cor. 13:9,10).

The *citizenship* of the city will be insured by redemption. Only those whose names are enrolled in the Lamb's book of life will be admitted. The book of Hebrews speaks of "the general assembly and church of the firstborn who are enrolled in heaven"(Heb. 12:23). If the very hairs of men's heads are numbered, assuredly the list of the saved must be known by God and must be kept in mind by Him. A restricted citizenship means a controlled society where no uncleanness, idolatry, or falsehood will ever find a place. There can be no degeneration of that society, because weakening elements will have no entrance into it. Redemption precludes deterioration.

In this vision the "throne of the Lamb" is connected with service rather than with judgment (Rev. 22:3). The *occupation* of God's servants will be a joyous obedience performed in the constant memory of Calvary. It will not be an aimless idleness, however pleasant, but it will be a purposeful devotion to Him who "loveth us, and loosed us from our sins by his blood" (1:5). The nature of that service has not been disclosed, and speculation would be profitless. It is sufficient to know that eternity will bring a new unfolding of constructive activity.

THE EPILOGUE: CHRIST CHALLENGING (22:6-21)

Ending as it does with the remote future, the words of Revelation would seem vague and impractical were they not given immediate application by the Epilogue. This application is a personal appeal by the Lord Himself, thrice repeated: "Behold, I come quickly . . ." (22:7, 12, 20). Each appeal is addressed to a different group. The first is probably intended for the church universal, since it links with the initial address of the book as a whole: "Blessed [are] . . . they that hear the words of the prophecy, and keep the things which are written therein . . ." (1:3). The beatitude of 22:7 virtually repeats the clause, thereby connecting it with the group to whom the words were initially spoken.

To humanity at large the words, "I come quickly," are a declaration of judgment, for He will come "to render to each man according as his work is" (22:12). The separation of men into the evil and the good will then become complete. At present it is partial and progressive; but from the eternal city evildoers will be permanently excluded. The work of judgment is personal, and will be administered by the Lord Himself.

To the individual believer also Christ's utterance is a warm personal promise. The spontaneous reply of the seer, "Amen: come, Lord Jesus," (22:20) shows how readily and gladly the normal heart responds to the prospect of the Lord's return. The Apocalypse does not end with a note of dread but of longing and anticipation. The seer, returned to earth after his visions "in the Spirit," echoes the feeling of all true followers of Christ.

CHAPTER XIII

THE CHRONOLOGICAL APPROACH

The most intriguing approach to the study of Revelation is chronological. If the content of the book, whether symbolic or literal, can be fitted into some definable era of history, it can then be integrated with reference to known persons, events, and trends. As long as it cannot be connected with any particular happenings in the world, it remains an unsolved enigma; but if only part of its strange prophecies can be interpreted by history, the rest may be explained in turn.

The deterrent to a strictly dated interpretation of Revelation is the failure of all such schemes that have hitherto been proposed. No matter how the figures and intervals in it have been pressed and twisted to yield results, no clear parallel to the current era has yet been devised. Dogmatism is out of order even though it may be temporarily satisfying. On the other hand, the book contains a definite order of events beginning with "the things which are," and concluding with the descent to earth of the city of God.

The most obvious point at which to start is the time of writing of the book, which furnishes the *terminus a quo*. The message which was given to the seer was calculated to meet the need of his own day. "Blessed is he that readeth, and they that hear the words of the prophecy, and keep the things which are written therein: *for the time is at hand*" (Rev. 1:3, italics ours). This declaration that the fulfilment of some of its events would take place in the near future indicates that at least part of the sequence of its prophecy would begin shortly after the book was written and circulated. They are "things which must shortly come to pass" (1:1), and are consequently not remote from the days of John and his readers.

The immediacy of these predicted events is confirmed partially by the letters to the churches. Each church is a present historic institution, with its problems and potentialities. The Lord of the churches addresses them concerning present needs, and calls for action lest He visit them with future judgment. The first three chapters of Revelation deal chiefly with existing facts, though they contain a number of allusions to events that are impending.

How shall the remainder of the book be interpreted? Is it genuine prediction, or is it a cipher code of the Christian evaluation of the present or of the foreseeable future, put forward under the guise of prediction? To be specific, is the beast of Revelation 13 a figurative description of the contemporary Roman emperor, or is it a prophetic sketch of an antichrist who is, from the viewpoint of the writer, yet to come, and perhaps unrealized even in our own day?

THE PRETERIST VIEW

The preterist view of interpretation takes the former position, and holds that Revelation is simply a sketch of the conditions of the empire in the first century, written by some Hebrew Christian who revolted against pagan tyranny. He saw the empire as a gigantic machine, the opponent of the gospel in the social, political, and religious realms, and bent on stamping out the Christian movement. In the apocalyptic symbols of this book he voiced his protest against the whole system of evil, and his hope of ultimate victory.

The first systematic presentation of the preterist viewpoint originated in the early seventeenth century with Alcazar, a Jesuit friar, whose work was not free from controversial bias.[1] The Reformers had identified Babylon with the Roman church, and had succeeded in making the Revelation a powerful controversial weapon in their favor. In order to offset this interpretation, Alcazar attempted to show that Revelation had no application to the future, but that its prophecy could be divided into two major sections (chs. 1-12, 13-19) which dealt respectively with the church's conflict against Judaism and against paganism. Alcazar thus cleverly nullified the attacks upon the Roman church which the Reformers had made so successfully by using the language of Revelation.

Alcazar's suggestion was followed by some Protestant expositors, but the rise of the modern preterist school came with the prevalence of the technique of historical criticism. Since preterism did not necessitate any element of predictive prophecy or even any conception of inspiration, it could treat the Revelation simply as a purely natural historical document, embodying the eschatological concepts of its own time. Sir William Ramsay in his *Letters to the Seven Churches*[2] follows this principle, and in more recent days Shailer Matthews' work on *The Apocalypse of John* treats the Revelation in the same way.[3]

There is an element of truth in the preterist method, for the book undoubtedly did strike its roots into its own times. A predictive work which is totally unrelated to its own day could have no meaning for its readers because they would be unable to bridge the gap of thought between themselves and its prophecies. One might as well give a textbook on thermo-nuclear fission to a medieval monk and expect him to understand it as to present a work of complete prediction of the future to a man of any era and assume that he would profit by it unless some means were established by which he could connect his own times with the events which were to come. The preterist interpretation stresses the historical background of Revelation. As Ramsay has shown, the meaning of the letters to the churches is made much clearer when one knows the story of the founding and of the development of the seven Asian cities in which they stood.

The preterist position acts also as a sane balance for those who might make the Revelation a vehicle for all kinds of wild schemes concerning the future. It establishes the continuity of Scripture, and ties the voice of revelation to the living church.

The limit of the preterist view is the plain declaration of Revelation 4:1: "Come up hither, and I will show thee the things which must come to pass hereafter." "Hereafter" means after the present moment; hence, the future. If it means the future, then not all of Revelation can be reduced to an account of contemporary events. The city of God, described in the last chapters of the book, is obviously unrealized. Even if it be regarded as a symbol of some perfect state of human society, it has not yet been achieved. The preterist view simply does not account adequately for the claim of Revelation to be a prediction of the future if one intends to take its claim seriously.

THE HISTORICIST VIEW

The historicist view, sometimes called the continuous-historical view, contends that Revelation is a symbolic presentation of the entire course of the history of the church from the close of the first century to the end of time. The argument for the view is founded on the fact that two termini are mentioned: the day in which John the seer lived, and the ultimate day of God's victory and the establishment of the Holy City. No point between them can be identified with certainty as making a break in the sequence; therefore the process must be continuous.

By this interpretation the various series of the churches, the seals, the trumpets, and the bowls are made to represent particular events in the history of the world that are related to the history of the church. For example, Elliott, in his *Horae Apocalypticae*,[4] holds that the trumpets (8:6-9:21) cover the period from A.D. 395 to A.D. 1453, beginning with the attacks on the Western Roman empire by the Goths and concluding with the fall of the Eastern empire to the Turks. The first trumpet was the invasion of the Goths under Alaric, who sacked Rome; the second was the invasion under Genseric, who conquered North Africa; the third was the raid of the Huns under Attila, who devastated central Europe. The fourth was the collapse of the empire under the conquest of Odoacer. The locusts of the fifth trumpet were the Moslem hordes that poured into the west between the sixth and eighth centuries, and the sixth judgment of the four angels bound at the Euphrates (9:14) was the growth and spread of the Turkish power.

Although many of the advocates of this view agree among themselves about the method, there is no general agreement about the details. Many of the interpretations have to be strained in order to preserve the proper sequence of the events which they are supposed to foreshadow. Elliott argues that the "hail and fire" in Revelation 8:7 must refer to the Goths because hail comes from the north, as did the Goths. The historicist is constantly confronted with the dilemma of a far-fetched spiritualization in order to maintain the chain of historical events, or else if he makes the events literal in accordance with the language of the text he is compelled to acknowledge that no comparable events in history have happened.

There have, however, been many champions of this theory in the ranks of evangelical Christianity from the Reformation down to modern times.[5] Their interpretation has been sufficiently literal to warrant taking the chronology of Revelation seriously. In the various judgments and woes they have seen the rise and fall of nations and the persecutions and warfare of the church. They have generally identified the beast with Rome, political and ecclesiastical, and the harlot Babylon with the apostate church.

There are several objections to an interpretation of Revelation by a complete historicist view. First, the exact identification of the events of history with successive symbols has never been finally achieved, even after the events occurred. It is reasonable to suppose that during the lapse of 1900 years at least a portion of the predictions would have been fulfilled. If they were to be of value to the reader of Revelation as an indication of where he belonged in the total historical process, they should be identifiable with certainty. Such, however, seems not to be the case. The points of interpretation on which the majority of the doctrinal interpreters agree can be interpreted as trends quite as intelligibly as events. Since trends may be evident in any period of history, such prophecies do not point to any one era.

Second, historical interpreters have not satisfactorily explained why a general prophecy should be confined to the fortunes of the western Roman empire. The historical interpretation stresses chiefly the development of the church in western Europe; it takes little cognizance of the East. Yet in the first few centuries of the Christian era the church increased tremendously in the East, and spread as far as India and China, though it did not gain a permanent foothold in all sections of those countries. If a continuous-historical method is to be followed, it must have a broader scope.

Third, if the continuous-historical method is valid, its predictions would have been sufficiently plain at the outset to give the reader some inkling of what they meant. If the fire and hail of the first trumpet (8:7) really did refer to the Gothic invasions, it is hard to see how any first-century Christian could have understood the prediction in such a way as to give it any value for his thinking. It may be conceded that sometimes the most obvious interpretation of a passage is not the correct one. The prophets did not always comprehend what the Spirit gave them. Daniel was told that the words were "shut up and sealed till the time of the end" (12:9). On the other hand, the seer of Revelation was commanded not to seal the words of the prophecy, because the time was at hand (22:10). Evidently the prophecies were intended to be sufficiently plain for the average Christian to understand at least a part of them, and to apply them to his thinking. On the procedure of a purely continuous-historical method it is difficult to see how he could do so.

THE FUTURIST VIEW

The third general method of interpretation on a chronological basis is the futuristic approach. The futurist generally believes that all of the visions from Revelation 4:1 to the end of the book are yet to be fulfilled in the period immediately preceding and following the second advent of Christ. The reason for the view is found in the comparison of Revelation 1:1,19, and 4:1. Revelation 1:1 states that the book as a whole is concerned with "the things which must shortly come to pass," and which are thus identified as belonging to the future as far as the seer is concerned. Revelation 1:19 contains a threefold or perhaps a twofold command:

> Write therefore the things which thou sawest, and the things which are, and the things which shall come to pass hereafter;

or, as it is sometimes rendered:

> . . . . the things which thou sawest, both the things which are, and the things which shall come to pass hereafter.

In either case, the visions are divided into two general sections: one, the things that fall within the actual lifetime of the seer, the first century, and second, the things which were future to his period.

The introduction to the fourth chapter seemingly identifies the future visions as beginning at that point, for the heavenly voice summoning the seer said:

> Come up hither, and I will show thee *the things which must come to pass hereafter*. (Italics ours)

On this ground the futurist has a good claim for the validity of his method. If the events of Revelation 4 through 22:5 are all in the future, they may or may not have taken place yet, and their strange statements may still be taken either literally or figuratively. If they are literal, they can refer to events such as the world has not witnessed hitherto, and such as it shall witness only in those times of the end when cosmic issues are at stake and when supernatural forces shall be let loose.

Many futurists hold that the period described by this part of Revelation begins with the removal of the church from the world as described in I Corinthians 15:52-54 and in I Thessalonians 4:13-18. Some, like Seiss, argue that the summons to the seer in Revelation 4:1,2 is the counterpart to the removal of the church.[6] Newell suggests that the more literal translation, "After these things," would give a clearer understanding of the meaning of the passage, since it would indicate that the events of 4:1 and of the text following came *after* the church age mentioned in 1:9-3:22.[7] While it is undoubtedly true that the word "church" does not occur in Revelation after 3:22, there is no sure proof that the church is not to be identified with any of the groups mentioned in the context.

Without disputing whether or not the church is removed from the world at the beginning of final judgment, one can say that this passage does not require either conclusion. There is no convincing reason why the seer's being "in the Spirit" and being called into heaven typifies the rapture of the church any more than his being taken into the wilderness to view Babylon indicates that the church is there in exile. The phrase relates only to the experience of the seer, and not necessarily to that of the church. Furthermore, "after these things" is used so frequently in Revelation that it has lost the exactitude of "after these events which I have just mentioned," and means rather, "next in order."

Many if not most futurists interpret Revelation 1:9-3:22 as the historicists do the rest of the book. For the futurists the letters to the churches represent successive periods of church history, beginning with Ephesus, the apostolic church, and continuing with Smyrna, the martyr church, Pergamum, the worldly church, Thyatira, the apostate church, Sardis, the church of the Reformation, Philadelphia, the live church, and Laodicea, the lukewarm church. Although certain broad parallels with the successive epochs of church history may be drawn, the letters to the seven churches do not call for such an alignment of periods, but seem to depict naturally seven contemporaneous churches of Asia Minor whose internal affairs were singularly well known to the writer. Their significance did not cease with the end of the apostolic age, for they are seven different types of churches that may be found in any period of the world's history since Pentecost. If they are understood as trends that divide the church age horizontally rather than as eras that divide it vertically, fewer difficulties will be encountered in interpreting them.

Ephesus is typical of the zealous church whose initial love is cooling but whose works are maintained. Smyrna, the suffering church, clings to its faith under persecution. Pergamum has become worldly, yielding to the pressure of its environment. Thyatira has retained its religious forms and works, but has been corrupted by apostate teachers with evil practices. Sardis is the church of hollow reputation, essentially dead in spirit. Philadelphia, small, struggling, and faithful, is unimpressive in appearance but totally loyal. Laodicea, the cultured and wealthy church, is successful but

indifferent. Taken together they illustrate the differing attitudes
to be found in almost every country and era where the church has
existed.

Two further observations concerning the futurist view may be
proffered. One should note carefully that the phrase "after these
things" is indefinite. It does not specify after *what* the predicted
events will take place, nor does it say how long afterward. Theoretically, the events of the Apocalypse could all have transpired
after the time of the seer, and yet prior to the present year of 1957.
They could occur any time after the year 100 and still be future
to the writing of the book. In that sense the historicist is a futurist, since he holds that the Revelation predicts what will come to
pass after the lifetime of its writer. Again, the *terminus a quo*
of this book is not easy to fix by the symbolism. If it be agreed
that the events of Revelation begin to unfold after the Lamb takes
the book from the hand of the enthroned Deity, when does that
happen? Is it identical with the ascension of Christ to the heaven-
lies after the resurrection? If so, then the seals must have already
been opened and the work of judgment begun. If this initial event
is to be placed in the future, then the present age is largely a parenthesis in the chronology of Revelation, and the investiture of the
Lamb with the authority to open the seals is yet to come. The
settling of this terminus is one of the crucial problems in the interpretation of the book.

In favor of the futurist view, one may say that the *terminus ad
quem* is unmistakable. However one may interpret the symbols,
the action of the book leads to and includes the last judgment of
earth and the final establishment of the city of God. As the events
lead up to this terminus in close succession, one may reason back-
ward and say that the bulk of these events must still be future,
since the consummation with which they are associated has not
yet been attained and since the symbols seem to call for a rapid
succession of acts rather than for a protracted process.

The more literal an interpretation that one adopts, the more
strongly will he be construed to be a futurist. The object like a
burning mountain cast into the sea (8:8), the opening of the bot-
tomless pit (9:2), and many other episodes must be interpreted
symbolically if they are to be taken as applying to current or to
past history. If they are yet to come, they may be a more accurate description of actual phenomena than most expositors have
realized, for the physical and psychical researches of recent years
have opened to the mind of man worlds that in John's time were

completely unknown.   The atom bomb, guided missiles, and the
scientific devices of modern warfare have made the Apocalypse
seem much less apocalyptic than it did fifty years ago.

THE IDEALIST VIEW

A fourth interpretation of the Revelation may be called the
idealist or spiritualist view.   The latter name has no connection
with spiritualism as a cult; it means simply that the whole book
is interpreted "spiritually." According to this view, the Revelation
represents the eternal conflict of good and evil, which persists in
every age, although here it may have particular application to the
period of the church.   The symbols have no immediate historic
connection with any definite social or political events.   The general
tenets of this view have been well stated by Raymond Calkins in
his work on *The Social Message of the Book of Revelation* :[8]

> If we understand the emergency which caused the book to
> be written, the interpretation of it for its time, for our
> time, and for all time, it becomes as clear as daylight. In the
> light of this explanation, how far from the truth becomes
> that use of it which finds the chief meaning of the book in
> the hints it gives us about the wind-up of creation, the end
> of the world, and the nature of the Last Judgment . . . . To
> use Revelation in this way is to abuse it, for the book itself
> makes no claim to be a key to the future.

Calkins affirms that the chief message of the book can be sum-
marized in five general propositions :

1.   It is an irresistible summons to heroic living.
2.   The book contains matchless appeals to endurance.
3.   It tells us that evil is marked for overthrow *in the end*.
4.   It gives us a new and wonderful picture of Christ.
5.   The Apocalypse reveals to us the fact that history is in
     the mind of God and in the hand of Christ as the author
     and reviewer of the moral destinies of men.

To all of these propositions almost any interpreter of Revelation could give assent regardless of the school to which he belongs.   The idealist view does contain much that is true.   Its flaw
is not so much in what it affirms as in what it denies.   Many
idealists could be classed as preterists, since they hold that the
imagery of the Apocalypse is taken from its immediate world, and
that the prevailing conditions of Domitian's reign are reflected in
the symbolic episodes that fill its pages. They refuse to assign to

them any literal historical significance for the future, and they deny all predictive prophecy except in the most general sense of the ultimate triumph of righteousness.

Which of these foregoing chronological schemes is correct? In varying measure they have all been held by evangelical Christians, the validity of whose personal experience and whose devotion to Christ cannot be challenged. In each of them there is some element of truth, yet in many respects they are mutually exclusive. Where can a solution be found?

A return to the Biblical text is the only recourse in this strife of opposing theories. The truth in each is drawn from its accord with the statements of Revelation; the error in each arises from an overextension of the truth or from an exaggeration of some one interest.

For the preterist view one may say that the book of Revelation begins with "the things which are" (1:19). The seer was writing for the immediate use of his own generation, represented in seven actual churches of Asia whose locations and characteristics are adequately described by the text. There can be no doubt that this book is rooted in a concrete historical situation. The island of Patmos, the cities where the churches were located, the commerce, corruption, and power of Rome, the "kings of the east" beyond the mysterious border of the Euphrates (16:12), the use of a seal to enforce economic sanctions (13:16,17), governmental insistence on united worship of the head of the state (13:12) were all common in Domitian's day. Insofar as he contends that contemporary conditions illustrate the Apocalypse and give it a field of immediate application the preterist is right.

The weakness of this view is its terminal limitation. Obviously the judgments predicted have not been fulfilled, and however figuratively one may interpret the conquest of the world by Christ and the picture of a final judgment, neither has appeared yet. The preterist has an interpretation which has a firm pedestal, but which has no finished sculpture to place on it.

The view of the historicist is harder to assess. He does take into consideration the fact that "the things which shall come to pass hereafter" (1:19) should be interpreted as future to the writing of the book, and he attempts to identify them one by one. Because he believes that the *terminus a quo* commences with the end of the first century, he is consequently compelled to stretch the symbolism in successive stages over the remaining period of history until Christ's return, and he is forced to make arbitrary identification of symbols with definite events. The result is a framework of guesses on which no two independent historicists agree completely, and which involves making the identifications on very uncertain clues. One wonders whether the original intention of the book was to convey as particularized a prediction of history as the historicists have found in it. Many seem to have insisted on a larger amount of detail than the text would warrant.

Continuity and an appreciation of the hand of God in the historical process are the chief contributions of the historical method, and these may surely be retained. The book of Revelation is not just a snapshot of one short period of time, however important it may be as the gateway of eternity. Revelation was calculated to impart to its readers a criterion for estimating the spiritual progress of their own times in the light of the divine process that was leading to a climactic consummation.

The futurist school of thought, because of its insistence upon an interpretation as literal as possible, has been a healthy antidote to an overbalanced symbolism that has tended to make Revelation mean everything except the obvious. Whereas other views have attempted to attach to symbols a significance that was arbitrary at best and ridiculous at worst, the futurists have generally tried to achieve a consistent interpretation. Along with the historicist view they have accepted the validity of predictive prophecy in Revelation. They have taken seriously the order and character of the prophecies, and have attempted to connect them with the personal return of Christ.

The idealist view has made some contribution to the methods of interpretation by showing that the book must be understood in terms of trends as well as by episodes. Movements of thought and of spiritual power are more important than the individual events that are part of them. It is silly to quarrel over the identification of a single figure of speech and to miss the meaning of the whole passage in which it occurs. Undoubtedly the Revelation does reflect the conflict of Satan and of God, of evil and of good, that has been going on in the world ever since Eden; but it predicts also that evil will have a definite end and that Christ will ultimately be victorious at a specific time and place.

All of these views contain some good. Can one be adopted to the exclusion of the others?

The preterist viewpoint does not do justice to the predictive element in Revelation. If its premises are accepted, the book is directed only to the day in which it was written, and has no real

significance for the succeeding centuries, except as the principles
of truth which were applicable then may still be valid.

The idealist view, which is often associated with the preterist,
assumes a "spiritual" interpretation, and allows no concrete significance whatever to the figures that it employs. According to
this viewpoint they are not merely symbolic of events and persons, as the historicist view contends; they are only abstract symbols of good and evil. They may be attached to any time or place,
but, like the characters of *Pilgrim's Progress*, represent universal
qualities or trends. In interpretation the Apocalypse may thus
mean anything or nothing according to the whim of the interpreter.

The final conclusion on the chronological methods of interpretation is that all contain some elements of truth, and that all are
in a measure overstrained. The Revelation was written for its
own day, and its imagery is to be understood in the figures used
by the public to whom it was written. It does give light on the
future of the church, and it forecasts the end of the age and the
beginning of the kingdom of Christ. Probably the bulk of its
judgments are still unfulfilled. The focus of the book is on the
return of Christ, for which the judgments are preparatory.
Throughout the Revelation are spiritual principles which are
eternally true, but which come to their perfect fulfilment in the
conflict depicted here. Thus all four types of chronological interpretation have their place, though the dominant idea of a coming crisis keeps the focus of the book in the future.

The soundest conclusion seems to be that its sequence must be
organized around the return of Christ at some indefinite time in
the future, whether close to the present day or remote from it.
Subsequent to the victory of Christ is His reign with His saints
upon the earth, the last judgment, and the eternal glory of the
Holy City. Prior to His return is the final consummation of evil
in its political, social, and religious organization — a consummation in which are concentrated all the elements of evil that existed in the world of the first century and that have persisted ever
since. Revelation depicts the future intensification and completion of these tendencies in one vast structure that will be destroyed forever by the righteous wrath of God.

CHAPTER XIV

THE ESCHATOLOGICAL METHOD

The eschatological method of interpreting Revelation is based partly upon the exegesis of one passage in the book and partly upon the teaching concerning the future that can be found in the rest of the Bible. If Revelation is only one unit in a larger complex of Biblical prophecy, all of which is the prophetic revelation of God, it must accord with the whole in general purpose and scheme. The eschatological framework supplied by the whole will condition any or all of its parts.

There are three general types of eschatological interpretation current in the present thought of the church: the postmillennial, the amillennial, and the premillennial. All three take their names and their point of departure from Revelation 20:1-8, in which is mentioned the reign of Christ for a thousand years, generally known as the millennium.

The word itself does not occur in the New Testament, but it is a convenient means of referring to the concept. According to this passage there is a period in the future at the first of which there will be a resurrection of saints, followed by their reign with Christ of a thousand years. Satan will be bound and inoperative. At the end of this period will come the temporary release of Satan, a rebellion followed by the resurrection of the wicked dead, the final judgment, and the establishment of the eternal city of God.

POSTMILLENNIALISM

The postmillennial school interprets the passage as figurative, and asserts that a return of Christ to judge the earth and to set up the eternal kingdom comes at the end of the millennium. Its teaching assumes that the gospel of Christ will slowly but surely subdue all nations; that the kingdom of God is identical with the church; and that when the church has done its work of extending the spiritual sway of Christ over the entire earth that His personal advent may be expected.

The postmillennial school had its roots historically in the teaching of Augustine, bishop of Hippo, who in the fifth century sought a new philosophy of history with which to meet the puzzling crises of his own day. The Roman empire, which had been the organizing and stabilizing power of the world, was slowly tottering to its complete collapse. The sack of Rome by Alaric in 410 and the subsequent invasion of North Africa, Augustine's own country, by the barbarian hordes prompted Augustine to rethink the whole position of the Christian church. In his famous work, *The City of God*, he advanced the doctrine that the city or commonwealth of the world was doomed to perish, whereas the "city of God," the church, was continuing and taking its place. He taught that the "city of God" was identical with the church, and that as the latter grew in power and influence it would gradually bring all men under its sway and would introduce the reign of righteousness.

This doctrine of Augustine became the basis for the temporal claims of the Roman church. If the kingdom was to grow irresistibly until it dominated the earth, and if the visible church was identical with the kingdom, then the visible church could rightfully assume political power, and could make its conquests by force.

A second consequence of Augustine's teaching was the concept that the church must gradually increase in numbers and in possessions until it should achieve world dominion. The fact that it had become the state religion of the empire seemingly corroborated this thought. When the political structure of the empire crashed, Augustine felt that stability and survival could be achieved by the church as the "city of God." The system of the world might be passing away, but the church, being divine in origin, would endure.

To reach this conclusion Augustine had to employ an allegorical method of interpretation that divested Scripture of literal meaning and that emptied it of any certain significance. He taught that the millennium is the era beginning with the first advent of Christ and continuing to the second advent; that the "first resurrection" is spiritual; that the binding of Satan has already been completed; and that the reign of Christ is now in progress.[1]

Since Christ must reign "till he hath put all his enemies under his feet" (I Cor. 15:25), from this philosophy one would deduce logically that the present era must continue until the church is triumphant. Augustine's view was later adopted by Thomas Aquinas, and became the official teaching of the Roman church.[2]

The form of postmillennialism which is more familiar today began in the eighteenth century with Daniel Whitby, a Unitarian commentator who shared in the production of the *Paraphrase and Commentary on the New Testament* published in London in 1703 in collaboration with Patrick, Arnold, Lowth, and Lowman. Whitby's principles can be stated in four general propositions:

1. The "first resurrection" is not to be taken as a literal physical resurrection of the dead. It is a revival of the genuine spirit of the martyrs in the church, and is ecclesiastical, spiritual, and national.

2. The millennium is yet to come. It will be preceded by a triumph over the papacy and heathenism in general, and will begin with the conversion of the world at large. At this point Whitby differed from Augustine, who identified the millennium with the present age. In this respect Augustine was more nearly an amillenarian than Whitby.

3. Satan will no longer trouble men. He will be bound and inactive.

4. The church will triumph completely, and will fill the earth with its benevolent rule. At the close of the period there will be a short rebellion; the final judgment will take place; and Christ will establish His eternal kingdom.

Whitby's view, although admittedly a new hypothesis, became very popular and prevailed in American Protestantism throughout most of the nineteenth century.

To those living in that "Great Century" from the close of the Napoleonic wars in 1815 to the opening of the first world war in 1914, the postmillennial view seemed to be justified by historical events. The increase of colonies and protectorates established by "Christian" nations in Africa and in Asia opened new doors for propagation of the Christian faith. The growth of a sense of missionary responsibility led to the founding of new societies and to expansion into the South Sea Islands, China, India, Africa, and other places. The agitation for the international peace table at the Hague convinced many people that war would shortly be outlawed, and that the settlement of disagreements by force of arms would cease. Literacy and education increased. All of these factors produced a feeling of optimism which was embodied in the preaching that "the kingdom is coming."

The liberal wing of Christianity that had adopted the philosophy of evolution modified the postmillennialism of its orthodox forbears by substituting social change and a general triumph of righteousness for the personal return of Christ. Judgment was interpreted to be the inexorable working of the social process by which evil would be surmounted and ultimately discarded. On both sides of the theological fence men felt that the age of righteousness was about to be ushered into existence.[3]

Neither of these views did justice to the command of the New Testament to "watch" for the return of Christ. If according to their theology His advent is to be preceded by at least a thousand years of peace and righteousness, which in turn are the result of a long process of spiritual or social evolution, it could scarcely be of imminent concern to the Christians of New Testament times or of today. Nevertheless they *were* concerned with the prospect of the Lord's return. The whole emphasis of Revelation is upon the fact that "he cometh with the clouds; and every eye shall see him" (1:7), and the book ends with the promise, "Yea: I come quickly" (22:20). Even though the fulfilment did not come in their time, the interpretation which would necessarily defer that coming was alien to the spirit of the book and to the understanding of the church.

Uncertainty about the time of the return of Christ is reflected in several passages of the New Testament. Paul in II Thessalonians 2:1-5 reassures his readers that the day of the Lord has not yet come because the predicted apostasy and the revelation of the man of sin had not yet occurred. II Peter 3:3-10 reflects the opposite attitude: disappointment that the prediction of the Lord's coming had not yet been fulfilled. Nowhere is a date set, nor was there any definite promise that the consummation would occur within the lifetime of the first century Christians. Nevertheless, the possibility of the Lord's advent was always present; and if the possibility were live, it could scarcely be admitted in the postmillennial program.

Apart from lack of Scriptural support for this interpretation, its optimism suffered a severe blow with the opening of the first world war in 1914. Hardly had the peace table at the Hague been established when the assassination of the Austrian archduke at Sarajevo precipitated a conflict that plunged all of Europe and several countries of the western hemisphere into armed conflict. The revolutionary struggle that followed with its sequel in the even bloodier second world war of 1939-1945 destroyed the illusion of inevitable progress and of the gradual conquest of the world by the gospel. The spectacle of so-called

Christian nations bent on the destruction of each other, the curtailment of missionary endeavor which was the inevitable result of war, the rise of Communism in Russia which transformed a former "Christian" nation into an atheistic state and which has brought 800,000,000 people behind the iron curtain, the wholesale murder of entire populations such as the Jews in Germany and the farmers of the Ukraine in Russia, demonstrate quite clearly that human nature has not become Christian and that the millennium has not yet arrived.

Furthermore, the birthrate of the world does not support postmillennial teaching. More heathen are born every year than are converted to Christ. Simple arithmetic shows that the population of the world is not becoming increasingly Christian. The old optimism has been eclipsed by a hopelessness that is quite its opposite, and the postmillennial concept of a world rapidly on its way to realizing the kingdom of God as the latter is defined in the New Testament has proved illusory. One does not have to be an incurable pessimist to admit that the world is not becoming progressively better, nor must he renounce all optimism if he believes that the only remedy lies in the intervention of God according to the program which He has provided.

AMILLENNIALISM

Because of the obvious failure of the postmillennial interpretation to meet the prescribed conditions of New Testament eschatology either exegetically or socially, the position of amillennialism has been developed. The amillennial interpretation holds that the passage in Revelation 20:1-8 does not refer to a period to come *after* the conquest of the world by the gospel, but that it is either a description of the current period before the return of the Lord, or else that it has no particular significance. The argument of the amillenarians is that the passage in Revelation is highly figurative, that it occurs only in one place in the most symbolic book of the Bible, and that its main concept of the thousand years is never found elsewhere in Scripture. It is therefore a relatively unimportant aspect of eschatology which cannot be used to establish any chronological sequence of events or any very definite scheme of the last things.

Amillennialism has been adopted in the last twenty-five years by those who have not found the postmillennial position tenable, but who are not fully satisfied with premillennialism. Amillennialism is not strictly novel, either. It can be traced back as far as Augustine, and perhaps earlier. It asserts the personal return of Christ to claim His church, to overthrow antichrist, and to judge the world, but it does not regard the millennium as a period of definable length intervening between the appearing of Christ and the establishment of the eternal state. Augustine contended that it was equivalent to the present era, in which Satan is restrained while the gospel is preached.[4] Mauro advanced the theory that it represents the spiritual triumph of the martyrs who are now reigning with Christ,[5] an opinion echoed by others including Hamilton, [6] who adds that the believers are now reigning upon the earth.

The defense of the amillennial position is both negative and positive. Negatively the amillenarian objects to what he calls the crass materialism of the premillennial system. Some of the advocates of the latter view have represented it as an earthly rule of the saints who indulge their appetite to the full and find their joys chiefly in material pleasures. From Eusebius [7] to Robinson[8] this has been a standing criticism, perhaps warranted by the extravagances of some exegetes.

Positively, the amillenarian position is presented in a series of arguments which are drawn partly from the text of Revelation and partly from other Scriptural and theological sources. According to this teaching, amillennialism fits better the *structure* of Revelation. Hamilton avers that the various sections of the Apocalypse are not successive chronologically, but that each one includes the one preceding it and goes beyond it in detail. On this assumption he says :[9]

> The sixth section either includes the twentieth chapter, or the seventh section begins with the twentieth chapter, but in any case the premillennialist declares that the twentieth chapter describes events that are *subsequent* in time to the events described in the nineteenth chapter, thus causing a break in the symbolic structure of the book. In view of the almost geometrical structure of the book, the outline of the premillennialist would seem to be less likely to be correct.

Hamilton's assumption that the various sections of Revelation are concurrent rather than successive may or may not be correct, but a more basic question would be whether he has divided the book according to its proper segments. A different scheme of divisions would invalidate his argument. The structure cannot be held to support exclusively the amillennial view. The divisions established by the repeated phrases of the text do not give support to Hamilton's contention. The vision of 17:1-21:8 which seems to be a unit conveys the impression that the events which it chronicles are successive. Even though the terms may be symbolic, they represent a series of acts which take place in the order listed. If so, the millennium has a definite place in the program of the future, and cannot be dismissed as negligible.

A second argument for amillennialism is its definition of the kingdom as a present reality rather than an exclusively future reign. The kingdom in Revelation is treated as already existent (1:6,9), and should not therefore be relegated to the distant future, subsequent to the return of Christ. Jesus came "preaching the kingdom" (Mark 1:14,15; Matt 4;23; John 3:5), a ministry which was continued by His successors, notably Paul (Acts 20:25). From this the amillenarian argues that Jesus did establish the kingdom in a spiritual sense, and that the reference to "reigning" in Revelation 20 is to be understood in the same way.

It may be conceded that the kingdom is essentially spiritual in its origin and nature. Jesus Himself said to Pilate, "My kingdom is not of this world: if my kingdom were of this world, then would my servants fight . . . " (John 18:36). "Spiritual," however, means that it is not the product of material necessity nor sustained by material force; but it does not mean that it may not have an outward and tangible manifestation. In the sense that the person of the King has been manifested on earth and that He has already received the allegiance of many devoted subjects, the kingdom has already come. Such realization, however, does not completely fulfil all the predictions of Scripture nor does it satisfy the meaning of Jesus' own words: "I [will] drink it new with you in my Father's kingdom" (Matt. 26:29). Jesus' declaration of a future phase of the kingdom makes clear that it is not all realized at present, and that its final realization is still in the future. That realization allows for the establishment and development of a literal millennial kingdom.

The amillenarian customarily interprets the "first resurrection" of Revelation 20:5 as figurative. Obviously, if it is literal, it means that the resurrection of the righteous dead is separated from the resurrection and judgment of the wicked dead by an interval of at least a thousand years.

> The amillennialist . . . believes that the first resurrection is the new birth of the believer which is crowned by his being taken to heaven to be with Christ in His reign during the inter-adventual period. This eternal life which is the

present possession of the believer, and is not interrupted by
the death of the body, is the first resurrection and participation in it is the millennial reign.[10]

Thus the second resurrection of Revelation 20:12-15 becomes the
final physical resurrection of all the dead, righteous and unright-
eous alike, from all eras in the history of the world. This argument is supported by reference to John 5:24-29, Daniel 12:1,2,
Acts 24:15, where the Scriptures state that "there shall be a resurrection both of the just and unjust."

The prediction of resurrection for the just and for the unjust
does not necessarily presuppose that the two are simultaneous.
The writers of Scripture did not always put all of their distinctions of thought into every statement that they made. The texts
mentioned above were not concerned chiefly with distinguishing
times and seasons, but they were dealing with the general principle of resurrection which they state quite adequately. Revelation, however, says: "The rest of the dead lived not until the
thousand years should be finished" (20:5). The word "rest" implies that the group here mentioned are in the same category of
the dead as those in verse 4. The word "lived" applies equally
well to both,[11] and if it means a spiritual resurrection in the first
instance, it does in the second. Since the second instance is generally understood by all schools to refer to a literal physical resurrection, it is only reasonable to assume that the same is true
of the first instance. If this is so, there must be a real interval
between them, however one defines its exact duration. It may be
one thousand literal years, or it may denote a period of unde-
termined length; but in any case it is a separate period of history
subsequent to the second coming of Christ. The plain teaching
seems to be that it intervenes between the resurrection of the
martyrs and the last judgment.

In all fairness it should be said that the advocates of the amillennial view generally believe in the personal return of Christ,
and that they are much less likely than the postmillenarian school
to equate it with the achievement of an evolutionary goal or with
the acme of social progress. Amillennialism does not necessarily
reject the concept of a real return of Christ at the consummation
of the age.

PREMILLENNIALISM

The premillennial interpretation of eschatology in general and
of Revelation in particular holds that the passage in Revelation

20:1-8 should be treated as a definite link in a chronological chain of text, and that it should be interpreted as literally as possible. Chapter 19 is the climax of the present age, when the Lord Jesus Christ returns in person to judge the earth and to defeat the armies of the antichrist who have received his mark and who have worshiped his image. At the consummation Satan is bound, and is cast into the abyss of darkness for a period of one thousand years, while the antichrist and his religious associate, the false prophet, are remanded to the lake of fire. The saints, now triumphant, will reign with Christ upon the earth, and the martyrs will be resurrected to share in the victory.

At the end of the thousand years Satan will be loosed from his imprisonment to test the strength of the new order. He will succeed in gaining a following from those nations on the periphery of the kingdom who have perhaps never given to Christ more than a grudging obedience. Their invasion of the kingdom and their siege of the capital city, presumably Jerusalem ("the beloved city"), will be terminated by swift and summary retribution. The utter doom of Satan and the judgment of the dead at the great white throne will follow immediately, and the descent of the eternal city of God will conclude the process of redemption.

The history of the premillenarian position is at least as old as either of the other views and in general it seems to accord better with such eschatological allusions as can be found in the earliest writings of the church fathers, and even earlier in some of the apocalyptic books of Judaism. Schurer points out [12] that the Apocalypse of Baruch and IV Esdras, both of which belong to the Old Testament Apocrypha that were known to the church, contain predictions of the end-time closely in accord with the content of Revelation. There will be a period of tribulation in which the entire world will be plunged into physical and moral confusion. All governmental control will be abolished; wars and lawlessness will be rampant. Elijah and Enoch ("the two witnesses"?) are expected to return. The Messiah will appear, and will repel and crush the last attack of hostile nations against the people of God. Jerusalem will be cleansed and reestablished as the center of the kingdom; the dispersed of Israel will be regathered; the theocratic kingdom will be renewed. In this period of the Messianic reign war and discord shall cease and perfect peace shall ensue.   Wealth and progress shall prevail among men.   The span of human life will increase greatly.   The traditions differed as to the duration of the kingdom.   Some held it to be everlasting;[13] others regarded it as of finite length, "until the end should come, the day of judgment."[14]   At the end of this kingdom will come the opening of the eternal age.   A general resurrection of the dead was predicated at the day of judgment, although the idea of a resurrection of the righteous dead to share in Messiah's kingdom, with the resurrection of the rest at the end, was not unknown.[15]

The resemblance between these Jewish traditions and the teaching of Revelation is obvious.   The explanation has been advanced that the early Christians did not shake themselves free from fanciful ideas of popular eschatology, but that they incorporated them into their thinking.   The Lord Jesus Christ, however, did not base His eschatological teaching on tradition but on His own authority.   He accepted His identification with the Messiah (Matt. 26:63-64) and asserted under oath that He would return on the clouds of heaven.   His teachings agree with the Old Testament and were linked closely to it.   Whatever resemblances exist between His teachings and the Apocrypha may be regarded as coincidental, since He, not they, is the final authority.

In the first three centuries of the church's life the premillenarian interpretation flourished, although it seemed to have no consistent formulation and was sometimes grotesque in form. Papais (*circ*. A. D. 116), the bishop of Hierapolis in Asia, and a friend of the writer of Revelation, was distinctly premillenarian.   Eusebius says:[16]

> . . . he [Papias] says that there would be a certain millennium after the resurrection, and that there would be a corporeal reign of Christ on this very earth, which thing he appears to have imagined, as if they were authorized by the apostolic narratives, not understanding correctly those matters which he propounded mystically in their representation.

Eusebius treated Papias' views as an aberration from normal interpretation, and suggested that Papias was ignorant.   Papias, however, was not alone in his convictions, and apparently represented a fairly large body of opinion.   It is just as possible that Eusebius was swayed by prejudice as that Papias was the victim of ignorance.

Justin Martyr (c. 140-160), a Syrian Greek, and the first prominent apologist of the Christian church, was a premillenarian. He asserted that

> I and others, who are right-minded Christians in all points, are assured that there will be a resurrection of the dead, and a thousand years in Jerusalem, which will then be built, adorned, and enlarged, [as] the prophets Ezekiel and Isaiah and others declare.

In addition to dependence on the teachings of the prophets, he affirmed that[17]

> . . . there was a certain man with us, whose name was John, one of the apostles who prophesied by a revelation that was made to him, that those who believed in our Christ would dwell a thousand years in Jerusalem; and that thereafter the general, and, in short, the eternal resurrection and judgment of all men would likewise take place.

Justin Martyr believed in the restoration of the nation of Israel and the rebuilding of Jerusalem, although he conceded that not all "pure and pious Christians" held that view. Apparently he did not make his eschatological position a complete criterion of orthodoxy.

Irenaeus, bishop of Lyons (178-202), seems to have followed Papias in his concept of a material kingdom subsequent to the coming of the antichrist and the destruction of all nations under his rule. Although his language is not always unmistakably clear, the general eschatological program which he advocated was premillennial.[18]

The premillennial expectation faded away during the post-Nicene period. When the church became the state religion its conquest of the empire seemed assured, and many thought that the kingdom had already come. Only occasional exegetes down through the Middle Ages and into the Reformation retained this interpretation. It was revived in modern times by a host of commentators of the eighteenth and nineteenth centuries whose scholarship and devotion cannot be questioned.[19]

The merits of these several views will never be settled by a numerical vote of commentators nor by accord with the exegetical trends of the time. There are fads and fashions in theological thought just as there are in other branches of human learning. The real answer will be decided by the literary interpretation of Revelation itself, and by the relation of its prophecies to the others of the whole Bible.

While no one of these three views can be made the final touchstone of evangelical eschatology nor the criterion of Christian fellowship, the author believes that the premillenarian interpretation of Revelation is correct. Not all views held by premillenarians are necessarily endorsed; but the general scheme of the Apocalypse is regarded as demanding a personal return of Christ to establish His kingdom, the actual maintenance of such a kingdom on the earth for an appreciably long period of time, and its ultimate transference to the eternal state following the last judgment of the wicked.

If this interpretation is applied to the Revelation as a whole one can easily see that the book has two termini: the opening vision on Patmos which occurred before the end of the first century, and the eternal state of indefinite duration at the end of time. The subdivisions indicated by Revelation are: (1) the course of the present age of the church up to the advent of the beast and the beginning of his rule; (2) the short period during which the kingdom of the beast is under the fearful judgments of the trumpets and the bowls, culminating in the personal appearance of Christ; (3) the establishment of the kingdom in which Satan is bound and the saints, especially the martyrs, are resurrected and share in the personal rule of the Messiah; and finally (4) the closing of the period of judgment and the city of God in which unchanging righteousness will abide.

The validity of this view is confirmed by several considerations. It is the only one of the three given above that provides for an equally literal or an equally figurative presentation of the text of Revelation as a whole. Undoubtedly many parts of Revelation are symbolic in language; but the symbols are intended to carry a definite meaning. For instance, the picture of an angel binding Satan may not mean that the devil is chained with literal iron links in a dungeon which has no floor. The premillennialist concedes that the material concept used as a medium of expression is of secondary value. He does, however, insist that the expression implies a period of measurable length during which Satan will be forcibly restrained by divine power from exercising his usual influence on the earth, and that this enforced absence from human affairs will do away with many of earth's evils in that time. Furthermore, he holds that since evil is so powerful at present, Satan has not already been remanded to that pit which shall keep him from the scene of human action.

If the premillenarian view is to be discredited because the first eight verses of the twentieth chapter are figurative and because they contain allusions that are difficult to understand, the same objection can be brought against any other passage of the book. The relation of this passage to the totality of Revelation seems to demand that it should be treated as referring to a definite period in the sequence of time which the prophecy projects.

Premillenarians should remember that although the importance of the millennium should not be underestimated, it should not be exaggerated. Although the book of Revelation marks it as an era in human history, it is only one era, and does not constitute the final goal. In the text where it is described it is part of the consummation which begins with the advent of Christ and which terminates with the destruction of the wicked and with the descent of the New Jerusalem to earth.

The millennial interim, then, is the kingdom over which Christ presides and by which He demonstrates His theocratic government over the nations. It can be the fulfilment of a dual purpose: the completion of God's promises for the restoration of Israel and her deliverance from Gentile oppression, and the demonstration of His sovereignty over the nations in the temporal affairs of earth. The former of these purposes is not plainly mentioned in Revelation because the book was not directed to an exclusively Jewish constituency. Since it was addressed to the seven churches of Asia it is concerned chiefly with the fate of a Gentile church in the Roman world, and it treats the Jewish people as they affected that church (Rev. 2:9, 3:9). By implication, however, the entire book is connected with Old Testament prophecy through the numerous quotations and allusions that it employs.

An example of the implied meaning may be found in the opening theme of Revelation. "Behold, he cometh with the clouds; and every eye shall see him, and they that pierced him; and all the tribes of the earth shall mourn over him" (1:7). The verse relates the entire content of the book to the closing chapters of Zechariah, which contains a prediction of the final siege and deliverance of Jerusalem from the besieging armies of a Gentile world that has found Jerusalem "a burdensome stone for all the peoples" (Zech. 12:3). The prophecy is directed to a specific time or period, for there are no less than seventeen occurrences of the expression "in that day" in Zechariah 12 through 14. These chapters predict that Jerusalem will be besieged by Gentile armies (12:3, 14:2); that a revival shall come to Israel through the visible appearance of "me whom they have pierced" (12:10); that the siege shall be lifted by the appearance of "Jehovah my God" (14:5). His arrival will be followed by the founding of a kingdom centered at Jerusalem, where a universal worship will be established (14:16,17). The correspondence of order between this passage and the twentieth chapter of Revelation is apparent, although the latter does not emphasize local detail as does Zechariah. In both a future reign of God upon the earth is asserted; and if the literal sense of the text be accepted, the reign must follow the advent of Jehovah in power to deliver His people.

A similar passage occurs in Isaiah 10:33 to 12:6. Its setting lies in the Assyrian invasion that threatened the kingdom of Judah in Isaiah's day, but its scope is much greater than the immediate situation. Isaiah predicted that the "shoot out of the stock of Jesse" (11:1) would bear fruit. The royal line would be renewed after the main stem had been cut down, and the new scion of the royal house would inherit the kingdom. Restoration from exile for Israel and universal knowledge of God for the nations would follow (11:11,9).

These two passages present the coming kingdom in terms of the future of Israel. The literal concept of this kingdom was not abandoned by the preachers of the New Testament, as Peter's speech in Solomon's porch shows:

> Repent ye therefore, and turn again, that your sins may be blotted out, that so there may come seasons of refreshing from the presence of the Lord; and that he may send the Christ who hath been appointed for you, *even* Jesus: whom the heaven must receive until the times of restoration of all things, whereof God spake by the mouth of his holy prophets that have been from of old (Acts 3:19-21).

Peter called on the nation to repent in order that God might complete the purpose which He had declared in the prophets. The important point in Peter's speech for this study is that Peter identified Jesus with the Deliverer of the Old Testament predictions, thereby accepting the fact that a kingdom would follow His advent.

From the standpoint of the church a similar comparison is possible, although the aspect of the kingdom in the New Testament is less terrestrial and political than in the Old Testament. Paul, in writing to the Corinthian church about the resurrection of the body, had something to say about the kingdom:

> But each in his own order: Christ the firstfruits; then they that are Christ's at his coming. Then *cometh* the end, when he shall deliver up the kingdom to God, even the Father; when he shall have abolished all rule and all authority and power. For he must reign, till he hath put all his enemies under his feet . . . . And when all things have been subjected unto him, then shall the Son also himself be subjected to him that did subject all things unto him, that God may be all in all (I Cor. 15:23-25, 28).

A listing of the events in this passage will show that the resurrection of Christ was the initial act of redemption in this present era. The next event to be expected is the coming of Christ, at which time those who are Christ's will be resurrected (23). Following His coming, He will deliver up the kingdom to God as a completion of His work after He has subjugated all His enemies, including death. Between the first two events more than nineteen hundred years have already intervened, and the period has still not come to its close. Is it improbable that between the advent of Christ and the delivery of the kingdom to the Father there may be another period of indeterminate length?

The surrender of the kingdom to the Father implies that the work of redemption is complete. Nothing remains to be finished. The roll of Christ's redeemed is full; the devastation brought by sin has also been undone; and the eternal state is about to begin.

It may be objected to the premillennial interpretation of this passage that the "reign" (25) of Christ refers to His present enthronement at the right hand of God, and that at His advent, when the dead are raised, death shall be destroyed. If His work is perfected at that moment, there would be no need for a millennium, since the victory would be instantly complete.

The order of this passage is determined by three words that indicate a sequence of action: "firstfruits" (23), "then" (23), "then" (24). The two "then's," although differing slightly in the Greek text, mean substantially the same thing: a further step in procedure or in point of time. Paul uses this same combination in the earlier part of the chapter where he is recounting the appearances of Christ after the resurrection. In that context the "then's" mark successive happenings separated from each other by an undefined lapse of time. Similar usage appears in I Timothy 2:13 and 3:10, where the adverbs unquestionably mean that one act or event follows another after an appreciable interval. If the same principle is applied to this passage under discussion, the "reign" and the "kingdom" fall between the return of Christ and the final consummation. It is not at all impossible on the basis of the language that a millennium can intervene between the time when Christ claims His own at His coming and the final delivery to the Father of the kingdom which He has redeemed.

This conclusion is at least partially supported by another consideration. I Corinthians 15:25, 26 says:

> For he must reign, till he hath put all his enemies under his feet. The last enemy that shall be abolished is death.

A more accurate translation would read:

> For he must go on reigning, until the moment when he shall put all his enemies under his feet.

The verb implies a continuation of His reign, not simply a sudden assumption of the throne. Here is the answer to those who contend that Christ is reigning now. He is even now King of kings and Lord of lords, but His reign has not been made manifest outwardly. When He is manifested in power, He will go on reigning until the last enemy is destroyed. Since that last enemy is death, His reign must continue until all death is abolished. Its conquest may be progressive, beginning with His own resurrection and continuing with that of the saints (15:20, 23), but it will not end until death itself is eliminated. According to Revelation, death and Hades are not destroyed until after the millennial reign (20:14), so that "the end" comes after the millennium.

This consideration gives a new value to "the end." Paul's general use of the term is confined to the meaning of terminus, goal, or destiny. He uses it with reference to the outcome of sin (Rom. 6:21), of holiness, (Rom. 6:22), or to the end result of life (II Cor. 11:15, Phil. 3:19). It is therefore not an exclusively eschatological term in the Pauline writings. In this passage (I Cor. 15:24, 26) it may be used in an absolute sense, because the temporal clauses that modify it, "when he shall deliver up the kingdom to God . . . ," and "when he shall have abolished all rule and all authority and all power" may be non-restrictive. In other words, "the end" may have a meaning all its own, not defined by the "when" clauses.

If so, "the end" may be a technical eschatological term to be equated with Jesus' identical expression, "the end," mentioned in the parallel Synoptic passages of Matthew 24:6, Mark 13:7, and

Luke 21:9. Matthew adds one other usage of it in 24:14. Even in these passages where the word is not specifically qualified one may legitimately ask, "The end of what?" Does it mean the terminus of the world as a whole, or only the end of an age? Assuredly it implies the return of Christ, but a study of the context will show that when He does appear He will have further business to transact on earth, and that He will bring in His kingdom.

Just how the process of judgment will be related to the reign and what will take place among the nations while He is reigning is not disclosed by the Gospels. Perhaps the future reign is as obscure to contemporary Christians as the progress of the last few centuries was to those who studied the prophecies concerning His birth and who welcomed Him when He first came.

It is safe to conclude that the language of the Gospels and of the Epistles does not preclude a millennial reign of Christ. Even if no particulars concerning it are given, the hints of the coming of His kingdom and the interim between resurrections confirm the predictions of the Apocalypse.

This presentation of premillennialism does not minimize the fact that Christ has already been exalted to the right hand of God as sovereign Lord of the universe. The Scripture states that He is even now in that position of authority, waiting until His enemies shall be made His footstool (Heb. 1:13, 10:12, 13; Acts 2:29-36). The apostolic explanation of the prophetic one hundred and tenth psalm, given in the foregoing references, connects the resurrection and ascension of Christ with His position on the throne of David. It does not, however, remove any possibility of a future earthly reign, nor does it mean that the subjugation of His enemies need not include just such a manifestation of the kingdom which Revelation 20 and kindred passages imply.

APPLICATION

Which of the three systems sketched above best fits the structure and content of Revelation?

From the evangelical viewpoint any one of them may admit that the ultimate coming of Christ is personal and literal. On this point there can be no clash with the obvious prophetic intent of Revelation. The orthodox postmillennialism of the past believed firmly that the world process would end with the visible return of Christ who would come to judge the evil, to reward the believers, and to introduce the eternal state of restored Paradise. The system, however, did not explain completely the body of Revelation. Either the critical events of the book had to be treated as only figurative of great crises of history (Historicist view) or else they had to be simply material emblems of the perpetual clash of moral forces in the present world, (Idealist view). Neither of these interpretations of history is wholly satisfactory. There is no thread of unity in the former, because the figures have not sufficiently distinctive features to identify them clearly with known historic events. The second view does not take into sufficient account the chronology in the structure of Revelation. Furthermore, Revelation indicates that the conquest of evil will be a crisis and not a process, nor will the evil be removed by the gradual improvement of civilization. The outward manifestation of the kingdom will occur only when Christ Himself returns.

Amillennialism avoids the undue optimism of postmillennialism and is much more realistic. Its interpretation of Revelation assigns positive values to the successive scenes in the book, and some amillennial expositors espouse the historical interpretation in an attempt to provide for a definite expository sequence. They do preserve the concept of imminency, as postmillenarians do not. Although they give great weight to a "spiritual" interpretation of Revelation they do not eliminate the literal aspect completely. According to this method the moral deterioration of civilization, the cataclysmic intervention of God in the affairs of earth, the resurrection and translation of the saints, the judgment and the final heavenly kingdom are likely to come without warning. In this respect the amillenarian and premillenarian views are somewhat alike.

The premillenarian view seems to do fullest justice to the structure of Revelation. It provides for a period of the conflict and growth of the church in the present era, during which time the people of God shall be gathered together and shall be preserved through increasing pressure and persecution until the time of the end. It predicts the rise of an organized hostile world state under the "beast" (13:1-10) who is energized by Satanic power. The conflict for supremacy ends with an apparent material victory for the "beast," since he achieves the union of all earthly forces under his banner. His rule creates an unprecedented trial for the people of God, many of whom are martyred. The assertion of Christ's kingly rights, His appropriation of the throne of the visible world, and His administration of the earth with His saints until such time as He abolishes all evil and presents the finished kingdom to the Father seems to be accounted for best by this system.

Premillennial thinkers do not agree on all subordinate points of interpretation within their own system any more than other schools agree on theirs, nor can it be said that no objections can be raised against it. It seems, however, to have fewer weaknesses and a greater general Scriptural strength than the other two schools of thought.

By the premillennial eschatology Revelation is given a fuller and stronger place in the canon. It becomes the prophetic guide for the future. The first section of the book presents the churches of the current era as they confront the event of Christ's imminent return forecast in the words, "I come quickly" (3:11). The present sovereignty of Christ is emphasized by the throne in heaven which occupies so prominent a place in the first chapters of the second section (4, 5). With the series of the seals, trumpets, and bowls begin the progressive judgments which conclude with the appearing of Christ in person to judge the earth and to consummate this age (6:16; 11:15-18; 16:17-21; 19:11-16). The period of His rule on earth, generally called the millennium, precedes the events which occupy the fourth vision of Revelation (21:9-22:5).

Subordinate to the general premillennial scheme is the question whether Revelation shall be applied to the total historic process of the Christian dispensation, or whether it covers only the last few years before the advent of Christ, called "the great tribulation." If the former is the correct interpretation, the exegete will be under obligation to identify the various symbolic judgments with events that have occurred already. Such an interpretation has been generally unsatisfactory because of the uncertainty in the identifications. If the futuristic interpretation be adopted, then the content of Revelation, with the possible exception of the first three chapters, has no immediate relevance for the present. The expectation of the believer is less likely to be directed toward the development of evil rather than toward the advent of Christ, since His coming will be the judgment on the system of antichrist whose advent has preceded Him.

Revelation was written toward the close of the first century when the churches had already become settled institutions and were recognized as an effective movement. Confronted by the growing hostility of the Roman empire which saw in them a political and social rival, they were naturally apprehensive of the coming struggle and its outcome. If they were to lose, their faith would be futile and their doctrine would be proved only another vain will-o'-the-wisp. If they were to win, what would be the divine program before them, and how would it eventuate?

The Revelation was intended to answer these questions, for it was given by God "to show unto his servants, *even* the things which must shortly come to pass" (1:1).

The first vision (1:9-3:22) deals with the evaluation of the church and the preparation for the crisis to come. Each of the promises given to the overcoming believers bears some relation to the kingdom or to the Paradise of God. A few of these seem to fit closely the idea of a millennial reign. For instance, in the letter to Thyatira, the Lord says:

> And he that overcometh, and he that keepeth my works unto the end[20] to him will I give authority over the nations: and he shall rule them with a rod of iron, as the vessels of the potter are broken to shivers (2:26, 27).

To the Laodiceans He said:

> He that overcometh, I will give to him to sit down with me in my throne, as I also overcame, and sat down with my Father in his throne (3:21).

The passage alludes to Christ's present position on the throne of the Father to which He has been elevated by the resurrection (Acts 2:32, 33; Eph. 1:20, 21). There He is exalted far above all opposing powers, and He possesses sovereign rule over the universe.

This position He has agreed to share with those who overcome evil through His strength. He has promised to give them power over the nations, and although His throne and the nations themselves will still be existing in the new heavens and the new earth (Rev. 21:24, 25; 22:1, 2), the initial part of the reign commences with the thousand years (20:4). The kingdom is part of the reward of those who have fought well in the conflicts of the present age.

To the idea of the kingdom in the second vision of Revelation the millennium forms a fitting climax. The song of the four living creatures states the keynote for this division of the book:

> Worthy art thou to take the book, and to open the seals thereof: for thou wast slain, and didst purchase unto God with thy blood *men* of every tribe, and tongue, and people,

and nation, and madest them *to be* unto our God a kingdom and priests; and they reign upon the earth (5:9, 10).

The judgments that follow this song culminate at the seventh trumpet, when voices from heaven announce:

> The kingdom of the world is become *the kingdom* of our Lord, and of his Christ: and he shall reign for ever and ever (11:15).

The resumption of action with the two signs of the conflict of the woman with the dragon and the judgment of the seven bowls (12:1, 15:1) leads logically to the climax of chapter 20, in which the dragon is bound (12:3, 20:2), the beasts are remanded to destruction (19:20, 21), the winepress of God's wrath is trodden out (14:17-20, 19:15), and the judgments of the bowls usher in the great day of God, the Almighty (16:13, 14; 19:6). All lines of progressive thought in the second section of the book lead up to the point at which the millennium is introduced. It constitutes the climax of terrestrial judgment.

The third vision of Revelation, in which the millennial passage itself occurs, is devoted almost wholly to judgments. The overthrow of Babylon (17:1-18:23), the consequent rejoicing in heaven (19:1-10), and the succession of episodes that lead up to the dénouement include the millennium as one of their number. It marks a distinct period in the succession, and cannot be explained away without doing violence to the scheme as a whole. It divides the present age from the eternity to come, and is itself part of the process of judgment (20:4).

The fourth vision of Revelation is the consequence of the millennium. The city of God is the perfection of the kingdom which the millennium began, and which will be continued after the last judgment has purged the earth of all rebellion. Into that city the nations bring the glories of their culture (21:26); the throne of God and of the Lamb are in the midst of His people (22:1), and the servants of God reign with Him forever (22:5).

While the millennium is not all there is in the Revelation, nor even perhaps the most important feature, it is a factor that affects the interpretation of the book as a whole. To misinterpret it throws the book out of perspective; to neglect it or to dismiss it fails to do justice to the total eschatological scheme. Even though it may be obscure to present understanding, it has a legitimate place in the prophetic program which must be acknowledged.

CHAPTER XV

THE TERMINOLOGY OF REVELATION

In the Apocalypse appear a number of terms which are frequently repeated. Many of them have a technical meaning, and several of them are closely related to the structure of the book by their usage. A closer definition of these terms and a study of their usage by the author may explain more clearly the meaning of the message.

There are at least three classifications of these terms: (1) those that deal with institutions or objects, such as "churches" and "throne"; (2) those that represent personalities or places, like "Lamb," "beast," and "Babylon"; and (3) those that constitute formulae, like "I was in the Spirit," "Blessed is . . . [or "are"],," "thunders, voices, and lightnings." A sharp distinction between classes is not always discernible. For instance, "beast" may mean an institution to some interpreters and an individual personality to others. Whether the "beast" is the Roman empire, the papacy, or a personal antichrist yet to come is not the immediate problem of this study. The procedure will be inductive, and will not begin with the assumption that any given term represents any other reality than can be defined by the language of its own context.

These recurring terms do have an important bearing on interpretation. Some of them appear to belong to a technical apocalyptic vocabulary. Their occurrence in Revelation and in other works of similar nature will identify leading concepts in the eschatology of the first century. Their relation to the Old Testament projects the main lines of past prophecy into the future and helps to unify the entire body of Messianic prediction. Within the book of Revelation itself there are integrating lines of thought that provide a framework to which seemingly unrelated episodes can be connected. Several of these topics will be considered in the following pages, and their contribution to the understanding of Revelation will be noted.

INSTITUTIONS AND OBJECTS

The first and most obvious reference to an institution is the word "church" or "churches."[1] Of the twenty uses in Revelation all except one are in the first three chapters. These uses refer to the bodies of Christians located in the seven different Asian cities to whom the Apocalypse was addressed. The other single instance is in the Epilogue (22:16) and refers back to the initial address, so that it introduces no new concept.

In all of these passages the word "church" is used only of a local body of believers. Unlike Ephesians, Revelation does not speak of the universal church under this designation. It may be that the great unnamed multitude (7:9) or "the bride of the Lamb" (19:7) or the New Jerusalem (21:9, 10) is a symbolic description of the entire congregation of the redeemed; but no certain identification is given. Insofar as the concept of the church is presented, it concerns a group of men and women who live in a definite place, and who unitedly profess the name of Christ.

The emphasis on the local use of the term does not preclude the possibility of its having a general and collective meaning elsewhere, nor does it mean that there was no connection between the several groups that are mentioned in Revelation. The uniformity of the letters to the churches indicates that the Lord thought of them as equals who were engaged in the common task of representing Him before the world. Together they constitute the active body of His disciples in Asia, but each is treated separately and its specific faults and virtues are evaluated.

This method of approach implies that Revelation was designated for the use of individual churches, and that its predictions and warnings should be applied to their individual needs. It was not just a general note of alarm to the church as a whole, but its admonitions were to be applied to particular groups. Furthermore, the allusion in the Epilogue to "the churches" shows that the entire book was addressed to them, and not just the first chapters. Although the remaining chapters never mention the churches in their terrestrial surroundings, their existence is taken for granted. They are involved in the developments of God's plan for the world, and they will share both in its tragedies and in its triumph. The Revelation makes the churches a part of that plan, and attempts to show them where they fit into it.

The relation of the churches to the kingdom has long been a difficult question in eschatology. The two concepts are not synonymous, yet they cannot be completely separated from each other. The address to the churches in Revelation 1:4 shows that they are included in the "us" of 1:5, 6, since together with the author they are the antecedent for the first personal plural pronoun. If so, the logical deduction is that they are to be included in the kingdom, since the text says, "Unto him that loveth us and loosed us from our sins by his blood; and he made us *to be* a kingdom . . ." (1:5,6). There can be no dispute that "loveth us" and "loosed us from our sins" apply to the churches. Should not the last clause apply to them also? The church is at present a visible manifestation of those whom God has saved and whom He has constituted as local groups for purposes of witness to the world. Ultimately the churches will be absorbed into the all-embracing kingdom which the Son will present to the Father, and which shall be called the city of God.

A confirmation of this deduction appears in the letters to the churches. Each of these with one exception contains some promise that finds its counterpart in the final consummation:

CHURCH	CONCEPT	CONSUMMATION
2: 7	The tree of life	22:2
2:11	The second death	21:8
2:17	The white stone	
2:27	The rod of iron	19:15
3: 5	The book of life	20:12
3:12	The temple of God	21:3, 22
3:21	The throne of Christ	22:3

All the promises to the overcomers from the various churches will be completed in the eternal city which is the perfected heavenly kingdom.

A second word that is important in Revelation is "throne." From the first of this book to the last it stands for the seat of authority. Three times it is used of evil authority (2:13, 13:2, 16:10); in three passages it applies to the thrones of the elders or of believers (4:4, 11:16, 20:4) who have had authority delegated to them, but in most of the passages it denotes the throne of God. Beginning with the second vision and continuing through to the end of Revelation the throne is the central point around which all the features of the vision are organized, and from which the major action of the book proceeds. Twenty times it is used with prepositions such as "before," "around," "out of," "in the midst of," "from." The celestial world with its widening circles of lamps of fire, living creatures, elders, angels, and all creation has its focus at the throne, to which praise is offered and from which the power of redemption emanates.

Even God Himself is characterized eleven times as He "that sitteth upon the throne" (4:2,9,10; 5:1,7,13; 6:16; 7:10,15; 19:4; 21:5). The phrase may have been borrowed from the Old Testament (Isa. 6:1, Ps. 47:8), but it is not simply a religious cliché. In connection with other uses of "throne" it emphasizes His sovereignty and affirms His rulership over the world as a whole. However chaotic the political and social scene may become, God remains unshaken and His will must prevail.

The throne is especially prominent in the scene of chapters 4, 5, and 7, which open the rapid action of judgment. Less is said about it in succeeding chapters, but it is mentioned often enough to remind the reader that it is still in the center of the background and that the content of those chapters is related to what has preceded. The entire plot of Revelation is constructed on the triumph of God over Satan, of right over wrong, and of order over chaos. However far the detailed episodes of the book may digress from its central thought, the recurring allusions to the throne keep the central theme within the mind of the reader.

The throne is the source of judgment. From it proceed the lightnings, voices, and thunders (4:5) that mark the culmination of retribution upon evil. The sudden plea of men for rocks and mountains to cover them is evoked by the fear of the wrath of God who sits on the throne (6:16). The terminus of the three series of seven judgments is declared by a great voice from the throne of God, saying, "It is done" (16:17). The regal seat of deity is the center of worship for the saved, and is the source of fear for all the lost.

Another object mentioned in Revelation is the temple of God (7:15; 11:19; 14:15,17; 15:5,6,8; 16:1,17). The Greek word is *naos*, a term which means a shrine or sanctuary in which deity dwells rather than the whole of the sacred building (Greek: *hieron*). In at least one passage it is equated with the tabernacle of the testimony (15:5), the name given to the portable building which the Israelites carried with them in their wilderness journeys (Exod. 38:21). Since the tabernacle of the Old Testament and the temple worship that followed it were modeled on a heavenly pattern given to Moses (Exod. 25:9,40), Revelation, literal at this point, may be speaking of the divine original which was the pattern that God showed to Moses in Mt. Sinai. In any case, the concept of the temple or tabernacle is related to the method of worship for which both stood, and features of the worship appear in Revelation.

In this heavenly temple are the ark of the covenant (Rev. 11:
19) and an altar (6:9; 8:3,5; 9:13; 14:18; 16:7). The term
(Greek: *thusiasterion*) which denotes it does not of itself determine whether it alludes to the altar of sacrifice or to the altar
of incense, which is described in Exodus 30:1-10. The description
given in Revelation seems to fit the altar of incense better than
the great altar of sacrifice which stood near the door of the tabernacle. The altar in Revelation is connected with the prayers of
the martyrs (Rev. 6:9), its fire is used to light the incense of the
golden censer (8:3,5), and its location is "before God," which
would accord much more closely with the place of the altar of incense that stood on the border between the Holy Place and the
Holy of Holies, the inner shrine of the tabernacle. The reference
in Revelation 14:18 is ambiguous, and does not demand either
altar to make its interpretation clear.

R. H. Charles comments[2] that it shares in the characteristics of
both altars, but since there is only one altar in heaven, this is probably the altar of incense. The altar of sacrifice (Exod. 40:6), the
laver of cleansing (40:7), the lampstand (40:24), and the table
of shewbread (40:22,23) have all been fulfilled and superseded in
the person of Christ. His sacrifice has put away sin (Rev. 1:5),
His people have been cleansed for fellowship (19:8). The light
of the lampstand has been succeeded by the seven lamps of fire that
burn before the throne (4:5), and the shewbread is hardly necessary where worshipers "hunger no more" (7:16). Prayer and worship such as were offered in the Holy of Holies in the tabernacle
and temple will always be acceptable; hence the ark with its open
mercy seat and the golden altar of prayer remain.

The heavenly temple-tabernacle is the refuge for the redeemed
of all nations who are brought out of earth's tribulation into the
presence of God (7:14-17). Even this heavenly temple, however,
will not remain permanently. The eternal city has no temple, "for
the Lord God the Almighty, and the Lamb, are the temple thereof"
(21:22).

In Revelation the heavenly temple is the source from which judgments emanate. The angel that introduced the seven trumpets stood
at the golden altar and flung his censer into the earth, typifying
the answer to the prayers of the saints for vindication. At the
seventh trumpet "there was opened the temple of God that is in
heaven; and . . . there followed lightnings, and voices, and thunders, and an earthquake, and great hail" (11:19). The final harvest of evil and its removal from the earth is announced by two

angels coming "out of the temple" (14:15, 17), the seven angels bearing the seven last plagues come "out of the temple" (15:5,6,8; 16:1), and "a great voice out of the temple" (16:17) announces the conclusion of the judgments.

PERSONALITIES AND PLACES

Revelation applies to God a title that is almost exclusive to the book: "the Lord God the Almighty" (1:8; 4:8; 11:17; 15:3; 16: 7, 14; 19:6,15; 21:22). It appears in one other passage in the New Testament where it is quoted from the Septuagint. The quotation, however, is composite, and cannot as a whole be traced to any single passage. The last phrase, "saith the Lord Almighty," may be a line from Amos 3:13. "Almighty" in the prophets (Septuagint version) is a translation of *Jehovah Sabaoth,* "the God of hosts," or Jehovah Militant." In Job the same word is a translation of *El Shaddai,* the sufficient God. If the title conveyed to the hearers of the Revelation the force of the Hebrew originals, it meant both the God who creates and sustains the hosts of creation and the God whose sufficiency is inexhaustible.

The first occurrence defines the person and authority of the Revelator: "I am the Alpha and the Omega, saith the Lord God, who is and who was and who is to come, the Almighty" (1:8). Eternity, omnipotence, and purposefulness are implied by these words. "Almighty" means "the one who masters or controls all things." The title is in keeping with the symbolism of the throne, and indicates that the entire operation of judgment which the book chronicles is carried on by the power of a God who can do all things.

In five of the nine uses of "Almighty" in Revelation it is connected with a song or a formal ascription of praise (4:8, 11:17, 15:3, 16:7, 19:6). Each of them is offered by some members of the celestial chorus: the living creatures, the twenty-four elders, the victorious multitude, the voice of the altar, and finally the great multitude in heaven. These correspond roughly to the circles of praise (5:11-13) that constitute the worshiping universe. Every class of being recognizes the greatness and power of God, and worships Him under the title of Almighty.

Two uses stress the aspect of judgment: "the war of the great day of God, the Almighty" (16:14), and "the winepress of the fierceness of the wrath of God, the Almighty" (19:15). The futility of warring against God, and the finality of His vengeance are assured by the fact that He is all-powerful.

One remaining passage connects the title with the bliss of the New Jerusalem. "The Lord God Almighty and the Lamb are the temple thereof" (21:22). The power of God is not terrible to those who love Him, but is their refuge and spiritual solace. They can enjoy perfect worship because they have an all-powerful God.

Another very important title of a person is "Lamb." There can be no question of its identification with Christ. It stresses particularly His redemptive aspect, since it is modified by the phrase "as though it had been slain" (5:6,9,12; 13:8). Never is the exact word "Lamb"[3] used of Christ outside of Revelation, although a similar word[4] meaning "sacrificial lamb" occurs in four passages elsewhere (John 1:29,36; Acts 8:32; I Pet. 1:19).

The lamblike qualities of meekness and gentleness seem strange in the stormy setting of Revelation, and the phrase, "the wrath of the Lamb" (6:16) does not accord with the facts of zoology. Nevertheless this title is the one most frequently used of Christ. By His blood He has purchased unto God men out of every tribe and tongue and people and nation (5:9). He has made them into a kingdom, and He is preparing to set up His rule upon the earth. The entire book of Revelation is the fulfilment of the redemptive purpose of Christ's sacrifice.

Because of that sacrifice He is worthy to take the sealed book and to open the seals that summon the forces of judgment against His enemies (5:7,9; 6:1ff.). Because of His great love for His people, He can become their shepherd to guide them to the fountains of living water (7:17). Because He has suffered for sin He is the arbiter of righteousness, and His wrath against unrighteousness is dreadful (6:16). Those whom He has saved are enrolled in "the book of life of the Lamb" (13:8, 21:27) which is the ultimate basis of appeal in the judgment. The people who are preserved from the final cataclysm of earth and who are to share in the fruits of redemption are called "the wife of the Lamb" (19:7, 21:9), and their reunion with Him is the "marriage supper of the Lamb" (19:9). The Lamb is the temple, the light, the ruler, and the center of worship of the everlasting city of God (21:22,23; 22:1,3).

The figure of the Lamb dominates the last three main sections of Revelation. Not once is the title used in the letters to the seven churches, but in the scenes of judgment there is constant reference to Christ's redemptive work. Revelation is the story of His active consummation of the work begun at Calvary. There righteousness was manifested in love and mercy; in the future, righteousness will be manifested in judgment. Afterward will come the peace of a completed salvation, in which the redeemed people will enter into the eternal joy of His presence.

In sharp contrast to the Lamb, who is delegated by the Lord God Almighty to be the executor of judgment, is the dragon or Satan. Again the symbolism is plain, for he is explicitly identified as "the Devil and Satan, the deceiver of the whole world" (12:9). He is the rival authority to Christ, his opponent in the battle for universal dominion, and he is the source of all evil. In the letters to the churches Satan appears as the inspirer of paganism. Pergamum, where the great temple and altar of Zeus and other large centers of heathen worship were located, was called "Satan's throne," "where Satan dwelleth" (2:13). Apostate or perverted Judaism was labeled as "the synagogue of Satan" (2:9, 3:9). The reality of Satan in spiritual conflict with the churches is affirmed at the outset of Revelation.

The symbol of the dragon or serpent is universal in pagan mythology. Usually it represents wisdom, power, or destroying might. The New Testament employs the idea, but does not deny the reality of the personality which it depicts. Satan is the accuser of the brethren (12:10), the persecutor of God's people (12:13), and the authority that energizes evil political, social, and economic power (13:2). He desires and accepts worship (13:4). The demonic spirits whom he controls agitate enmity against God and seek to organize the world for a campaign against Him. Satan's doom is certain, for he will be imprisoned during Christ's reign on earth, and will be remanded subsequently to the lake of fire (20:10).

Revelation does not treat the origin and career of Satan in any detail. It takes his existence for granted, and discloses enough about him to show that he is a very real and fearsome figure. He is the power behind the scenes of this world, the evil intelligence that makes war on the saints of God. The conflict between the Lamb and the dragon shows that the whole historical process can be interpreted in terms of a warfare which does not end in a hopeless dualism, but in a victory for God and for His Christ. The supernatural elements on both sides become increasingly evident as the plot progresses, until at last in the final climax God removes the dragon from the scene of earth by one great cataclysmic judgment.

Two other personages allied to the dragon are "the beast out of the sea" and "the beast out of the earth" (13:1-18). They are closely associated with each other, for the second "exerciseth all the authority of the first beast in his sight" (13:12). The power of the first seems to be chiefly political and social; the power of the second is religious and economic. The rule of this pernicious pair extends over "every tribe and people and tongue and nation" (13:7). Worship of the first beast will be universal, except for those whose names are written in the roster of heaven (13:8). The language of Revelation 13 is sweeping in its scope. "The whole earth wondered after the beast" (13:3). "All that dwell on the earth shall worship him . . ." (13:8). "No man should be able to buy or to sell, save he that hath the mark" (13:17). Under these two personages there will rise a dominion of evil that will seek to crush every vestige of godliness and virtue, and that will elevate evil to the place of good.

Whereas the former beast is a political and military leader, the latter is a religious leader. He has the appearance of a lamb, but his words are those of the dragon. Supported by the political power of the first beast, he enforces a false worship on the world. The first beast suffered a deadly wound that was healed — a parody on the resurrection of Christ. The second beast possesses supernatural powers with which to propagate his cult of state-worship, and even makes the image of the first beast to speak as if it were alive. He demands that no man shall be allowed to buy or sell unless he carries the mark of the beast on his person. The result of this joint misrule of evil is a frightening totalitarianism. Apart from supernatural intervention the worship and even the knowledge of God could be wiped out in one generation.

The effect of this diabolical rule is described in chapters 13 through 19. The kingdom of the beast is universal; the civilization of culture, trade, and religion is utterly corrupt (17:4) and loses the support even of its own political leaders (17:16). The kingdom of the beast becomes a military organization whose sole objective is the destruction of the people of God. Its devastating power will be overthrown at the appearing of Christ, after an interim of three and one half years (13:5).

The continuity of the career of these "beasts" shows that the content of chapters 13 through 19 is a unit. Chapters 15 and 16 might be regarded as a recapitulation of former judgments were they not plainly stated to be designed for those "that had the mark of the beast, and that worshipped his image" (16:2). In similar fashion the fall of Babylon, which belongs in a separate division of

Revelation, is related to the beast (17:12,16). The last unit comprises the final tribulation that bursts upon the world when evil is unchecked and when Satan tries to establish his kingdom by crushing completely the city that stands for God's purpose and for God's people (11:2; 14:19, 20; 19:15,19-21). The last battle between organized evil and the armies of heaven will be fought for the possession of Jerusalem and for the preservation of all for which the city has stood.

Two geographical names occur in Revelation that have a definite bearing on its interpretation as a whole: Babylon and Jerusalem. They are contrasted in the two final sections of the book, for the fall of Babylon occupies 17:1-21:8, and the coming of the New Jerusalem is described in 21:9-22:5. The two sections are already related both by contrast and by connection. The first eight verses of the twenty-first chapter could belong to either. By literary division they belong to the fall of Babylon; by content they should accompany the text that follows them.

Both names, though taken from historical cities, are symbolical. Although Jerusalem still existed when the Apocalypse was written, it may not have been flourishing. There is an allusion to it in the measuring scene in 11:2:

> . . . . measure it not; for it hath been given unto the nations: and the holy city shall they tread under foot forty and two months.

A further reference to it in the same context speaks of it as " . . . the great city, which spiritually is called Sodom and Egypt, where also their Lord was crucified" (11:8).

These passages are less important than the figurative reference to the New Jerusalem. Each time it is mentioned its celestial character is stressed, for it comes down out of heaven (3:12, 21:2, 10). As the earthly Jerusalem was the center of worship for Israel, and the delight of every devout Jew, so the heavenly city becomes the desire of every Christian and the destination which he aspires to reach. It is the eternal fulfilment of all the hopes and desires that have been kindled and encouraged by redemption.

The meaning of Babylon has already been discussed at length, and needs no further elaboration. (See pp. 82-87.)

FORMULAE

Throughout Revelation are scattered a number of phrases which are related to each other, but which have no definite connection with concrete persons or objects. They are formulae which by their repetition show a sequence of thought and which mark like milestones the progress of the book.

The first of these, "I was in the Spirit," has already been treated in detail. It provides division points for the main sections of Revelation (1:10, 4:2, 17:3, 21:10), and keeps in the mind of the reader that the book is primarily a vision. Each pair of uses contrasts two localities. The first pair contrast the action of the church on earth and the action of the Lamb in heaven. The second pair contrast Babylon and the New Jerusalem. Each differs in its scene: the first is in Patmos, the second in heaven, the third in a wilderness, and the fourth in a high mountain. Such a uniform sequence cannot be a literary accident. It was designed; and the design shows that the author of the book followed a purpose in chronicling these successive visions.

A second phrase which is repeated at least four times is "thunders, lightnings, and voices" (4:5, 8:5, 11:19, 16:18). The first of these instances is a general statement: "And out of the throne proceed lightnings and voices and thunders." It does not refer to any particular moment, but describes the awesome phenomena attending the manifestation of God. The other three, however, relate to specific occasions.

Revelation 8:5

And the angel taketh the censer; and he filled it with the fire of the altar, and cast it upon the earth: and there followed thunders, and voices, and lightnings, and an earthquake.

At end of seventh seal (8:1)

Revelation 11:19

And there was opened the temple of God that is in heaven; and there was seen in his temple the ark of his covenant, and there followed lightnings, and voices, and thunders, and an earthquake, and great hail.

At end of seventh trumpet (11:15)

Revelation 16:18

And there were lightnings, and voices, and thunders; and there was a great earthquake, such as was not since there were men upon the earth, so great an earthquake, so mighty.

The seventh bowl (16:17)

The problem for the expositor presented by these phrases is whether they refer to an identical event which marks a common terminus for all judgments, or to three similar events in a succession. If the former is true, they substantiate to some degree the futuristic view, because all of the phenomena of Revelation would thus be connected with the time of the end. If they mark three successive stages of judgment, they might be interpreted either by the futuristic or by the historical method.

The former of these alternatives is a temptingly neat solution. If the three series of seven judgments each are coterminous, and somewhat simultaneous in action, one may interpret them with a high degree of literality and assign them to the period immediately preceding the Lord's return. They belong to the period of the final tribulation in which the supernatural becomes ordinary and in which anything can happen. The seals could symbolize the general preparation of the world for a climax; the trumpets could represent the more severe physical judgments prior to the end; and the bowls would be the climactic punishments just before the last cataclysmic act.

The other alternative makes the series successive, not simultaneous. The "thunders, lightnings, voices, and earthquake" mark the end of a process. Such a conclusion seems justified on the basis of the language in the eighth chapter:

And when he opened the seventh seal, there followed a silence in heaven about the space of half an hour.

And I saw the seven angels that stand before God; and there were given unto them seven trumpets.

And another angel came and stood over the altar, having a golden censer . . . .

And he filled it with the fire of the altar, and cast it upon the earth; and there followed thunders, and voices, and lightnings, and an earthquake.

And the seven angels that had the seven trumpets prepared themselves to sound (8:1-6).

The uninterrupted train of "and's" indicates that the series of the seven trumpets follows the "thunders, and voices, and lightnings, and an earthquake" (8:5) rather than recapitulating the previous judgments. The effects of each series may be concomitant with the series following it, but on this scheme the total period of judgment is longer than would be necessitated by the preceding alternative.

A similar phrase, "voice of thunder," (6:1, 14:2, 19:6) seems to have no particular chronological significance. It is used only for defining the quality of the sound that marks the majesty of the heavenly announcement of judgment or of the volume of the songs of praise.

Another phrase used only twice in Revelation is "It is done" (16:17), or in the plural "They are come to pass" (21:6). It is derived from the Greek verb *ginomai* which means "become," "happen." These two instances are in the perfect tense, which denotes that an event has taken place, and that the results of it are fixed in a state.

"It is done" is the announcement of the great voice from the throne which declares the completion of God's work of judgment at the seventh trumpet. It ends the second vision of Revelation with the battle of Har-Magedon (16:16) and the fall of Babylon (16:19). The course of evil is finished, and God's punishment of it has been put into effect.

"They are come to pass" (21:6) is the conclusion of God's announcement, "Behold, I make all things new" (21:5). Not judgment, but the fulfilment of the promises and purpose of God is predicated by this phrase. Both uses indicate the finality of the overthrow of evil and the establishment of righteousness.

Quite different in scope and usage are the seven beatitudes of Revelation.

1. Blessed is he that readeth, and they that hear the words of the prophecy, and keep the things which are written therein: for the time is at hand.   (1:3)

2. Blessed are the dead who die in the Lord from henceforth: yea, saith the Spirit, that they may rest from their labors; for their works follow with them. (14:13)

3. Blessed is he that watcheth, and keepeth his garments, lest he walk naked, and they see his shame.   (16:15)

4. Blessed are they that are bidden to the marriage supper of the Lamb.   (19:9)

5. Blessed and holy is he that hath part in the first resurrection: over these the second death hath no power; but they shall be priests of God and of Christ, and shall reign with him a thousand years.   (20:6)

6. Blessed is he that keepeth the words of the prophecy of this book.   (22:7)

7. Blessed are they that wash their robes, that they may have the right *to come* to the tree of life, and may enter in by the gates into the city.   (22:14)

The beatitude as a literary form is generally associated with the teaching of Jesus. It does occur in the Old Testament (Ps. 32:1) and in a few passages in the New Testament (e.g. Rom. 14:22, Jas. 1:12, I Pet. 3:14, 4:14). These latter may well have been allusions to Jesus' beatitudes, or at least an imitation of His style.

The beatitudes in Revelation are not an index to the structure of the book. They do not appear at any precise point in their respective sections, nor do they seem to be related to the turns of thought. One belongs to the introduction; the next two belong to the second vision of Revelation; the fourth and fifth occur in the third vision; the sixth and seventh are in the Epilogue. They are not uniformly distributed at all.

The purpose of these beatitudes is hortatory. They make a personal appeal to the reader on the basis of the implied teaching of the context in which they are embedded, and put into a proverbial form the truth which the symbols seek to convey.

The first beatitude (Rev. 1:3) concerns the reading of the book itself. Doubtless many spurious apocalypses were circulated in the early church, so that the people were wary of any works of that type. In order to ensure a hearing for the book, the first blessing is pronounced upon the leader who would read it publicly and upon the members of the church who would accept and heed its precepts.

The beatitude on "the dead who die in the Lord" is included in the account of the reign of the beast, to whom was given power "to make war with the saints, and to overcome them" (13:7). The apparently unlimited power of the beast and his steady victory over the saints of God would tend to be utterly discouraging to them. How could they continue to believe in the sovereignty and goodness of God if He let them suffer without atttempting to rescue them? What difference would there be between their fate and the death of anybody else? The beatitude asserts that they will be compensated by rest and reward. It is intended to encourage those who are under persecution.

The third beatitude (16:15) fits the same situation. In a world prevailingly evil, controlled by demonic influences, God's servants are exhorted to "keep their garments." Vigilance is needed to avoid the accidental errors that may expose the believer to shame and contempt. He must maintain his personal holiness even under stress.

The fourth, fifth, and seventh beatitudes (19:9, 20:6, 22:14) are alike in one respect: they speak of the destiny of believers.

The marriage of the Lamb, the first resurrection and priesthood before God, and entrance into the eternal city are blessings which only the Christian can enjoy. These are the hope that keeps him persevering through hardships to the end of the present age.

The sixth beatitude is much like the first except that it is singular instead of plural. The appeal of the Revelation is individual rather than collective. Whereas the opening sentences of the book are addressed to the churches, or to a collective congregation, the closing appeal is for the individual hearer: "he that keepeth . . . ."

Collectively, all seven beatitudes summarize the holiness and hope of the Christian as he approaches the end of this age. They are an antidote both to fear and to laxity, because they focus his attention on the provision of God for his future.

Like the beatitudes, there are a number of songs or poetic expressions of praise to God scattered through Revelation. All of them, except for the "Four Hallelujahs," belong to the second vision of the book. They express the reaction of witnesses to the divine procedure of judgment, and thus help to explain the meaning of the action.

The first five constitute a group by themselves. Each is uttered by a different company of personages or by a different combination of companies. The first, spoken by the four living creatures around the throne, defines the character and power of God:

> Holy, holy, holy *is* the Lord God, the Almighty, who was and who is and who is to come (4:8).

God's holiness, omnipotence, and eternal being are given public recognition because they are basic to His rule.

The second "song," addressed to God by the living creatures, declares His worthiness to receive glory and honor and power because of His creative work.

> Worthy art thou, our Lord and our God, to receive the glory and the honor and the power: for thou didst create all things, and because of thy will they were, and were created (4:11).

The magnificence of God's creation is itself a tribute to His greatness, and makes Him worthy of the worship of His creatures. His ownership of creation gives the authority for His activity and obligates Him to rid the world of usurping evil.

The removal of this evil can be effected only through the redeeming power of the Lamb of God. The fourth song celebrates His effectual salvation.

> Worthy art thou to take the book, and to open the seals thereof: for thou wast slain, and didst purchase unto God with thy blood *men* of every tribe, and tongue, and people, and nation, and madest them *to be* unto our God a kingdom and priests; and they reign upon the earth (5:9, 10).

The song of the elders is called "new" (5:9), for creation is old, but redemption is recent. Creation began with the universe; redemption rescued it. The Lamb has effected deliverance from ruin, has given sovereignty in the place of slavery, and has brought order out of chaos. Consequently the angelic choir is saying:

> Worthy is the Lamb that hath been slain to receive the power, and riches, and wisdom, and might, and honor, and glory, and blessing (5:12).

He is exalted to the throne of the universe because He has retrieved the creation of God from unspeakable loss. All the created universe, therefore, joins in the formal paean:

> Unto him that sitteth on the throne, and unto the Lamb, *be* the blessing, and the honor, and the glory, and the dominion, for ever and ever (5:13).

These five songs or five parts of the heavenly anthem introduce the opening of the seals (6:1). They explain that because of the double authority of creation and redemption God alone is worthy of worship. All other worship is false, and has no place as a rival to the adoration of Him. The worship of the image of the beast is therefore a wicked parody of the reverence that should be paid to God.

Another song of worship rises from the redeemed themselves.

> Salvation unto our God who sitteth on the throne, and unto the Lamb (7:10).

It is chanted by the great multitude out of every nation, standing before the throne. They are earth's addition to heaven's citizens, brought there out of great tribulation. To their praise the heavenly host responds:

> Amen: Blessing, and glory, and wisdom, and thanksgiving, and honor, and power, and might, *be* unto our God for ever and ever. Amen (7:12).

By the arrival of this multitude in heaven the people of God have been removed from earth, and the final judgments commence. When the consummation is reached at the sounding of the seventh trumpet, there rises another song:

> The kingdom of the world is become *the kingdom* of our Lord and of his Christ: and he shall reign for ever and ever (11:15).

To this the elders add:

> We give thee thanks, O Lord God, the Almighty, who art and who wast; because thou hast taken thy great power, and didst reign. And the nations were wroth, and thy wrath came, and the time of the dead to be judged, and *the time* to give their reward to thy servants the prophets, and to thy saints, and to them that fear thy name, the small and the great; and to destroy them that destoy the earth (11:17, 18).

Once again out of the judgments emerges another group of those who have been victorious over the beast and over his image, joining in "the song of Moses the servant of God, and the song of the Lamb":

> Great and marvellous are thy works,
>   O Lord God, the Almighty;
> Righteous and true are thy ways,
>   Thou King of the ages.
> Who shall not fear, O Lord,
>   And glorify thy name?
>   For thou only art holy;
>   For all the nations shall come
> And worship before thee;
>   For thy righteous acts have been manifest.
>   (15:3, 4)

The song is expressive of supreme faith in the justice and in the triumph of God.

The last lyric expression in Revelation is in the nineteenth chapter. As Babylon falls and as the bride of the Lamb is prepared for her marriage, the great multitude and the elders and living creatures unite in one final paean of praise:

> Hallelujah!
> Salvation, and glory, and power, belong unto our God:
> For true and righteous are his judgments;
> For he hath judged the great harlot,
> Her that corrupted the earth with her fornication,

And he hath avenged the blood of his servants at her hand.
>   Hallelujah!
>   Amen: Hallelujah!
Give praise to our God, all ye his servants,
Ye that fear him, the small and the great.
>   Hallelujah!
For the Lord our God, the Almighty, reigneth.
Let us rejoice and be exceeding glad,
And let us give the glory unto him:
For the marriage of the Lamb is come,
And his wife hath made herself ready.
And it was given unto her
That she should array herself in fine linen, bright *and* pure:
For the fine linen is the righteous acts of the saints.

>   (19:1-3, 4-8)

In these Hallelujahs thanks are given for three great accomplishments:

>   He hath judged the great harlot.
>   He hath avenged the blood of his servants.
>   The Lord our God, the Almighty, reigneth.

God has vindicated His cause completely, and the victory is near.

These songs and expressions of praise rise above the undertones of judgment as a clear carol may be heard above the roar of a city street. They give a new optimism to a book of doom by showing that not once does the heavenly faith in God's power and goodness falter. He must be victorious.

CHAPTER XVI

THE SYMBOLISM OF REVELATION

The symbolical nature of Revelation is announced by the book itself at its very beginning. "Signified" (Greek: *semainein*), the word which describes the method by which the disclosure of truth was made known to the seer, was an ancient technical term for the pronouncements of the Delphic oracle in Greece. Plutarch, a classical author contemporary with the New Testament, says:[1]

> I suppose that you know the saying found in Heracleitus, that the ruler whose prophetic oracle is located in Delphi neither declares nor conceals, but communicates by symbols [*semainei*].

This term evidently meant a kind of communication that is neither plain statement nor an attempt at concealment. It is figurative, symbolic, or imaginative, and is intended to convey truth by picture rather than by definition.

Xenophon, who wrote earlier (434-358 B.C.?), used the word in the same way of the revelations of the gods, for he said that "Socrates thought that they know all things . . . : that they are present everywhere and grant signs [*semainein*]."[2]

If the language of Plutarch and Xenophon forms any fair index of the current meaning of the term in the first century, "signify" implies a divine communication to man in symbolic terms.

Because of this symbolism objection has been raised that Revelation cannot be definitely or finally interpreted. The figures of speech are foreign to modern thought, and are not set forth with any fixed equivalents. Revelation thus becomes much like a lock for which the key has been lost. It could be opened, and there must be a key, but without the key the possibility of correct interpretation seems almost hopeless.

However strange the symbolism may be, it is not completely impenetrable. There are several possible keys that can be used for unlocking the mysteries. They fall generally into three categories: (1) the symbols that are definitely explained by stated equivalents; (2) the symbols that are unexplained but that are drawn from Old Testament background; and (3) the symbols that have some connection with the apocalyptic literature or with pagan usage. There are very few that cannot be placed in one of these classes.

SYMBOLS EXPLAINED

Just why the writer explained some of the imagery that he employed and not all of it is an insoluble mystery. The symbols that are thus defined aid the scholar in understanding related figures that are not so plain. At least ten may be catalogued.

1. The seven stars — angels of the churches   1:20
2. The seven lampstands — the seven churches of
                                                  Asia   1:20
3. The seven lamps of fire — the seven spirits
                                                of God   4:5
4. The bowls of incense — the prayers of the saints   5:8
5. The great multitude — those who came out of
                                      great tribulation   7:13,14
6. The great dragon — the Devil, Satan   12:9
7. The seven heads of the beast — seven mountains   17:9
8. The ten horns of the beast — ten kings   17:12
9. The waters — peoples, multitudes, nations,
                                      and tongues   17:15
10. The woman — the great city   17:18

It would be fair to conclude that these symbols have a uniform meaning, and that wherever they appear in the book of Revelation they are used in the same way. The dragon, for instance, invariably refers to the devil. Some of the other symbols are not used more than once, but their value is fixed by the given definition.

SYMBOLS PARALLELED BY OLD TESTAMENT IMAGERY

Another series of symbols are not defined explicitly, but are obviously drawn from the Old Testament where their context helps to define them. The following list is fairly inclusive:

1. The tree of life   2:7, 22:2
2. Hidden manna   2:17
3. The rod of iron   2:27
4. The morning star   2:28
5. The key of David   3:7
6. The living creatures   4:7 ff.
7. The four horsemen   6:1 ff.

8.	The great angel	10:1 ff.
9.	The first beast	13:1-10
10.	The second beast	13:11-18

Some of these are objects; some are persons corresponding to others in the prophetic narratives. The use of the Old Testament imagery implies at least a connection between the two, whether it is continuous identity or similarity to be explained in terms of the concepts familiar from past knowledge.

Inasmuch as several of these symbols have already been explained in the treatment of the content of Revelation, only a few of the list will be treated here as samples.

In the class of identifiable objects is the tree of life, mentioned in Revelation 2:7 and 22:2. Its fruit is promised as a reward of the overcomer, who shall taste of the tree of life when he reaches the Paradise of God, and its leaves will be used for the healing of the nations who throng the city of God. Its very name makes it a figure of the fulness of life. Those who partake of it shall not experience death, but shall enjoy everlasting strength. The reference in Genesis undergirds this idea, for God expelled man from the garden of Eden "lest he put forth his hand, and take also of the tree of life, and eat, and live for ever" (Gen. 3:22). The tree is an emblem of eternal life which is the heritage of the child of God.

Another is the beast out of the sea, introduced in Revelation 13, and mentioned frequently in the following chapters. It is a composite of the four beasts of Daniel's vision (Dan. 7) and must be related to them. The difference in symbolism is a change of viewpoint. Daniel wrote from the standpoint of the Jewish people, whose fate under the Gentile empires to come would effect the first coming of the Messiah. Revelation, written under the fourth and last of these empires, presumably after the Jewish commonwealth had been crushed, takes this picture of Gentile world power from Daniel and combines these four empires into the picture of the future world-state. The magnificence of Babylon, the vastness of Medo-Persia, the dominating culture of Greek Macedonia, and the organizing might of Rome are united in one state that will aspire to world domination and that will achieve it. As Daniel gave a key to the interpretation of history in which Judaism awaited the first advent of Christ, so Revelation affords the key to the events preceding the second advent of Christ.

One cannot assert that the "beast" is finally to be equated with any single person or power that has yet appeared. Expositors have identified him with almost every sinister figure known, from Nero to Mussolini. Dogmatic pronouncements on this question are out of order; but as the concept of world government becomes more popular, and as world powers gain more territorial influence in every succeeding generation, it is easy to see that the Revelation points the way in which civilization is traveling. One government, materialistic in philosophy and absolutist in character, ruled by a single political and economic genius, is predicted in Revelation. Such a government, unthinkable a generation or two ago, now seems not too remote a possibility. The dictatorship of one man over the world might be welcomed if he could offer some assurance of universal peace and prosperity. What seemed a dream to statesmen of yesterday is prophesied in this book, and as the years roll by it comes closer and closer to fulfilment.

The correlation of the symbols of Revelation with their prototypes in the Old Testament can indicate the continuity of the spiritual principles or of the lines of prophecy that were first established in the revelation to the prophets and that are completed in Christ.

THE UNEXPLAINED SYMBOLS

Even when the symbols explained directly or by parallelism with the Old Testament are deducted from the total list of Revelation, there still remain a large number that are either novel in character or else unexplained by their context. A partial list is appended:

1.	The white stone	2:17
2.	The pillar	3:12
3.	The elders	4:4 ff.
4.	The seals	5:1, 6:1-17
5.	The two witnesses	11:3 ff.
6.	The woman clothed with the sun	12:1,2,14 ff.
7.	The winepress	14:20, 19:15
8.	The supper	19:6-9, 17
9.	The lake of fire	19:20
10.	The great white throne	20:11
11.	The city of God	21:2 ff.

Although these symbols are not identified clearly either by the immediate context or by exact correspondence with the Old Testament, they are not completely obscure. In a few cases they are to be interpreted in terms of local custom or usage which may be unknown to us, but which was obvious to the initial readers.

For instance, the "white stone" (2:17) has no precedent in the Old Testament, nor does the context define the meaning. It has been variously explained as the ballot used in a voting urn, or as the pebble which was sometimes given as a ticket for free entertainment,[3] or as the white pebble cast by a juryman for acquittal of a prisoner,[4] or as an amulet engraved with a secret formula,[5] possibly corresponding with the Urim and Thummim of the Pentateuch, (Exod. 28:30, Lev. 8:8). While each of these suggestions possesses some merit, it is more likely that the white stone is a pledge of friendship or keepsake on which God has inscribed the name that represents most adequately His relation to the believer. It is both a guarantee of divine favor and a key to divine fellowship.

The symbol of the pillar was taken directly from contemporary architecture (Rev. 3:12). Every city in the Roman world had temples adorned with colonnades which supported the roof of the shrine or which made the porches where the public assembled. Pillars were essential to the structure and stability of the building, and they added to its beauty. In this passage the individual believer is likened to a pillar in God's temple, built permanently into its structure and bearing its proportion of responsibility for the maintenance of God's worship.

"Elder was a title used for members of the governing body of Judaism (Matt. 26:57, Luke 20:1, 22:52) and of the church (Acts 14:23, 16:4, 20:17). The twenty-four elders were thus representative of the people of God, perhaps twelve from Israel and twelve from the church. Wherever they appear in the heavenly scene (Rev. 4:4, 10; 7:11, 13) they are worshipers along with the living creatures and the cherubim.

The seals of chapter 6 draw their meaning from documentary usage. The "book" which John saw in the right hand of the occupant of the throne (5:1) was not a volume with pages like a modern book, but was properly a scroll made of papyrus, a kind of paper. It may not have been very large, but it was peculiar because it was "written within and on the back, close sealed with seven seals" (5:1). Ordinarily papyrus scrolls were inscribed on one side only. The reverse side was used either because the writer had more material than he could put on one side of the sheet, or because he placed the title on the book where it could be seen readily. A scroll written on both sides and sealed with seven seals would be an unusually full and important document, possibly legal in character.

Roman wills were often written on bronze or wooden plates, with one copy on the outside and an original sealed within. While the document of Revelation 5 is a scroll, it is possible that the seven seals would connote a will to all who read the passage. If so, a new meaning is given to the text; for a will could be opened only by the heir and executor of the estate. In breaking the seals he avowed his rightful claim as heir and asserted his authority over the property. The opening of the sealed scroll would thus show that Christ was the heir of God, worthy to assume rulership over the universe by right of redemption and ready to exercise the authority necessary to reclaim for God the inheritance that had been usurped by Satan and his minions.

The two witnesses (11:3ff.), although they are not named directly, may be explained on the basis of their connection with the Old Testament. The seer identifies them with the candlesticks and the olive trees of Zechariah 4:11-14; but the description of them accords better with Elijah and Moses, who "have the power to shut the heaven, that it rain not in the days of their prophecy; and they have power over the waters to turn them into blood, and to smite the earth with every plague, as often as they shall desire" (Rev. 11:6). Their assumption into heaven (11:12) accords with that of Elijah (II Kings 2:11), and with that of Moses as stated in *The Assumption of Moses,* mentioned by Clement of Alexandria[6] and Origen.[7] In this instance the Revelation seemingly assumes the familiarity of its readers with apocryphal literature.

The two witnesses may be actual reappearances of these two great leaders of the past who championed God's cause against bitter opposition, or they may be symbolic of the law and the prophets. The former alternative seems more likely in the light of Malachi 4:4-6, where Moses and Elijah are coupled together as mentors of a decadent age, and where the prediction of Elijah's return to earth is plainly taught.

The "suppers" of Revelation 19:9,17 afford a startling contrast. The former is a supper of fellowship based on love; the latter is destruction brought on by rebellion. The former is the delight of the saints in Christ; the latter is the doom of those who have resisted Him. Festal meals were as common in the first century as they are now, and their significance needs no elaboration. Both celebrate the victory of Christ over evil.

Every inhabitant of the Mediterranean lands was familiar with the figure of the winepress in which the juice of the grapes was trodden out to be made into wine. Revelation likens the crushing of the fruit to the treading down of God's enemies in the winepress of His wrath. There is a possible allusion to Isaiah 63:2,3 in these passages (Rev. 14:20, 19:15), but it is indirect. They are probably to be interpreted on the basis of common knowledge rather than by allusion to the Old Testament.

The "lake of fire" (19:20; 20:10,14,15; 21:8) has no exact parallel in the Old Testament, but in heathen mythology and in apocalyptic literature there were corresponding figures. The use of the definite article with "lake" implies that the readers were familiar with the concept. The *Book of Enoch* says: "Because these waters of judgment minister to the healing of the body of the kings and to the lust of their body, therefore they will not see and will not believe that those waters will change and become a fire which burns forever".[8] In another context the same work says: "Know ye that their souls [the sinners'] will be made to descend into Sheol, and they will become wretched and great will be their tribulation. And into darkness and chains and a burning fire, where there is grievous condemnation, will your spirits enter."[9]

Judgment by a burning fire was an accepted concept in apocalyptic literature and would doubtless be known to the readers of Revelation. Perhaps the imagery was affected by the widespread knowledge of the eruption of Vesuvius in A.D. 79, when the city of Herculaneum perished in a flow of molten lava.

The "great white throne" is not primarily an Old Testament figure. Daniel speaks of the "Ancient of Days," whose throne was "fiery flames" (Dan. 7:9); but the *Book of Enoch* speaks of a mountain which "reached to heaven like the throne of God, of alabaster . . . ."[10] He further states, "This high mountain which thou hast seen, whose summit is like the throne of the Lord, is His throne, where the Holy and Great One, the Lord of Glory, the Eternal King will sit, when He shall come down to visit the earth with goodness."[10] The throne was a symbol of sovereignty and judgment, peculiarly the prerogative of God. Its whiteness is emblematic of purity against which all evil would be contrasted in bold relief. The books associated with it are the records of mankind, preserved by the mind of God and unalterable.   The total picture is the final triumph of truth in a judgment that is both just and relentless.

The city of God has already been discussed in the eighth chapter of this book, and needs no further elaboration.   The city is the symbol of a community, the organized life of a given people. The New Jerusalem is thus the representation of the people of God, who shall be associated with each other in happy union for all eternity.

The symbols as a whole are not taken from fanciful or imaginary sources, but are related to ideas that would be readily recognized by the readers.   The Old Testament, which was their source of revelation, current religious literature embracing the apocryphal works, and the common phenomena of everyday life provided the backgrounds for the figures of the book.   They are partially obscure to the modern world because they belong to a bygone day, but when they are explained for modern ears, they take on new meaning.

It would be presumptuous to claim that their meaning is perfectly explained by relating them to their original setting.   There will always remain an aura of mystery around them because one is never quite certain just what movements, events, or trends they denote.   Nevertheless, as the time of fulfilment approaches, they will become constantly plainer, and the final identification will be made by those who witness the scenes that the symbols prophetically describe.

Chapter XVII

THE MEANING OF REVELATION FOR THIS PRESENT AGE

Any attempt to identify the symbols of Revelation or its predicted events with the current happenings of the twentieth century must be made cautiously. For eighteen hundred years interpreters have tried to show that Revelation was written to describe the events of their own times. However sincere they may have been, the calendar has been a witness to their failure, for the end of the age has not yet come and their predictions have not been fulfilled. To assert that the present decade will see the opening of the great tribulation, or to state that Communism is the antichrist, or to hail any social or ecclesiastical movement as equivalent to the coming of the kingdom of God would be foolhardy indeed.

Even though the Revelation may not find its fulfilment in the events of the present day nor even within the next century, it may still be relevant to the present situation. The particular application of God's Word to some predicted event does not rob it of significance for the time preceding that event. The prophecies concerning the incarnation gave meaning to all the historical events preceding it, so that Paul could say, "When the fulness of the time came, God sent forth his Son, born of a woman, born under the law" (Gal. 4:4). They gave direction and coherence to the understanding of the social and political forces that surged in conflict across the Roman world. In similar fashion the declaration that "The kingdom of the world is become *the kingdom* of our Lord, and of his Christ" (Rev. 11:15) lends a new perspective to the apparently aimless though terrifyingly rapid drift of modern civilization.

One of the marvels of the written Word of God is its perennial relevance to every time and situation. Its principles are universally applicable, although its predictions may fit only one specific era. Yet if there is purpose in history, and if God is moving toward a climax, there must come a time when those who are living will say, "This is the end!" The fulfilment of Revelation comes nearer every day.

There are four ways in which Revelation may be meaningful for this present age: (1) by giving to us the divine estimate of history; (2) by predicting the future to a definite degree; (3) by contributing theologically to the structure of Christian thought; and (4) by offering a spiritual stimulus to daily living.

ITS HISTORICAL SIGNIFICANCE

Awareness of the flow of history has become peculiarly a property of modern man. His facilities for research and communication are far superior to anything possessed by his ancestors. Archaeology has compelled the silent centuries to yield up many of their secrets; the modern facilities of radio and telephone have enabled the newspapers and magazines to keep abreast of the whole world at a time, and have minimized provincialism. History is not now so much a part of what we study as a part of what we live. Even the remote past has a bearing on modern life, and one can realize that there is an unbroken chain of social cause and effect between Babylon and Washington, D. C.

If man is being borne alone on the tides of history, in what direction is he going? Only the disclosure of God's knowledge can tell him, for apart from revelation he cannot know the divine purpose, nor can he understand the application if he knows it. The book of Revelation helps to interpret the history of the past in several ways.

It shows that no human empire can endure permanently. When Revelation was written, Rome was at its peak of power, and the decline of the empire, though it had already begun, was not apparent for another century. Revelation declares plainly that "the great city that reigneth over the kings of the earth" was doomed to ruin. Its reign would be broken, and its prosperity would depart. Its evil power must have seemed invincible to the Christians of that day, and they would be tempted to think that their cause was hopeless; nevertheless Rome's dominion passed, and Christ remained.

The same principle applies today. Fascism, Communism, and other forms of government bid for the domination of the world and come close to attaining it. However powerful they may become, they cannot ultimately win. God must have the last word.

Historically also Revelation explains the church, "by schisms rent asunder, by heresies distressed." In the letters to the seven churches of Asia one may see that the typical Christian communities of the first century were not essentially different from those

today. The same virtues and the same evils that characterized
them are apparent now. If the Lord of the church was sufficiently interested in these groups to discipline them and to preserve
them, He has the same interest today. There will be apostate
churches whom He will reject utterly; there will be others whom
He will discipline severely: and there will be also those whom He
will cherish and develop. One thing is certain: He will bring out
of tribulation those who are His and who are loyal to Him.

Undeniably Revelation deals not only with broad historical
trends which may recur from century to century, but also with
the specific events of the end time. Their approach may be dis-
cerned in the trends that lead toward them.

Revelation predicts that in the end of time the world will be
under one government. To the beast, who is the head of the
kingdom of earth, will be given "authority over every tribe and
people and tongue and nation" (13:7). Such a concept existed
when the Apocalypse was written because Rome was the con-
trolling power in the Western world. There was not, however, a
"one-world government," because the Far East was under a totally different civilization and because the barbarian peoples beyond the borders of the empire had not been absorbed into the
commonwealth. Today the concept seems nearer realization, for
the peoples of the world are gravitating into two opposing camps
— the free states and the totalitarian state. Since such a division
cannot be permanent, it is obvious that one will try to conquer
the other. The ensuing conflict can lead only to domination of
the world by one side or the other, and the consequent establishment of the rule that Revelation describes.

Revelation predicts the development of urban civilization.
Babylon, the center of all commercial and social life, is "the great
city" (18:18). There were great cities in the empire of the first
century, but a larger portion of the population was agrarian than
today. The lament of the merchants in Revelation 18 shows that
Babylon was the key to the prosperity of the whole world; and
that its overthrow upset the economic structure. Unprecedented
prosperity ending in terrible calamity is foretold for the future.

A totalitarian system of unbelievable scope and power is also
predicted. Every new invention of man gives him one more tool
by which he can control others and enforce his will upon them.
These inventions under the power of an able leader could make

him the undisputed tyrant of the earth.   Such a rule is fore-shadowed for the beast whose image is made to speak (13:15), and who becomes not only the object of man's political allegiance but of his religious worship as well.

The political, economic, social, and even religious controls which have been exercised upon entire populations in recent years by the Communist, Fascist, and even in measure by democratic governments, illustrate the fact that the attempt to establish a world government and a world philosophy by force is not beyond imagination.   The second world war grew out of such an attempt, and the memory of the narrow margin by which it failed is still enough to provoke a shudder from those who cherish freedom.

Revelation predicts unmistakably a new world order founded on the redemptive work of Christ.   The concentration of evil in one vast system ruled by an antichrist who will be the most powerful potentate that the human race has ever produced will be overthrown by the manifestation of Christ in power.   His kingdom will succeed the kingdom of earth.   His righteousness will supplant the trickery and graft that have so long cursed human government.   The equity and justice of His rule will eliminate the miseries and injustices that have disfigured society.   In this prophecy the present world can see both its doom and its hope.

ITS THEOLOGICAL TEACHING

The teaching of Revelation is not concerned exclusively with eschatology.   Even though its main theme is the coming of Christ, there are in the book certain basic assumptions that are calculated to do more than to satisfy curiosity about the future. Revelation was written not only to reveal the things which must shortly come to pass, but also to stabilize the life and testimony of believing Christians.

Revelation offers a satisfying theism for a confused world. New cults appear with bewildering rapidity, each claiming to possess final truth and to be able to solve all human problems. War, with its train of attendant ills, disasters of nature that sweep good and bad indiscriminately into destruction, economic pressure that makes life a burdensome struggle for existence make men wonder whether there is a God who rules the world or whether it is just one vast mathematical accident.   If there is a God, has He any more interest in their affairs than a farmer has for the ants in a colony on his property?   If He has a control over their destiny, what will that destiny be?

These questions are vital to human thinking, for their answers determine human behavior. All purpose, all morality, and all hope depend upon man's concept of God and on his attitude toward God. If God's interest is real and if His purpose is sure there is reason for maintaining a struggle against evil, because sacrifice will be rewarded and hope will find freedom.

Revelation presents a sovereign God whose purposes must be victorious. He is almighty (1:8), everlasting (4:8), seated upon the throne of the universe (4:2), the Creator of all things (4:11). His authority is greater than that of evil (12:10), and His name is the security of those who trust in Him (14:1). Revelation emphasizes that God is not only "our help in ages past," but that He is "our hope for years to come, our shelter from the stormy blast, and our eternal home."

Revelation presents a high view of the person of Christ. There is no doubt of His real humanity, for He actually lived among men and actually died (1:5,18; 11:8). He is a member of the Jewish nation, and is the heir to their Messianic expectations (5:5). He is, however, equal with God, for He shares the attribute of eternity (1:18) and the throne of the Father (3:21, 5:6, 22:1). He is called the Son of God (2:18) and the Word of God (19:13), who by the authority of the Father speaks the Father's message. His chief work is redemption, of which the word "Lamb" is the symbol. The great stress of Christology in Revelation, however, is upon the activity of Christ rather than upon the nature of Christ. Throughout the book He is constantly engaged in superintending the churches, in ordering the events of the cosmos, appearing in judgment, and finally establishing the promised kingdom and bringing the affairs of earth to a victorious conclusion. Revelation paints Him in flaming colors and with startling imagery as priest, administrator, avenger, and comforter of His people. He is, nevertheless, not an icon but a person; and the book concludes not with a rapturous description, but with a direct appeal to Him.

Revelation affords a dual concept of sin that illumines the dangers of the last days. One aspect concerns the church. The seven letters reveal the evils that beset God's people as they confront a hostile and godless world, dominated by the philosophy of Babylon. A waning zeal (2:4), the infiltration of fleshly sins (2:14,20), incomplete works because of infirm purpose (3:1,2), indifference (3:15) are the chief dangers that rob the church of its effectiveness.   While these have always been a source of peril, they are doubly so in the end time, for the pressure of evil will increase, and the temptation to defection will be stronger. Each letter is a warning for the church today, for while the character of these perils may not have been changed, the crucial test of consummation will intensify them and the remedy which the Lord prescribed will be more pertinent than ever.

The sins of the world at large are vigorously denounced. Demonology, idolatry, murders, sorceries, fornications and thefts (9:20,21) are the chief offenses.   Their heinousness consists not only in the nature of the crimes themselves, but also in the accompanying attitudes: "they repented not" (9:21), and "they repented not to give him glory" (16:9).   Impenitence and unwillingness to recognize the sovereignty of God are the fatal aspects of sin.   Human decline began when man, "knowing God . . . glorified him not as God" and "worshipped and served the creature rather than the Creator" (Rom. 1:21,25).   Revelation shows the ultimate consequence of this act in the darkness of heart that worships the beast (Rev. 13:4,8,12), and that refuses utterly to respond either to God's appeal (Rev. 14:6,7) or to the severity of God's judgments (16:11).

ITS SPIRITUAL APPLICATION

The book of Revelation has been a definite source of spiritual strength for the church in all ages.   It is the one book in the Bible that is given wholly to the consideration of the plan of God for His people's future. Within its pages may be found the pattern for their behavior, warnings against the peculiar dangers that the last days will bring, and exhortations to godliness and zeal.   The preparation for "things which must shortly come to pass" (1:1) was not solely the provision of adequate information about the future, but was a direct appeal to the members of the churches of Asia to renew their spiritual life.   Revelation opens with a blessing on those who *keep* the things written in it, and ends with an invitation to the thirsty to come and take the water of life freely (22:17).   The book as a whole is a rebuke to complacency, and a powerful incentive to holy living.

Worship is one of its strongest emphases. The first vision of the book brought the writer prostrate before the figure of the living Christ who appeared to him on Patmos. Through the long series of visions that followed there are repeated references to worship.

The action of the book opens with the worship of heaven (4:9-11) and continues as group after group offers adoration to God and to the Lamb (7:9-11, 11:16-18, 14:3, 15:2-4, 19:3). Worship is the main occupation of the redeemed.

The implication of the book is that worship is a token of the genuineness of spiritual life now. The contrast between the saved and the lost in Revelation could be called a contrast in worship, since the latter worship the beast (13:4,8,12,15). Man is made to worship someone, and if he will not have the true God, he will inevitably turn to a false idol. Revelation offers the true God in His majesty and redemptive power as the only source of righteousness and of courage for men when evils multiply and judgment approaches.

Instruction in particular principles of individual spiritual life is given by the imperatives that appear in the letters to the churches. "Remember" (2:5), "repent" (2:5), "fear not" (2:10), "be faithful" (2:10), "hold fast" (2:25), "buy of me gold refined by fire . . . and white garments . . . and eyesalve (3:18). These injunctions, repeated in some instances, are the positive stimuli given by the Lord to His church for holy living. They are the great needs for the latter days in particular, when complacency, failure, fear, laxity, discouragement, and satisfaction with a mediocre set of values will imperil the church's very existence. The relevance of these principles for the latter days is made unmistakably clear by this statement: "Hold fast till I come" (2:25). All of the ethic enjoined upon the churches by the Lord is to be viewed in the perspective of His imminent return.

Injunctions and warnings are not the only spiritual stimuli in Revelation. There is also the note of comfort. At the conclusion of this book which contains such frightful pictures of apostasy and of judgment there is the promise of a restoration of Paradise, the coming of the final city of God. It will be the realization of all that for which believers have struggled and of all for which the martyrs have died.

> And I heard a great voice out of the throne saying, Behold, the tabernacle of God is with men, and he shall dwell with them, and they shall be his peoples, and God himself shall be with them *and be* their God: and he shall wipe away every tear from their eyes; and death shall be no more; neither shall there be mourning, nor crying, nor pain, any more: the first things are passed away (21:3-5).

In moments of disappointment and discouragement, whether they are caused by personal reverses or by the total outlook of the world conditions, this promise of God's ultimate victory can cheer His servants, and can cause them to lift up their hearts and heads in joy.

Where does the present generation stand in relation to Revelation? Is the book simply a chronicle in figurative terms of what is past, and therefore useful only as admonition by example? Is it a tapestry of the future, to be fitted into the blueprint of things to come? Should it be treated only as a helpful allegory, like *Pilgrim's Progress,* or should it be regarded as definite prediction, even though its meaning may not always be clear to the reader?

No good result can be achieved by setting dates or by insisting arbitrarily that the twentieth century is prefigured by some one of the seals, trumpets, or bowls. The history of such interpretation is its own best refutation. On the other hand, the passing years bring constantly nearer the consummation of which Revelation speaks. The converging trends of universal government, universal culture, centralization of economic and political power in fewer and fewer hands, the increasing ability of man to destroy himself and his world by the powers of nature which he has harnessed, all point to a climactic focus at which God must intervene if the world is to survive at all. Legislation and diplomacy, conferences and peace parleys cannot stay permanently the tides of destruction. These arise from within the heart of man, and until the heart is changed, the evils will persist and will increase in magnitude. Nothing but the advent of the King of kings and Lord of lords can save mankind.

Will that come within the present generation? Revelation does not say, but it may be possible. The world-process has accelerated greatly in the last fifty years. In knowledge, in communications, in political theory, in economic development man has made enormous strides. There was a greater difference between the civilization of 1950 and that of 1900 than there was between that of 1900 and that of 1800. If the acceleration is maintained, the internal tensions in the political, social, and economic realms will become greater. Such an acceleration could bring the consummation when man asserts his independence of God under the leadership of one genius, the beast, and when God manifests His ultimate authority through Christ, the redeemer and the conqueror.

The growth of good and evil trends keep pace with each other.

As the gospel reaches out to the uttermost frontiers of earth, rebellion against it becomes more widespread. The multiplication of the mechanical devices which aid the travel and work of the servants of God can be put to use in the service of evil. The return of Israel to its own land after banishment of nearly two millennia produces an international crisis. Widespread conversions resulting in the growth of the visible church may foster a superficial Christianity. As these conflicting tensions multiply, they prepare the way for a final crisis in which human destiny must be taken in hand by Deity to prevent the complete dissolution of the human race.

Nobody can say exactly in what generation the end will come; but it is obvious that an end must come, and that the swiftly passing years are bringing it constantly nearer. Perhaps within the life-span of many now inhabiting the earth the Lord may finish the work begun at Calvary. This is the Christian's hope, and the answer to the crowning prayer of the book of Revelation: "Amen: come, Lord Jesus."

NOTES

CHAPTER I

1. For specimens of Blake's poetry, see *The Complete Poetry and Selected Prose of John Donne and The Complete Poetry of William Blake.* First Modern Library Giant Edition. (New York: The Modern Library, 1946).

2. Irenaeus, *Against Heresies,* V, xxx, 3.

3. Justin Martyr, *Dialogue with Trypho,* 81.

4. Irenaeus, *Against Heresies,* IV, xiv, 2; xvii, 6; xxi, 3; V, xxviii, 2; *et al.*

5. Implied in Eusebius, *Historia Ecclesiae.* III, 39.

6. *Shepherd of Hermas,* Vision II, 4; III, 6-10.

7. Clement of Alexandria, *Stromata* VI, 106, 107.

8. For a good brief discussion of Marcion see C. R. Gregory, *The Canon and Text of the New Testament* (New York: Charles Scribner's Sons, 1912), pp. 81, 82.

9. Eusebius, *Historia Ecclesiae,* III, 25.

10. See Moses Stuart, *A Commentary on the Apocalypse* (Andover, Mass.: Allen, Morrill, & Wardwell, 1845), I, 257-282. Stuart's discussion of the ancient authorities on this question is thorough, though his work is old.

11. T. Zahn, *Introduction to the New Testament* (New York: Scribner's 1909), III, 444, 445.

12. Irenaeus, *Against Heresies,* V, xxx, 3.

13. Victorinus, *In Apocalupsi,* 10, 11.

14. Eusebius, *Historia Ecclesiae,* III, xviii, 1.

15. Jerome, *De Viris Illustribus,* 9.

16. For a complete discussion of this topic, see T. W. Davies, "Apocrypha," in *International Standard Bible Encyclopedia,* I, 178-183.

17. For allusion, see C. R. Gregory, *op. cit.,* p. 133.

18. Eusebius, *Historia Ecclesiae,* III, 25.

19. H. B. Swete, *The Apocalypse of St. John* (London: Macmillan & Co., Ltd., 1906). See pages xviii-xxviii for full treatment of the subject.

20. R. H. Charles, *The Revelation of St. John* (Two Volumes. New York: Scribner, 1929), Vol. I, pp. lxv-lxxxii.

21. Charles, *op. cit.,* I, lxxxiii ff.

CHAPTER II

1. In grammatical language, is "of Jesus Christ" an objective or subjective genitive? See Charles, *op. cit.,* I, 6.

CHAPTER III

1. For a more detailed consideration of these "songs" see pp. 182-185.

2. These are not formally listed by the author, but have been recognized by many exegetes. See *Scofield Reference Bible* (New York: Oxford University Press, n.d.), pp. 1340-1342, 1351, 1352.

3. *Ibid.,* pp. 1346-1350.

CHAPTER IV

1. Eusebius, *Historia Ecclesiae,* III, 25.

2. Justin Martyr, *First Apology,* lxvii.

3. Sir William Ramsay, *The Letters to the Seven Churches of Asia* (New York: Geo. H. Doran, 1905), p. 446.
4. Alfred Tennyson, *In Memoriam*.

CHAPTER V

1. Greek: *chalkolibano*. The translations given here are suggested by Riddell-Scott-Jones *Lexicon*.
2. Greek: *podērē*. See Exodus 25:6; 28:4, 27; 29:5; 37:8; Ezek. 9:2, 3, 11; Zech. 3:4.
3. Ramsay, *op. cit.*, pp. 269, 270.
4. *The Martyrdom of Polycarp*, xiii, in *Ante-Nicene Fathers*, I, 42.
5. Ramsay, *op. cit.*, p. 283.
6. *Ibid.*, 291-298 for details concerning Pergamum.
7. See Num. 22:1-25:9; II Pet. 2:15, 16.
8. Irenaeus, *Against Heresies*, I, xxvi, 3; III, xi, 1.

CHAPTER VI

1. Philip Mauro, *Of Things Which Soon Must Come to Pass* (Grand Rapids: Wm. B. Eerdmans Pub. Co., n.d.), p. 284.
2. Ramsay, *op. cit.*, pp. 97-108.

CHAPTER VII

1. *Supra*, p. 18.
2. Ford C. Ottman, *The Unfolding of the Ages* (New York: Baker & Taylor, n.d.), 385-401; W. R. Newell, *The Book of the Revelation* (Chicago: Grace Publications, 1941), pp. 263-291; J. A. Seiss, *Lectures on the Apocalypse* (10th ed.; New York: Charles C. Cook, 1909), III, 139-157.

CHAPTER X

1. Charles, *op. cit.*, I, 1, li.

CHAPTER XI

1. Swete, *op. cit.*, p. cxxxv. Swete gives a representative list in the Greek text.
2. Charles, *op. cit.*, I, 292.
3. See *supra*, pp. 83-87.
4. The word translated "tribes" in Rev. 1:7 is translated "families" in the Septuagint version of Zech. 12:14.
5. Wm. R. Newell, *op. cit.*, pp. 170-171.
6. Swete, *op. cit.*, p. 145.
7. Seiss, *op. cit.*, II, 319-324; G. H. Lang, *The Revelation of Jesus Christ* (London & Edinburgh: Oliphants, 1945), pp. 198-202.

CHAPTER XII

1. *Supra*, p. 51-55.
2. *Supra*, p. 68.
3. Swete, *op. cit.*, p. 74.
4. Seiss, *op. cit.*, I, 264-274.
5. See Adolf Deissmann, *Light from the Ancient East*. Transl. by Lionel M. Strachan (London: Hodder & Stoughton, 1911), pp. 357-359, 366, 367.

CHAPTER XIII

1. Swete, *op. cit.*, pp. ccix, ccx.
2. Ramsay, *op. cit.*, pp. 93-115.
3. Shirley Jackson Case, *The Revelation of St. John* (Chicago: University of Chicago Press, 1919), pp. 125-185.

4. E. B. Elliott, *Horae Apocalypticae* (3d ed.; London: Seeley, Burnside, and Seeley, 1847), I, 343-501.

5. The Historicist view was followed in the Reformation period by Luther, Zwingli, Knox, and later by Bullinger, Sir Isaac Newton, Bickersteth, and Elliott. In the last century it was defended by H. Grattan Guinness, A. J. Gordon, A. B. Simpson, and others.

6. Seiss, *op. cit.*, II, 234.

7. Newell, *op. cit.*, p. 90.

8. Raymond Calkins, *The Social Message of the Book of Revelation* (New York: The Woman's Press, 1920), pp. 3-9.

CHAPTER XIV

1. Augustine, *De Civitate Dei*, xx, 5. For the English translation see *The Nicene and Post-Nicene Fathers*, Series I, Vol. II, p. 424. It is significant that Augustine himself states that his teaching is a reaction against the millennialism of his time.

2. Leroy E. Froom, *The Prophetic Faith of Our Fathers* (Washington, D. C.: Review & Herald, n.d.), I, 659.

3. J. H. Snowden, *The Coming of the Lord* (2d ed.; New York: Macmillan, 1918), pp. 275, 276.

4. Augustine, *De Civitate Dei*, xx, 5, 6.

5. Mauro, *op. cit.*, pp. 616, 622.

6. Floyd Hamilton, *The Basis of Millennial Faith* (Grand Rapids: Wm. B. Eerdmans, 1942), p. 142.

7. Eusebius, *Historia Ecclesiae*, III, 39.

8. Wm. Childs Robinson, *Christ, the Hope of Glory* (Grand Rapids: Wm. B. Eerdmans, 1945), pp. 318-322.

9. Hamilton, *ibid.*, pp. 113-115.

10. *Ibid.*, pp. 117, 118.

11. Greek: *ezēsen*. This aorist form may be ingressive, and so be translated "come to life."

12. Emil Schürer, *A History of the Jewish People in the Time of Jesus Christ*, transl. by Sophie Taylor & Peter Christie (2d & rev. ed.; New York: Scribner, 1891), Division II, Vol. II, pp. 154-187.

13. Enoch lxii, 14.

14. IV Ezra xii, 34.

15. Josephus, *Antiquities* XVIII, 1, 3; *Wars of the Jews* II, 8, 14. Josephus' statements are not very clear.

16. Eusebius, *op. cit.*, III, 39.

17. Justin Martyr, *Dialogue with Trypho*, LXXX, LXXXI.

18. Irenaeus, *Against Heresies* V, xxxiii-xxxv.

19. Among these are: Bengel, Olshausen, Alford, Lange, Fausset, Seiss, Delitzsch, Ellicott, Darby.

20. Greek: *achri telous*.

CHAPTER XV

1. Greek: *ekklesia*.

2. Charles, *op., cit.*, I, 172, 226-231.

3. Greek: *arnion*.

4. Greek: *amnos*.

CHAPTER XVI

1. Plutarch, *Moralia*, 404E. (Original translation).

2. Xenophon, *Memorabilia*, I, i, 19.

3. Swete, *op. cit.*, pp. 39, 40.

4. Samuel Wills, *The Seven Churches of Asia* (New York: Edward H. Fletcher, 1852), pp. 157, 158.

5. Charles, *op. cit.*, I, 66, 67.

6. Clement of Alexandria, *Stromata,* VI, 15.
7. Origen, *In Josuam hom.,* 11, 1.
8. Enoch LXVII, 13.
9. *Ibid.* CIII, 8.
10. *Ibid.* XXV, 3.

BIBLIOGRAPHY

A complete bibliography of all works on Revelation would constitute in itself a large volume and would not be pertinent to the needs of the average reader. The following list is designed to serve three purposes: (1) to give a complete reference list of all works mentioned in the notes; (2) to suggest a general classification of the literature available; and (3) to indicate possible sources for further research and reading. These titles do not represent any single viewpoint exclusively, although the majority of commentaries are evangelical in theology. Brief annotations will serve as a guide to the student who is making his first venture into this field.

HISTORICAL BACKGROUND

The Ante-Nicene Fathers. Translations of the Writings of the Fathers down to A.D. 325. Alexander Roberts and James Donaldson, Editors. Revised and Chronologically Arranged with Brief References and Occasional Notes, by A. Cleveland Coxe, D.D.. Bibliographical Synopsis and Comprehensive General Index, and the Original Supplement by Allen Menzies, D.D. Ten Volumes. Grand Rapids: Wm. B. Eerdmans Publishing Co., 1951. Source for the teaching of the early church fathers.

Cambridge Ancient History. S. A. Cook, F. E. Adcock, M. P. Charlesworth, Editors. Vol. XI, *The Imperial Peace*, A.D. 70-192. New York: Macmillan, 1936. Pp. xxvii, 997. For the history of Domitian, see pp. 22-32.

Deissmann, Adolf. *Light from the Ancient East*. Translated by Lionel R. M. Strachan. London: Hodder and Stoughton, 1911. Pp. xl, 514.

Eusebius. *The Ecclesiastical History*. English Translation by Kirsopp Lake. Two volumes. London: W. Heinemann, New York: G. P. Putnam's Sons, 1926.

Froom, Leroy Edwin. *The Prophetic Faith of Our Fathers*. Four Volumes. Washington, D. C.: Review & Herald Publishing Association, 1950. An exhaustive history of eschatological thought, interpreted from the standpoint of an historicist.

Gregory, C. R. *The Canon and Text of the New Testament*. New York: Charles Scribner's Sons, 1912. Pp. 539.

Jones, Maurice. *The New Testament in the Twentieth Century*. London: Macmillan, 1924. Pp. xxxvi, 467. Chapter XI, "The Apocalypse of St. John," pp. 435-455, gives a history of the critical treatment of the Apocalypse up to date of publication.

Josephus, Flavius. *Antiquities of the Jews* and *Wars of the Jews*. English Translation by H. St. John Thackeray and Ralph Marcus. *Loeb Library Translation*. Eight volumes. London: W. Heinemann, 1926.

The Nicene and Post-Nicene Fathers. Series I, edited by Philip Schaff. Fourteen volumes. Grand Rapids: Wm. B. Eerdmans Publishing Co., 1956. Vols. I-VIII: Works of St. Augustine.

Plutarch. *Moralia*, with an English translation by Frank Cole Babbitt. Fourteen volumes. London: W. Heinemann, Ltd., N. Y.: G. P. Putnam's Sons, 1927-

Ramsay, Sir William. "The Flavian Policy Towards the Church" in *The Church in the Roman Empire*. New York: G. P. Putnam's Sons, n.d. Ch. XVI, pp. 252-278.

Rowley, H. H. *The Relevance of Apocalyptic*. London and Redhill: Lutterworth Press, 1950. Pp. 205.

Salmon, Edward T. *A History of the Roman World from 30 B.C. to A.D. 138.* New York: Macmillan, 1944. Pp. xiii, 363.

Stauffer, Ethelbert. *Christ and the Caesars.* Translated from the third German edition of *Christus und die Caesären* by K. and R. Gregor Smith. London: SCM Press, 1955. Pp. 293. New historical material on the background of Domitian's reign.

Schürer, Emil. *A History of the Jewish People in the Time of Jesus Christ.* Second and Revised Edition. Translated by John Macpherson, Sophia Taylor, and Peter Christie. Two Divisions, Vols. I-II, I-III. New York: Charles Scribner's Sons, 1891.

Stonehouse, Ned Bernard. *The Apocalypse in the Ancient Church.* A Study in the History of the N. T. Canon. Goes (Holland): Oosterbaan & Le Cointre, n.d. Pp. 160. Good bibliography; conservative.

Zahn, Theodor. *Introduction to the New Testament.* Translation from the Third German Edition, under the supervision of Melancthon Williams Jacobus, assisted by Charles Snow Thayer. Three volumes. New York: Charles Scribner's Sons, 1909. Reprinted, Grand Rapids: Kregel, 1953.

APOCRYPHA

Charles, R. H., Ed. *The Apocalypse of Baruch .* Introduction by W.O.E. Oesterley. London: Society for Promoting Christian Knowledge, 1918. Pp. xxxiii, 42.

——*The Book of Enoch.* Translated from Dillmann's Ethiopic Text. Oxford: Clarendon Press, 1893. Pp. xiii, 391.

——"Apocalyptic Literature" in Hastings' *Dictionary of the Bible,* I, 109a-110b. New York: Charles Scribner's Sons, 1902.

—"*The Apocrypha and Pseudepigrapha of the Old Testament in English, with Introductions and Critical and Explanatory Notes to the Several Books.* Vol. I, Apocrypha; Vol. II, Pseudepigrapha. Oxford: Clarendon Press, 1913. Contains full commentaries.

——*Studies in the Apocalypse.* Edinburgh: T. & T. Clark, 1915. Pp. 199.

——*Lectures on the Apocalypse.* The Schweich Lectures, 1919. London: Humphrey-Milford, 1922. Pp. 80. An attempt to reconstruct the order of the Apocalypse.

Davies, T. W. "Apocrypha" in *International Standard Bible Encyclopedia,* I, 178-183. Grand Rapids: Wm. B. Eerdmans Publishing Co., 1949.

GENERAL COMMENTARIES

Barrett, J. O. *The Book of the Revelation.* London: The Carey Press, 1947. Pp. 123.

Beckwith, I. T. *The Apocalypse of John.* New York: Macmillan, 1919. Pp. xv, 794.

Bowman, John Wick. *The Drama of the Book of Revelation.* Philadelphia: Westminster Press, 1955. Pp. 158. Organized into form of a drama, with a new translation. Not an extended commentary.

Boyd, Robert. "The Book of Revelation," in *Interpretation,* II (1948), 467-482. Contains some good suggestions on the structure of the Apocalypse.

Calkins, Raymond. *The Social Message of Revelation.* New York: The Woman's Press, 1920. Pp. xi, 190.

Carpenter, W. Boyd. *The Revelation of St. John the Divine.* Ed. C. J. Ellicott. London, Paris & New York: Cassell, Petter, Galpin & Co., n.d. Pp. 280.

Case, Shirley Jackson. *The Revelation of John.* Chicago: University of Chicago Press, 1919. Pp. xii, 419. Rationalistic; clear, and well outlined.

Charles, R. H. *A Critical and Exegetical Commentary on the Revelation of St. John,* with Introduction, Notes, and Indices; also the Greek Text and English Translation. Two Volumes. In *International Critical Commentary.* New York: Charles Scribner's Sons, 1920. Contains Greek text, exhaustive Introduction, grammar of Apocalypse, and critical treatment of text.

Davidson, F., Stibbs, A. M., and Kevan, E. F., Editors. *The New Bible Commentary.* Grand Rapids: Wm. B. Eerdmans Publishing Co., 1953. Pp. xii, 1199. For Revelation, see pp. 1168-1199. Most recent general conservative commentary.

Dean, John T. *The Book of Revelation* in *Hand-books for Bible Classes.* Edinburgh: T. & T. Clark, 1915. Pp. 191.

Elliott, E. B. *Horae Apocalypticae.* Third Edition. Four Volumes. London: Seeley, Burnside, & Seeley, 1847. One of the best examples of the historicist school. Postmillennial.

Gaebelein, Arno C. *The Revelation, An Analysis and Exposition of the Last Book of the Bible.* New York: Publication Office "Our Hope," n.d. Pp. 225. Futurist and premillennial.

Hengstenberg, E. W. *The Revelation of St. John.* Translated by Patrick Fairbairn. Two Volumes. Edinburgh: T. & T. Clark, 1851.

Ironside, H. A. *Lectures on the Revelation.* New York: Loizeaux Bros., 1930. Pp. 366. Futurist view presented in popular lecture style.

Kiddle, Martin. *The Revelation of St. John.* In *The Moffatt N. T. Commentary.* New York: Harper & Bros., n.d. Pp. 460.

Kuyper, Abraham. *The Revelation of St. John.* Translated by John De Vries. Grand Rapids: Wm. B. Eerdmans Publishing Co., 1935. Pp. 360. Futurist; amillennial. Some very good suggestions.

Lang, G. H. *The Revelation of Jesus Christ: Select Studies.* London: Oliphants, Ltd., 1945. Pp. 420.

Lange, J. P. *The Revelation of John.* Translated from the German by Evalina Moore. New York: Charles Scribner's Sons, Armstrong, 1874. Pp. vii, 446. Exhaustive in detail.

Mauro, Philip. *Of Things Which Soon Must Come To Pass.* (An enlarged edition of *The Patmos Visions*). Grand Rapids: Wm. B. Eerdmans Publishing Co., 1933. Pp. xxviii, 623. Attempted fusion of four main views. General abandonment of futurist position, with spiritualized millennium.

Milligan, William. *The Book of Revelation.* New York: Armstrong, 1889. Pp. viii, 392. Generally preterist-idealist.

Moorehead, Wm. C. *Studies in the Book of Revelation.* New York: Fleming H. Revell Co., 1908. Pp. 153.

Newell, Wm. R. *The Book of the Revelation.* Chicago: Grace Publications, 1941. Pp. 404. Verse by verse commentary; strongly futurist.

Ottman, Ford C. *The Unfolding of the Ages in the Revelation of John.* New York: Baker & Taylor, 1905. Pp. xxx, 511. One of the earlier premillennial commentaries.

Peake, A. S. *The Revelation of John.* London: J. J. Johnson, Primitive Methodist Publishing House, 1919. Pp. 390.

Pieters, Albertus. *Studies in the Revelation of St. John.* Grand Rapids: Wm. B. Eerdmans Publishing Co., 1950. Pp. 367. Amillenarian; good classified bibliography. For discussion of millennium, see pp. 278-311.

Plummer, A. *Revelation.* In the *Pulpit Commentary,* New York: Funk & Wagnalls, n.d. Pp. 585.

Preston, Ronald H., and Hanson, Anthony T. *The Revelation of St. John the Divine.* London: SCM Press, n.d. Pp. 145. Brief, up to date; literary rather than theological.

Robertson, A. T. *Word Pictures in the New Testament.* Vol. VI, *The General Epistles and the Apocalypse.* New York: Harper & Bros., 1933. Pp. xiii, 488. See Pp. 267 ff.

Scofield Reference Bible. New York: Oxford University Press, n.d.

Scott, C. A. *The Book of the Revelation.* New York: Doran, n.d.

Scott, Thomas Lucas. *The Visions of the Apocalypse and Their Lessons.* London: Skeffington & Son, 1893. Pp. xix, 341. Some good suggestions on structure of book.

Scott, Walter. *Exposition of the Revelation of Jesus Christ.* Fourth Edition. London: Pickering & Inglis, Ltd., n.d. Pp. 456. Futurist.

Scroggie, W. Graham. *The Great Unveiling.* Edinburgh & London: Oliphants, Ltd., n.d. Pp. 222. Good treatment of Christological approach and of symbolism.

Seiss, J. A. *Lectures on the Apocalypse.* Tenth Edition. Three volumes. New York: Charles C. Cook, 1909. One of the first popular premillennial futurist commentaries on Revelation, and perhaps the most influential.

Simcox, W. H. *The Revelation of St. John the Divine. Cambridge Bible for Schools & Colleges.* Cambridge: University Press, 1898. Pp. lx, 174.

Stevens, W. C. *Revelation: The Crown Jewel of Biblical Prophecy.* Two volumes. Harrisburg: Christian Alliance Publishing Co., 1928. Futurist.

Stuart, Moses. *Commentary on the Apocalypse.* Two volumes. Andover, Mass.: Allen, 1845.

Swete, H. B. *The Apocalypse of St. John.* The Greek Text with Introduction and notes. London: Macmillan, 1911. Pp. 348. Thorough treatment of content of Revelation.

Vaughan, C. J. *Lectures on the Revelation of St. John.* Fifth Edition. London: Macmillan, 1882. Pp. xvi, 548.

Zahn, Theodor. *Die Offenbarung des Johannes.* Erste bei dritte Auflage. Zwei Bände. Leipzig: A. Deicherstsche Verlagsbuchhandlung, 1924, 1926. Probably the best German commentary on the Revelation.

THE SEVEN CHURCHES

Crosby, Howard. *The Seven Churches of Asia.* New York: Funk & Wagnalls, 1890. Pp. 168.

Morgan. G. Campbell. *A First Century Message to Twentieth Century Christians.* Third Edition. New York: Fleming H. Revell Co., 1902. Pp. 217.

Plumptre, E. H. *A Popular Exposition of the Epistles to the Seven Churches of Asia.* Second Edition. London: Hodder & Stoughton, 1879. Pp. 218.

Ramsay, Sir William M. *The Letters to the Seven Churches of Asia and Their Place in the Plan of the Apocalypse.* New York: Doran, 1905. Pp. 446. Best volume for historical background.

Wills, Samuel. *The Seven Churches of Asia.* New York: Edward H. Fletcher, 1852.

ESCHATOLOGY AND THE MILLENNIUM

Blackstone, Wm. E. *Jesus Is Coming.* Chicago: Fleming H. Revell, n.d. Pp. 252. An influential premillennial presentation.

Brown, D. *Christ's Second Coming: Will It Be Premillennial?* Edinburgh: Clark, 1882. Pp. 499.

Bruce, F. F. "The Earliest Latin Commentary on the Apocalypse," *The Evangelical Quarterly,* X (1938), 352-366.

Case, Shirley Jackson. *The Millennial Hope*. Chicago: The University of Chicago Press, 1918. Pp. ix, 253. Strongly anti-millennial.
English, E. Schuyler. *Rethinking the Rapture*. Travelers' Rest, S.C.: Southern Bible Book House, 1954. Pp. 123.
Feinberg, Charles. *Premillennialism or Amillennialism?* Second and Enlarged Edition. Wheaton, Ill, Van Kampen Press, 1954. Pp. xx, 354.
Hamilton, Floyd E. *The Basis of Millennial Faith*. Grand Rapids: Wm. B. Eerdmans Publishing Co., 1942. Amillennial view.
Kromminga, D. H. *The Millennium in the Church*. Grand Rapids: Wm. B. Eerdmans Publishing Co., 1945. Pp. 359. A history of chiliasm in the church. Leans to the premillennial position; adheres to covenant theology.
——*The Millennium*. Grand Rapids: Wm. B. Eerdmans Publishing Co., 1948. Pp. 121.
Ladd, George E. *The Blessed Hope*. Grand Rapids: Wm. B. Eerdmans Publishing Co., 1956.
Murray, George L. *Millennial Studies: A Search for Truth*. Grand Rapids: Baker Book House, 1948. Pp. 207. Amillennial.
Robinson, William Childs. *Christ, the Hope of Glory*. Grand Rapids: Wm. B. Eerdmans Publishing Co., 1945. Pp. 324.
Silver, Jesse F. *The Lord's Return*. Fifth Edition. New York: Fleming H. Revell Co., 1914. Well-documented historical treatment of eschatology, and of the millennium in particular.
Snowden, Jas. H. *The Coming of the Lord: Will it be Premillennial?* Second Edition, Revised. New York: Macmillan, 1919. Pp. xvi, 288. Postmillennial. Excellent bibliography.
Stanton, Gerald B. *Kept From the Hour*. Grand Rapids: Zondervan Publishing House, 1956. Premillennial; dispensational; pretribulation rapture.
West, Nathaniel, ed. *Premillennial Essays of the Prophetic Conference Held in the Church of the Holy Trinity, N. Y. C.* Chicago: Fleming H. Revell Co., 1879. Pp. 528.
West, Nathaniel. *The Thousand Years in Both Testaments*. Chicago: Fleming H. Revell, 1880. Pp. 493.

INDEX OF SUBJECTS

213

INDEX OF SCRIPTURE